For Sarah and David
Your love and marriage is a true inspiration

Journey of Love

From my heart to yours.
May love always be your guide!

RASSOULI & RICHARD COHN

Richard Cohn

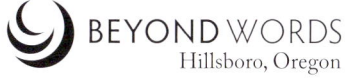
BEYOND WORDS
Hillsboro, Oregon

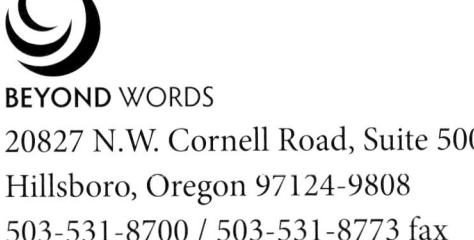

20827 N.W. Cornell Road, Suite 500
Hillsboro, Oregon 97124-9808
503-531-8700 / 503-531-8773 fax
www.beyondword.com

Copyright art © 2012 by Freydoon Rassouli
Copyright text © 2012 by Richard Cohn

All rights reserved, including the right to reproduce this book or portions thereof in any form whatsoever without the prior written permission of Beyond Words Publishing, Inc., except where permitted by law.

First Beyond Words hardcover edition February 2012

For more information about special discounts for bulk purchases, please contact Beyond Words Special Sales at 503.531.8700 or specialsales@beyondword.com.

Manufactured in the United States of America

10 9 8 7 6 5 4 3 2 1

Library of Congress Control Number:

Cohn, Richard.
　Journey of love / Rassouli & Richard Cohn; foreword by Jean Houston.—1st Beyond Words hardcover ed.
　　p. cm.
　I. Rassouli. II. Title.
　PS3603.O396J68 2012
　811'.6—dc23
　　　　　　　　　　　　　　　　　　　　　　　　　　　　2011048028
ISBN: 978-1-58270-271-1

The corporate mission of Beyond Words Publishing, Inc.: *Inspire to Integrity*

*"Poetry is formless imagery that we feel;
painting is formed imagery that we see.
Together, they become what we see and feel."*

RASSOULI

foreword

Richard Cohn has become the troubadour of love. In these exquisite verses he brings his heart song about the Beloved, whoever and whatever she may be. The depth of his feeling, the power of his longing, and the rapture of intimacy known and felt with such tenderness—these are the words of a poet who has taken up the robe of Rumi. His gift is enhanced and indeed embedded in the luminous paintings of Fusionartist Rassouli, a visionary painter who invites the viewer into the creative power of the heart and the radiance of the soul. A student of the mystical realm, he gives the poems the imagery of transcendent love.

    Together, the poet and painter show us that love changes everything. It changes the way we see, think, dream, act, engage the world, serve others and even transcend our local selves. Love is the source of most songs, poetry, writing, dreaming, human folly, and human glory. It is what wakes us up and keeps us going. As we love more, we honor more, we see and accept more: we honor pain, beauty, each other's paths, we honor each other. With love we become more intelligent and creative, for we are open to the patterns of intelligence from the whole network of life. We come to glimpse the wonder of life in its infinite forms, and the wonder that is within us. Quite simply, with love we exceed our local conditions, we evolve. Without love we probably would not have gotten beyond the primordial globules floating in an early ocean. No, even earlier, without love we would not have flung ourselves forward in the Big Bang, seeking partners and lovers in creation.

    In Plato's *Symposium* there is a wonderful passage where Aristophanes, the most comic of the dramatists tells the saddest tale. He says that human beings originally consisted of two persons in one body, with two heads and four arms and legs. These beings were shaped like a ball, and, in their completeness and satisfaction, they rolled along in

foreword

ecstasy, ready and able to do almost anything. The Titans, fearful of the enormous power available to these extraordinary double beings, feared for their own power and forced Zeus to split them in half, thus diminishing both their powers and their happiness. It is said that we spend our lives yearning to find our other half.

This tragic-comic tale shows the twinned but divided self to be the primary condition of the human race. What is so potent in these poems and paintings are the images that give new hope in our search for the Beloved. Herein, the meeting occurs, the dilemma is ecstatically resolved, we become whole again.

But the key to it all, the one that is the matrix of all manner of loving, and found in the visionary discoveries of this profoundly evocative book is the great Lure itself, the possibility of loving partnership with the Universe, the Infinite Spirit, the Divine Beloved. In giving energy, artistry and commitment to this spiritual partnership each man is building up loving capabilities to all the realms of existence, both visible and invisible. One expresses his experience in what has been called spiritual surrealism; the other uses words as wands to evoke the physical presence and eros of mystical union. Together, they show that the universe in all its parts is alive and love is its life force.

As we turn the pages, we come to realize that there are waves of thought, energy, color, form and emotion coming from everything in the universe toward us and we are offering the same--thus reality is a vast interplay in which everything is affected by everything in the most literal and loving sense.

Savor the book slowly and be led into rapture.

Jean Houston

Introduction by Rassouli

Poetry and painting are two art forms with their own unique expression of the artist's inner feelings and experience. Poetry uses words and sounds, and painting uses colors and forms. Each has its own impact on people's hearts and minds. Painters and poets often turn to one another for inspiration, and the dialogue is mutually beneficial to their art. Many writers have turned to paintings for their inspiration while painters and illustrators have frequently been inspired by literature. When the two are united, they become like two rivers that merge into a larger and more majestic flow.

Having been educated and trained in an environment of traditional Persian art, where painting is closely aligned with poetry, I was fortunate to enjoy both as closely connected art forms. Ultimately, I chose painting as the primary source of expressing my creativity, and poetry has been a source of inspiration for me. The focus of my paintings often centers around poetic themes. I enjoy the brilliant colors of nature, for they provide me with rich metaphors to develop my creative imagination in my paintings.

Since poetry is not separated from my painting, my collaboration with Richard Cohn was a natural development. The sensuality of his poetry and the power of his imagery evoke my imagination and invite me to look for the hidden concepts that are so closely tied to his emotions. After receiving a manuscript of Richard's poetry, my interest in his vision grew alongside the mystical poetry, which I have known since childhood. I found a common ground between the two.

It is interesting to note that I have not done a single painting to illustrate or try to reflect Richard's poetry, and he has not written a single poem that was inspired by my artworks, and yet, there is a strong parallel as they flow together. There is a natural alliance and closeness that exists between our two forms of artistic expression. This is a remarkable

Introduction by Rassouli

example of the journey of love and the way one enhances and expands the other and still preserves the contribution and beauty of the uniqueness and the creative flow of our different artistic forms.

This book, which I consider a delicious conversation between painting and poetry, evolved after I read Richard's collection of poetry. I was immediately drawn to the similarity of his poetic images with the symbolic images in my paintings. The content of his poetry, not unlike my painting, is created through the use of allegory, metaphor, and bringing the complexity of experience to life in a new way. They complement each other and bring out the intrinsic value of the two art forms.

I would describe Richard's poetry as soulful and as an expression of one who cherishes life. His poetry feels to me like a form of surprise, sometimes like a prayer, and as a way to respond to the challenges of life. The poems provide the stimulation of intimacy, comfort, pleasure, discovery, arousal, and offer a creative connection with another human being, which can expand the awareness of my own feelings.

The paintings in this book have been coupled with poetry through the connection experienced through the heart. Whatever the communication has been, each of us has received it in our own way, taken it in and reflected it in a creative way. I would open Richard's original manuscript to any page, and I would read each one of his poems again and again, both silently and aloud to hear the melodious sounds and feel the powerful rhythms in his writing. Suddenly, as I entered into the poetic experience, one of my paintings would come to mind. It was not so much a conscious experience as a feeling that might recall a shape or even a texture I created while I was painting.

The paintings and poetry represent a conversation, an inner dialogue with the poet and painter who created them, and hopefully with you, the viewer and reader of our combined experience. We all share in the meaning and value of creative expression, which I believe is both deeply solitary and profoundly communal.

Each page of this book contains a poem and a painting, which touch in an intimate and interior way, yet they have their own unique integrity and expression. We extend an invitation and invite you along to share the journey with us. It is a process of extending the creative act to allow you to see what you see, to feel what you feel as you join us on this journey of love. In doing this, we engage in the intimacy of the artistic sharing of our

Introduction by Rassouli

hearts with you. We are excited by the presence you bring to this communal experience of creating together.

The creation of this book professes a powerful belief in the arts. Imagination enhances our faith and strengthens our creative expression. Poetry and painting meet at the crossroads of imagination and reality and encourage us to dream. Sharing our vision and feelings can help us discover our profound connectedness with each other. Such is the journey of love.

Introduction by Richard Cohn

Creativity moved through me.
With a life of its own
My brush moved from hand to hand
From pallet to canvas
In a dance of color, bathed in blue,
Emotions welled
Longing for release
Time stopped
Minutes seemed like hours
How long they had waited
Years of judgment vanished like mist
When the brush stopped
Tears became the creative flow

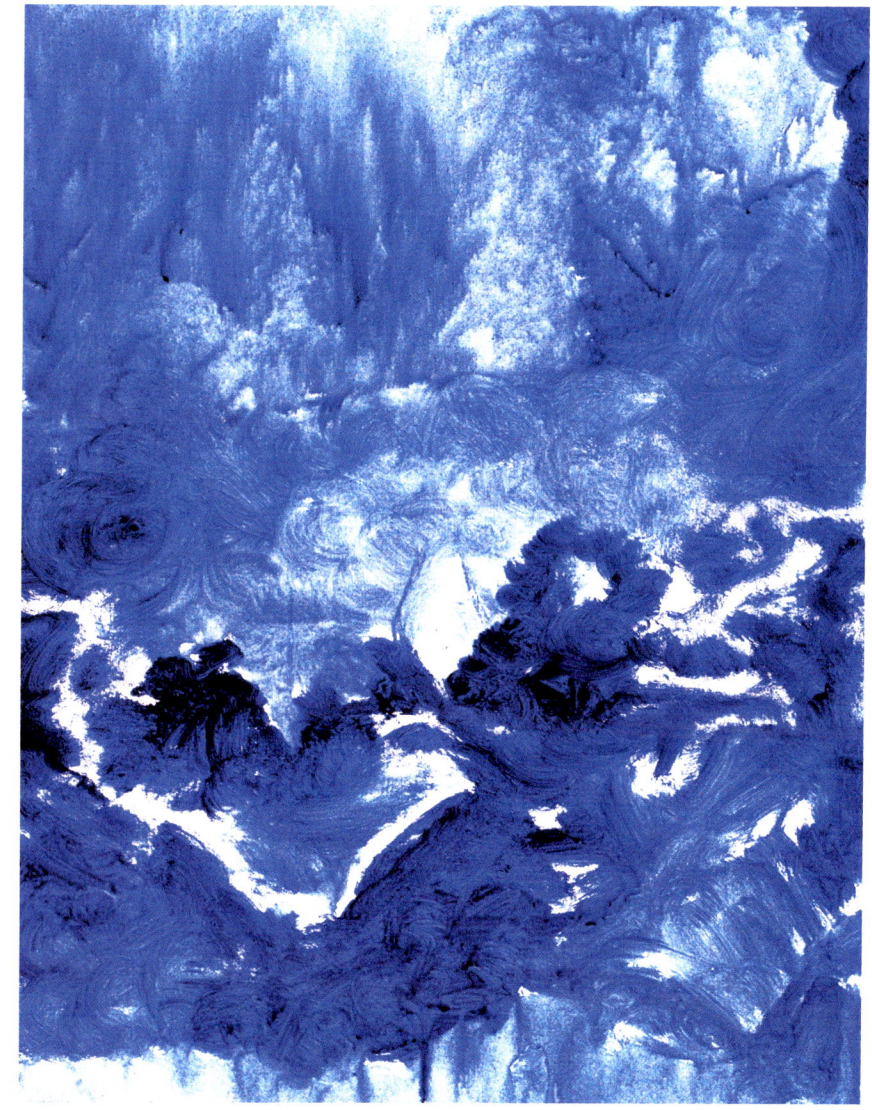

Painting by Richard Cohn

# Journey of Love

*Life unfolds in wondrous ways
and time together fills the days
with unexpected gifts,
beyond our wildest dreams
like open hearts as feelings start
to face the longing when we part
our souls know this is more than
what it seems.*

*In gratitude I offer prayer
with thanks for this love so rare
asking guidance on this sweet sojourn.*

*The answers come in tears that flow
emotions raw and smiles that show
becoming one is worth the wait
until
I can return.*

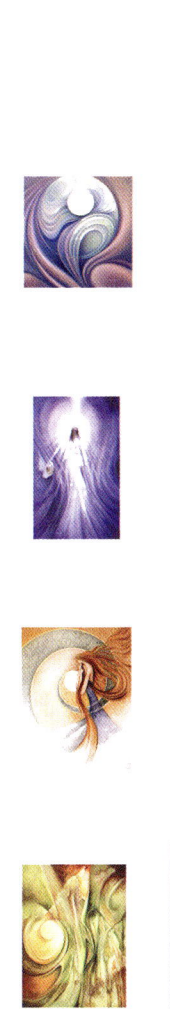

THE PEARL
2000

Oil on Canvas   30" x 30"

PAGE 95

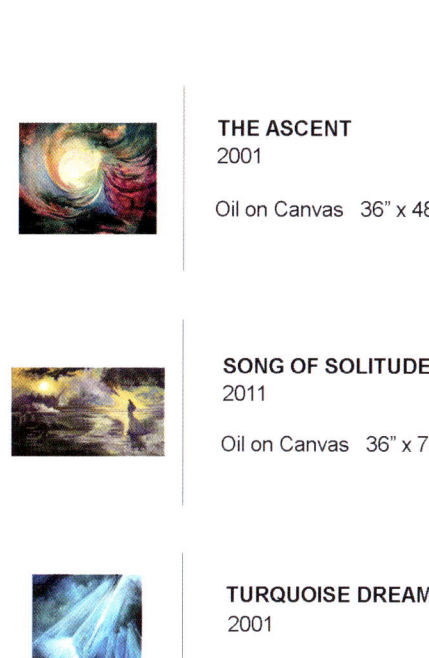

THE ASCENT
2001

Oil on Canvas   36" x 48"

PAGE 97

ASCENT TO LOVE
2004

Oil on Canvas   32" x 48"

PAGE 98

SONG OF SOLITUDE
2011

Oil on Canvas   36" x 72"

PAGE 101

ANTICIPATION
2000

Oil on Canvas   24" x 30"

PAGE 103

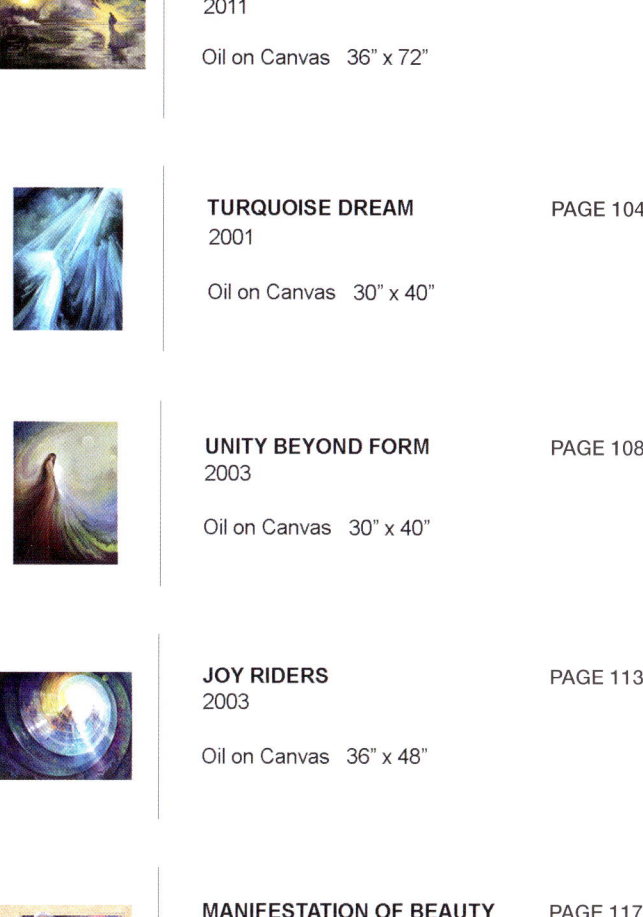

TURQUOISE DREAM
2001

Oil on Canvas   30" x 40"

PAGE 104

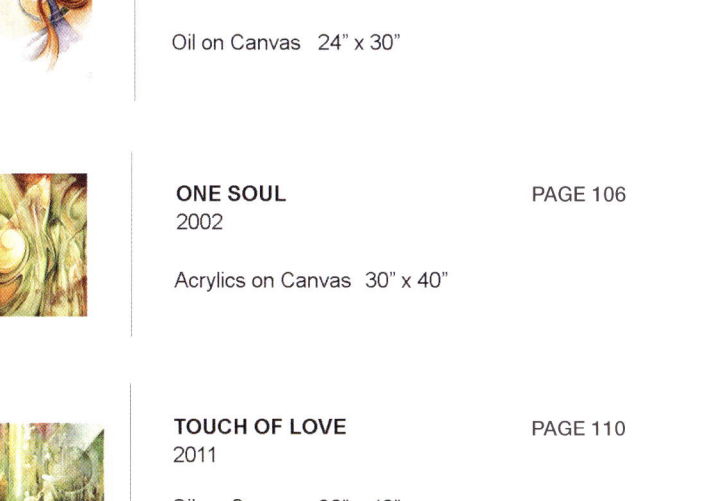

ONE SOUL
2002

Acrylics on Canvas   30" x 40"

PAGE 106

UNITY BEYOND FORM
2003

Oil on Canvas   30" x 40"

PAGE 108

TOUCH OF LOVE
2011

Oil on Canvas   30" x 40"

PAGE 110

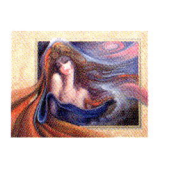

JOY RIDERS
2003

Oil on Canvas   36" x 48"

PAGE 113

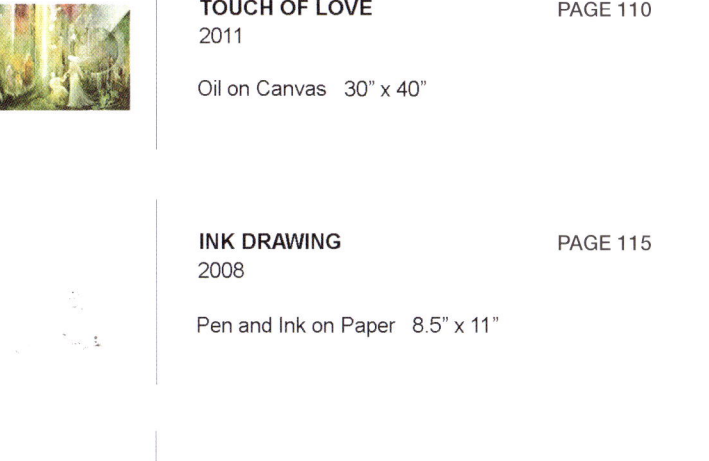

INK DRAWING
2008

Pen and Ink on Paper   8.5" x 11"

PAGE 115

MANIFESTATION OF BEAUTY
1996

Oil on Canvas   30" x 40"

PAGE 117

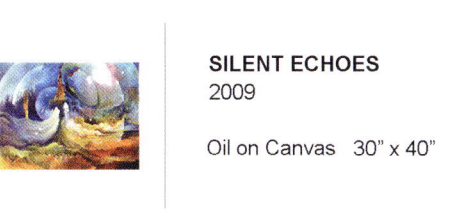

SILENT ECHOES
2009

Oil on Canvas   30" x 40"

PAGE 119

JOURNEY OF LOVE
2011

Oil on Canvas   36" x 72"

PAGE 121

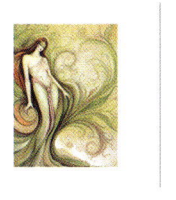

MATURITY
1998

Oil on Canvas   36" x 48"

PAGE 122

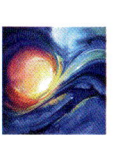

KINGDOM OF THE SUN
2001

Oil on Canvas   48" x 48"

PAGE 125

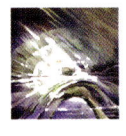
LOVE PREVAILS
2009

Acrylics on Canvas   36" x 36"

PAGE 126

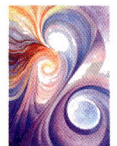
INVOKING THE MUSE
2002

Oil on Canvas   30" x 40"

PAGE 129

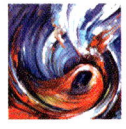
MYSTICAL ECSTASY
2004

Acrylics on Canvas   36" x 36"

PAGE 130

MYSTERY OF THE UNIVERSE
2001

Acrylics on Canvas   36" x 48"

PAGE 133

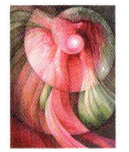
SKETCH NO. 486
2007

Water Color on Paper   5" x 5"

PAGE 134

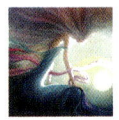
ECSTATIC DANCE
1997

Oil on Canvas   30" x 40"

PAGE 137

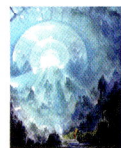
MEDITATION AT SUNRISE
2001

Oil on Canvas   32" x 32"

PAGE 138

MYSTERIOUS ENCOUNTER
2008

Oil on Canvas   30" x 40"

PAGE 140

For more information about the paintings, please visit:

Rassouli.com

About the Authors

Rassouli is an artist who paints from his heart—pouring out without limitation.

"I love to paint and this feeling is expressed through the poetry and the art. I recognize that we are all here to be the best we can and to always stay in a place of bewilderment. I don't see it as poetry. I feel it. I experience it where reading stops and words disappear."

Rassouli describes himself as a "madman" who is a drunk, an ogler and a libertine. His drunkenness comes from within to make him create, because he breaks away from his mind and rational thinking. As an ogler, he looks at places others don't see. This allows him to see through the veil, to see the heart of everything and the pearl that is hidden inside the shell. As a libertine, he is both an iconoclast and a freethinker who is constantly breaking the rules and creating new rules in his artwork.

As a poet, Richard is a creative listener with an inner knowing and the ability to see deep inside at things most people never see. His poetry reflects his innocence and benevolent nature in a harmony of creative celebration. And the harmony is more important than the poetry or art on its own. It is a blending, a creation of something new.

"I have spent a lifetime writing—creating a sculpture of words and feelings. Poetry is like a brush in my hand. It opens my heart to the river of love, to the flow, which allows me to express a deeper message that is not me, a message that comes through and touches the heart and the soul with feelings married in form and space, beyond the limits of time."

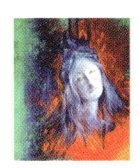

IN-LOVE   PAGE 62
2001

Acrylics on Canvas   18" x 24"

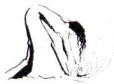

PICKING A ROSE   PAGE 64
2005

Ink on Cardboard   10" x 10"

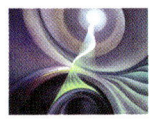

THEOPHANIC LIGHT   PAGE 67
1998

Oil on Canvas   30" x 40"

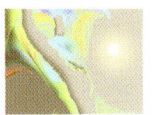

AWAKENING   PAGE 68
2011

Mixed Media on Canvas   30" x 40"

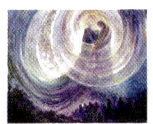

EMBRACE   PAGE 71
2006

Oil on Canvas   24" x 30"

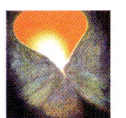

PSYCHE   PAGE 72
1998

Oil on Canvas   40" x 40"

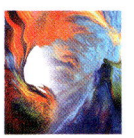

LOVE SONG   PAGE 75
1999

Acrylics on Canvas   36" x 36"

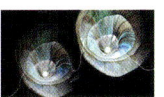

LOVE CONNECTS HEARTS   PAGE 76
2011

Mixed Media on Canvas   36" x 72"

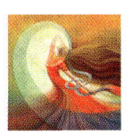

BORN FREE   PAGE 79
1999

Oil on Canvas   40" x 40"

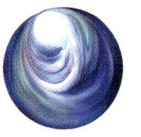

LUSTER OF JOY   PAGE 80
2000

Oil on Canvas   48" Radius

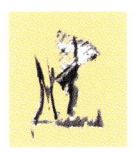

SKETCH No. 523   PAGE 83
2003

Watercolor on Colored Paper   6" x 8

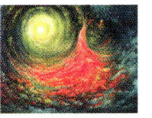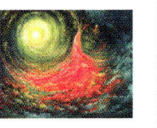

ENCHANTED GARDEN   PAGE 84
2001

Oil on Canvas   36" x 48"

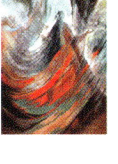

PRAYER FOR THE EARTH   PAGE 86
2001

Oil on Canvas   30" x 40"

COSMIC MOTHER   PAGE 89
1995

Acrylics on Canvas   36" x 48"

PENCIL DRAWING   PAGE 90
1996

Pencil on Paper   10" x 12"

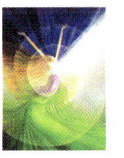

JOY OF FREEDOM   PAGE 92
2000

Oil on Canvas   30" x 40"

	SCHEHERAZADE 1995 Oil on Canvas 36" x 36"	PAGE 31		**TEMPLE OF LOVE** 2011 Oil on Canvas 36" x 36"	PAGE 33
	THE COMMANDER 1999 Oil on Canvas 24" x 30"	PAGE 34		**BREATH OF DAWN** 2008 Acrylics on Canvas 48" x 60"	PAGE 37
	FIRE OF LOVE 2001 Oil on Canvas 32" x 32"	PAGE 39		**COMING HOME** 2002 Oil on Canvas 22" x 34"	PAGE 41
	NEW DAWN 2000 Oil on Canvas 24" x 30"	PAGE 42		**SURRENDERING** 1998 Oil on Canvas 30" x 36"	PAGE 45
	GREETING THE DAWN 2003 Oil on Canvas 36" x 72"	PAGE 47		**CONCEPTION** 1994 Oil on Canvas 24" x 36"	PAGE 49
	LIGHT OF THE MYSTIC 1998 Oil on Canvas 30" x 40"	PAGE 51		**SERENITY** 2004 Oil on Canvas 30" x 30"	PAGE 53
	REVELATION 2001 Oil on Canvas 32" x 40"	PAGE 55		**PATH OF THE WAYFARER** 2007 Oil on Canvas 24" x 36"	PAGE 56
	QUEST FOR LIGHT 1994 Oil on Canvas 24" x 36"	PAGE 58		**SHORES OF HEAVEN** 2006 Oil on Canvas 36" x 48"	PAGE 60

Paintings Index

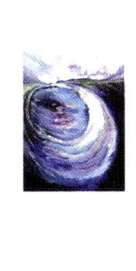
UNFOLDING
1996

Oil on Canvas 36" x 36"

PAGE 3

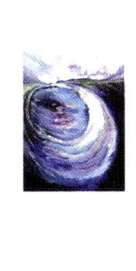
DREAM PASSAGE
2010

Oil on Canvas 30" x 40"

PAGE 4

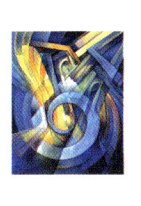
MESSIAH
2002

Acrylics on Canvas 42" x 62"

PAGE 6

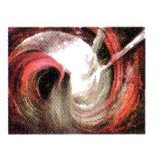
SKETCH NO. 864
2010

Black Ink on Cardboard 4" x 6"

PAGE 9

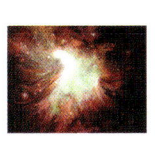
JOY OF UNION
2007

Oil on Canvas 30" x 40"

PAGE 11

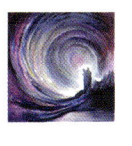
KINDRED SPIRIT
2001

Acrylics on Canvas 48" x 72"

PAGE 13

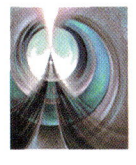
SYMPHONIC DANCE
1993

Oil on Canvas 40" x 50"

PAGE 15

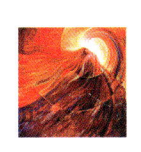
ENRAPT
2011

Oil on Canvas 30" x 40"

PAGE 16

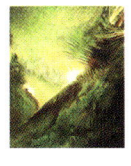
STAR DANCE
2001

Oil on Canvas 30" x 40"

PAGE 18

INTO DEEP SPACE
2009

Oil on Canvas 30" x 36"

PAGE 21

A MOMENT IN ETERNITY
2004

Oil on Canvas 30" x 40"

PAGE 23

SENSATION OF CRIMSON
2003

Acrylics on Canvas 30" x 30"

PAGE 25

EVOLUTION
2008

Oil on Canvas 30" x 40"

PAGE 27

SKETCH NO. 542
2010

Water Color on Paper 4" x 4"

PAGE 29

The sky ablaze with morning light
on silver wings of birds in flight

In gratitude a tear released
a knowingness embraced at peace

She speaks to those that gaze below
ancestral wings which call my soul
to open hearts
and soar above

In awe the winds
await this love

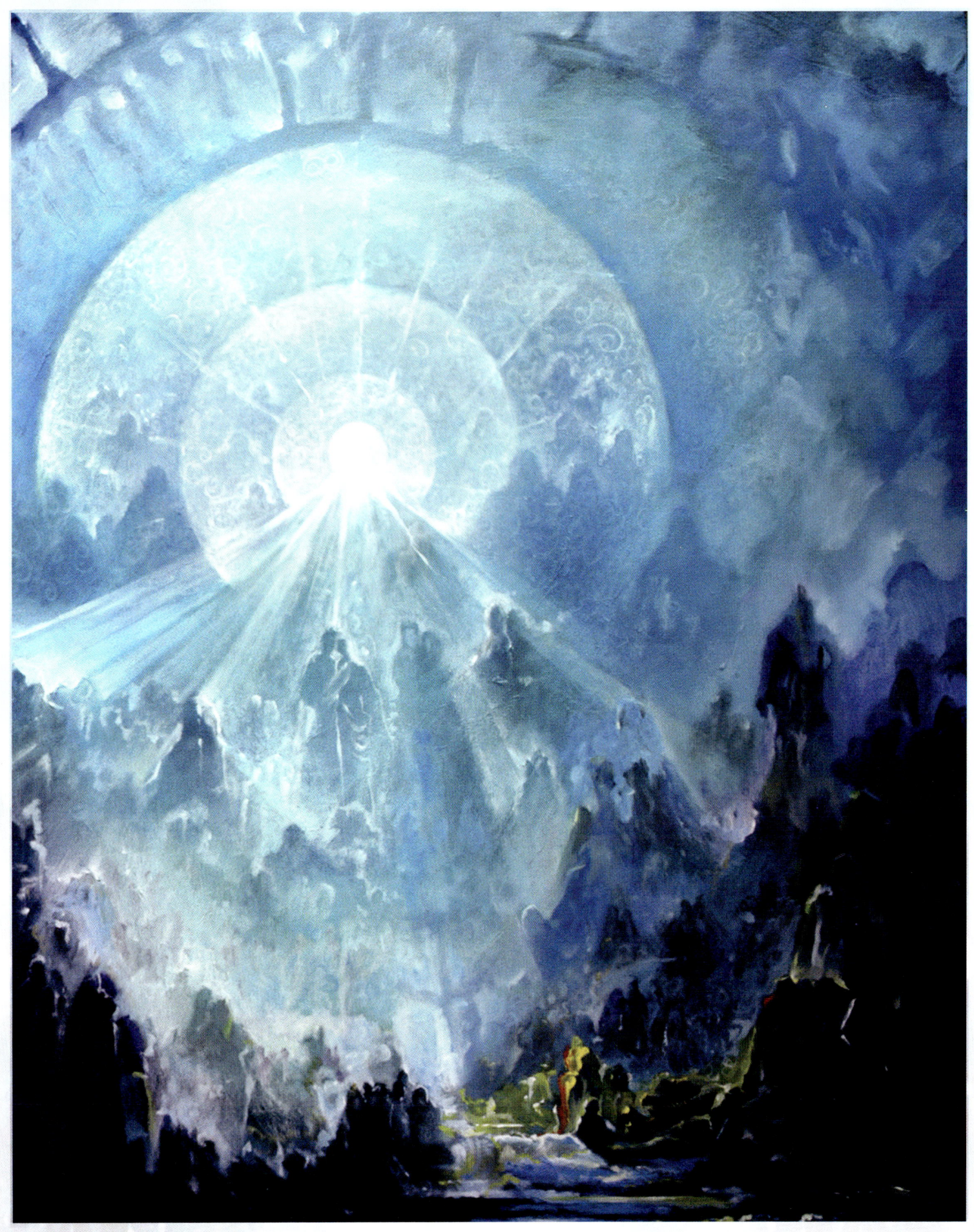

Patterns break through the night
in beams of light awakening
memories of walking on sand
moments, waves replace
waiting for another passerby

Reflections, time to look outward in
to find those hidden spaces
residing alone
waiting for a twin soul,
waiting for myself

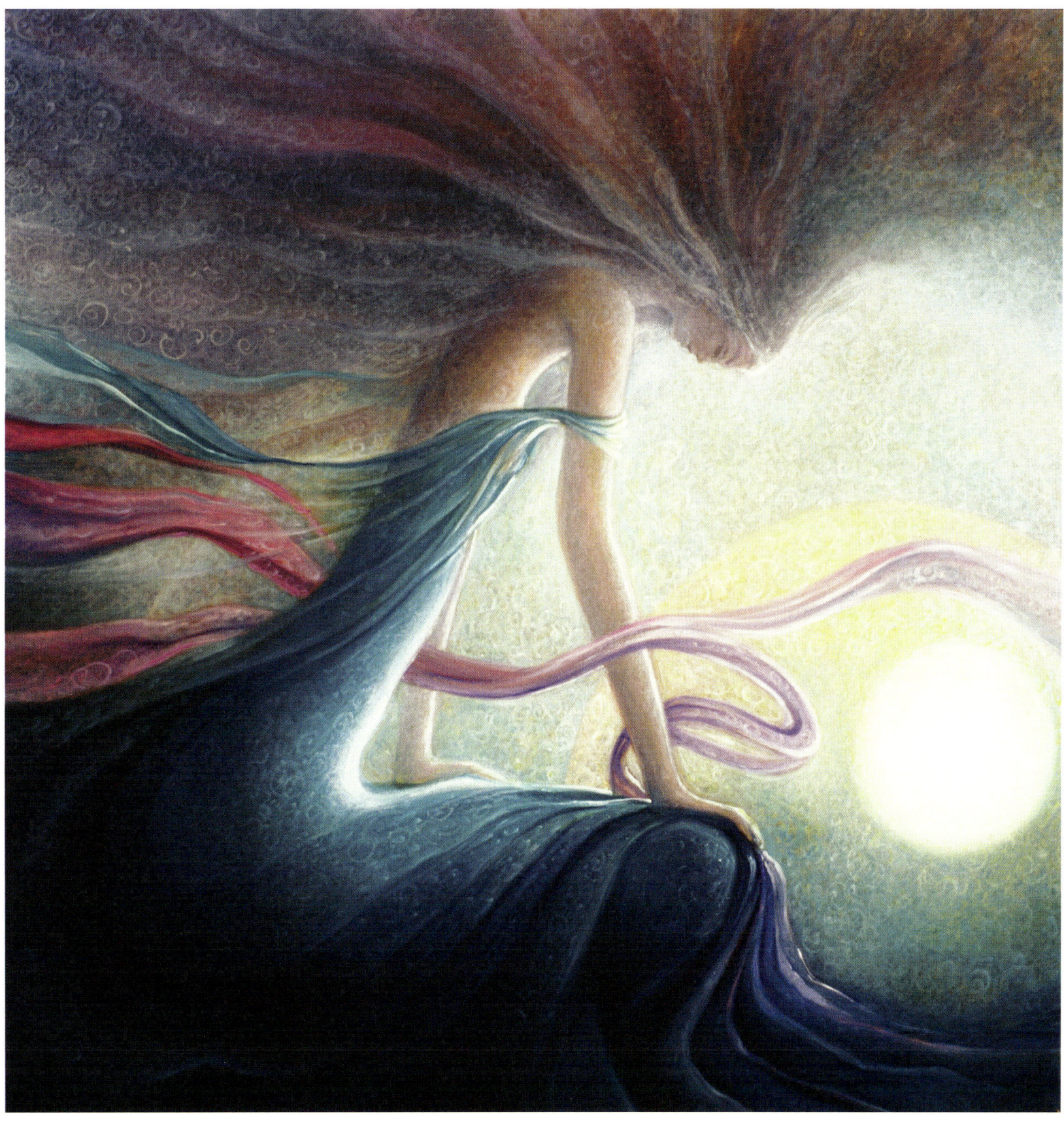

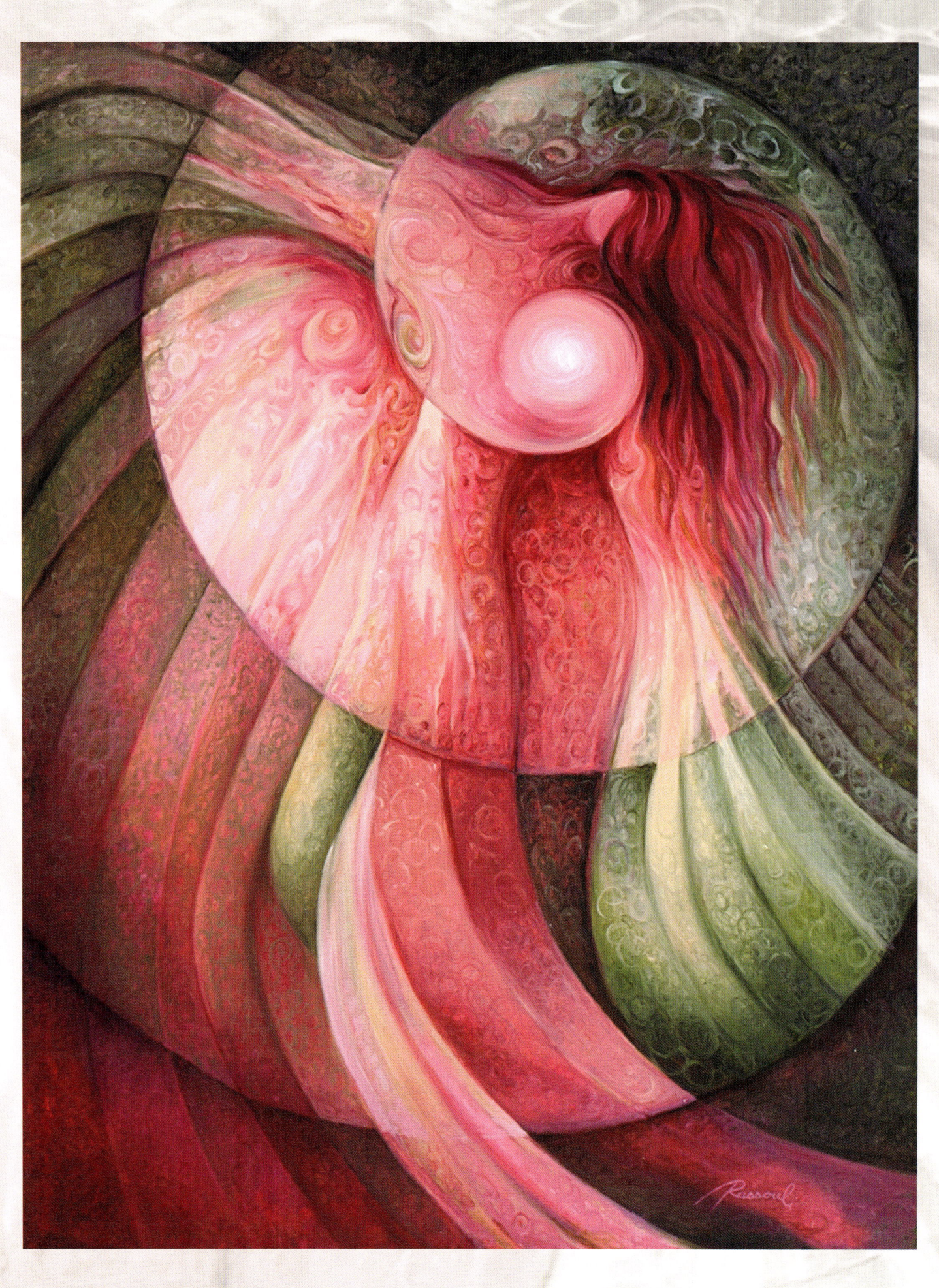

Longing

The dance to move beyond the feeling
    that draws me forward
        to a place born within
            that calls my soul
                to feel complete

*To love from afar
all we share are dreams
of what will unfold.*

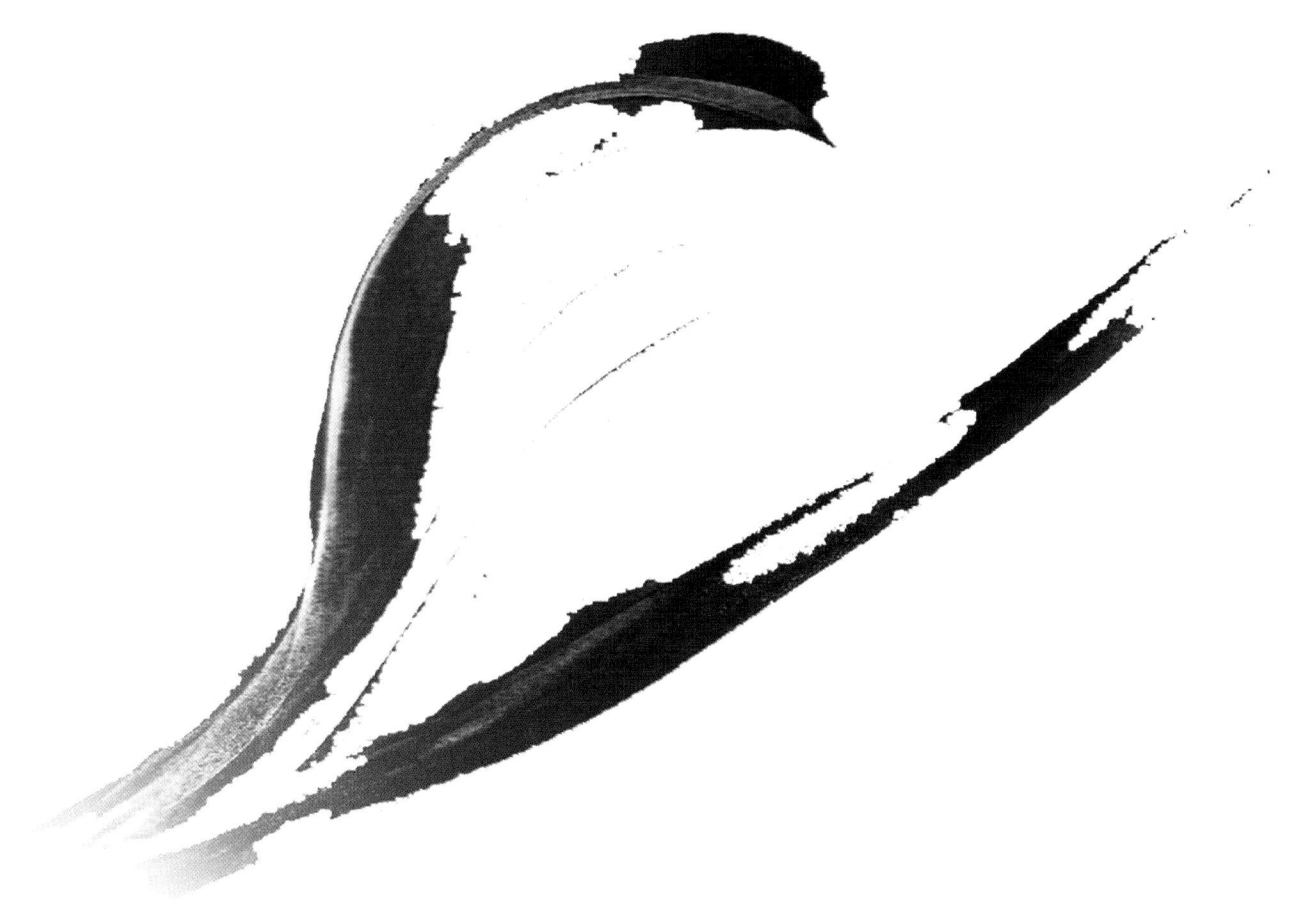

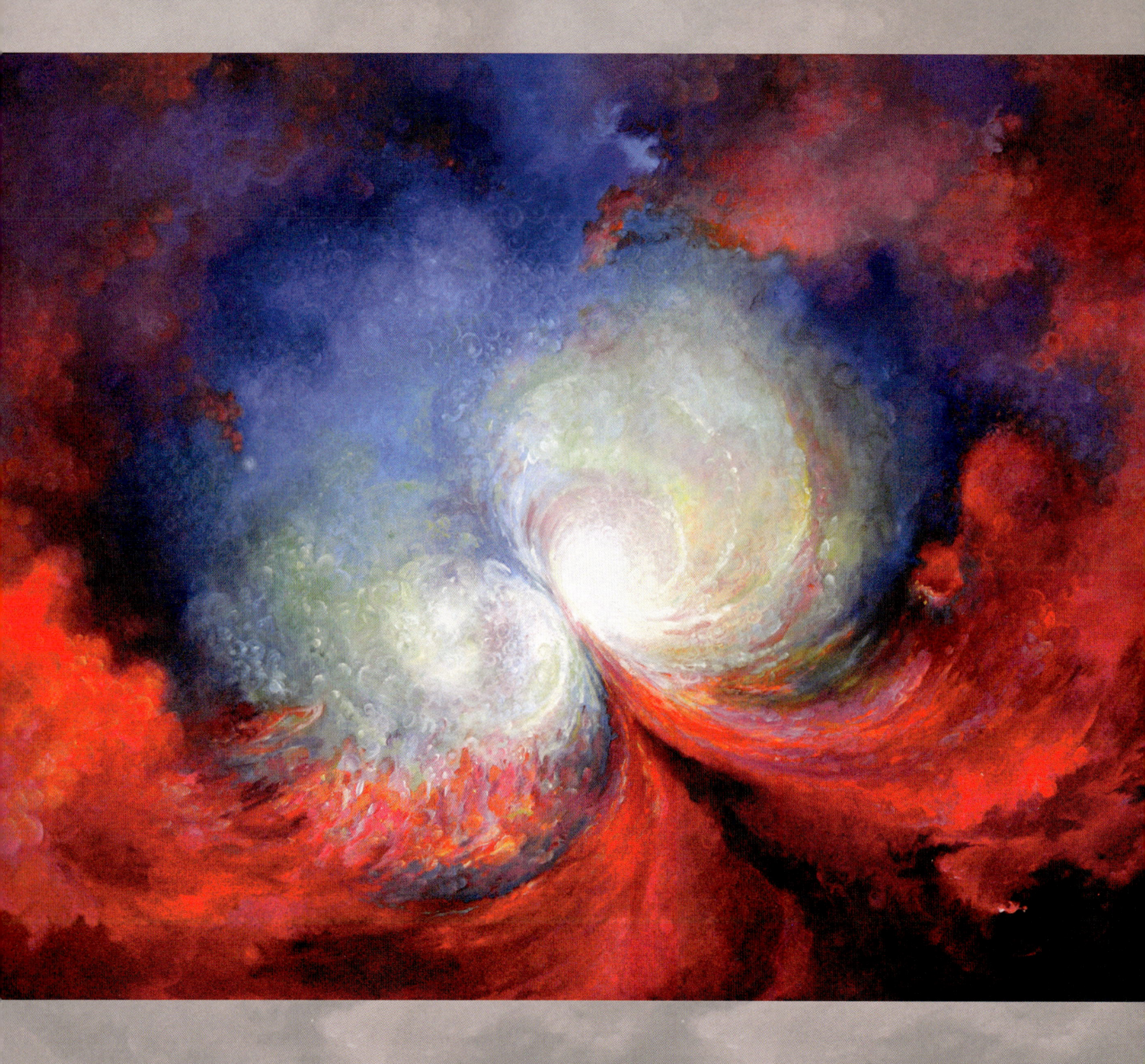

*Two energy patterns came together
a shared frequency in a field of possibilities
and there was* RESONANCE

Love

Love is a special closeness
that sings from the heart
that warms my days and nights
that feels good
that makes me smile
that makes me glad
to be,
alive

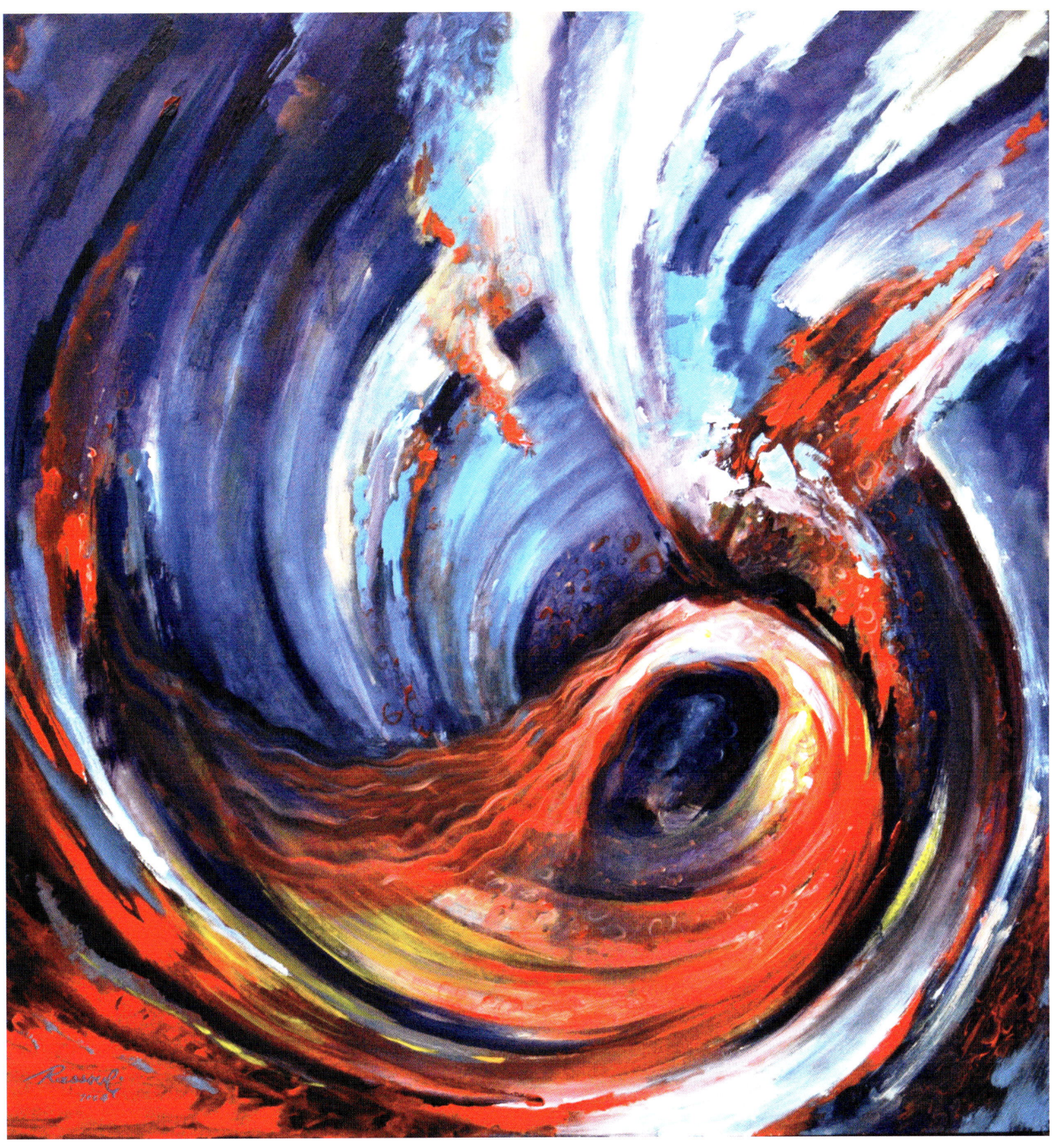

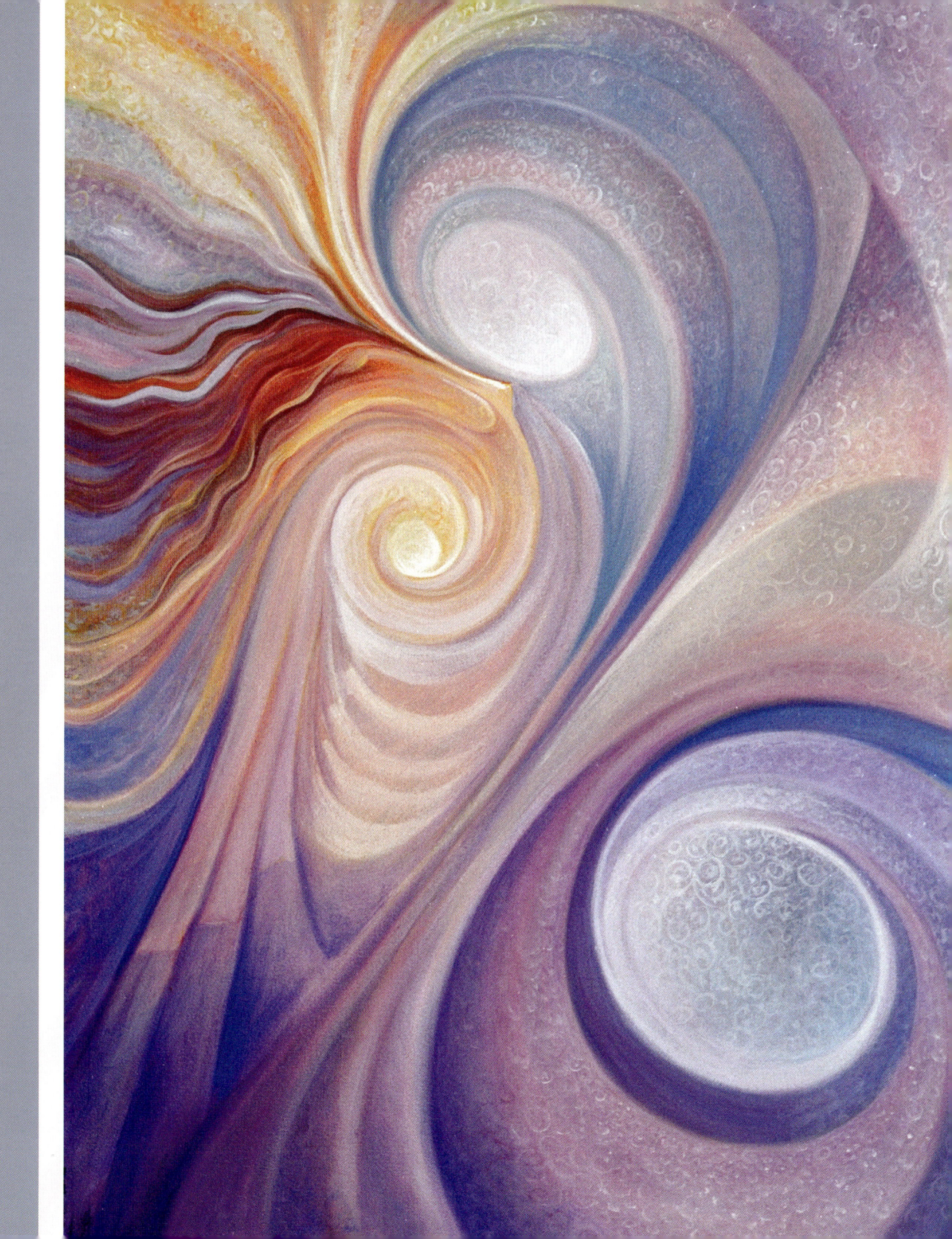

I dare not touch my heart's desire
that sings a melody so still
and lights within a yearning fire
a void that you alone can fill

I cannot say how my heart aches
nor speak the words as embers burn
such blessings come to those who wait
a love that asks naught in return

An open soul a risk must bear
to love without restrictions held
to reach another level rare
where two embraced as one are meld

To taste surrender's nectar sweet
by piercing through the veil so thin
and bathe in joy as tears release
a promised dance begins again

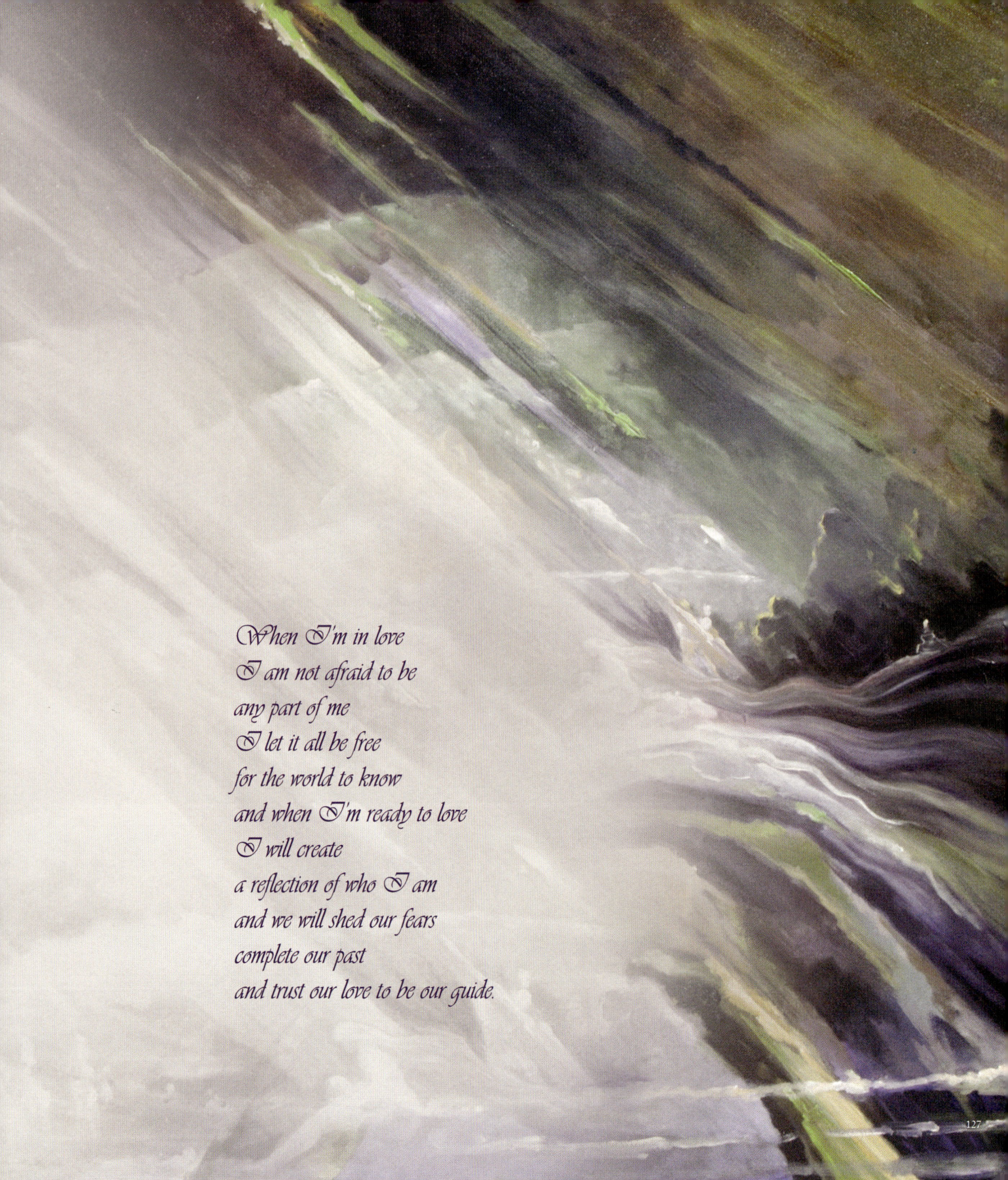

When I'm in love
I am not afraid to be
any part of me
I let it all be free
for the world to know
and when I'm ready to love
I will create
a reflection of who I am
and we will shed our fears
complete our past
and trust our love to be our guide.

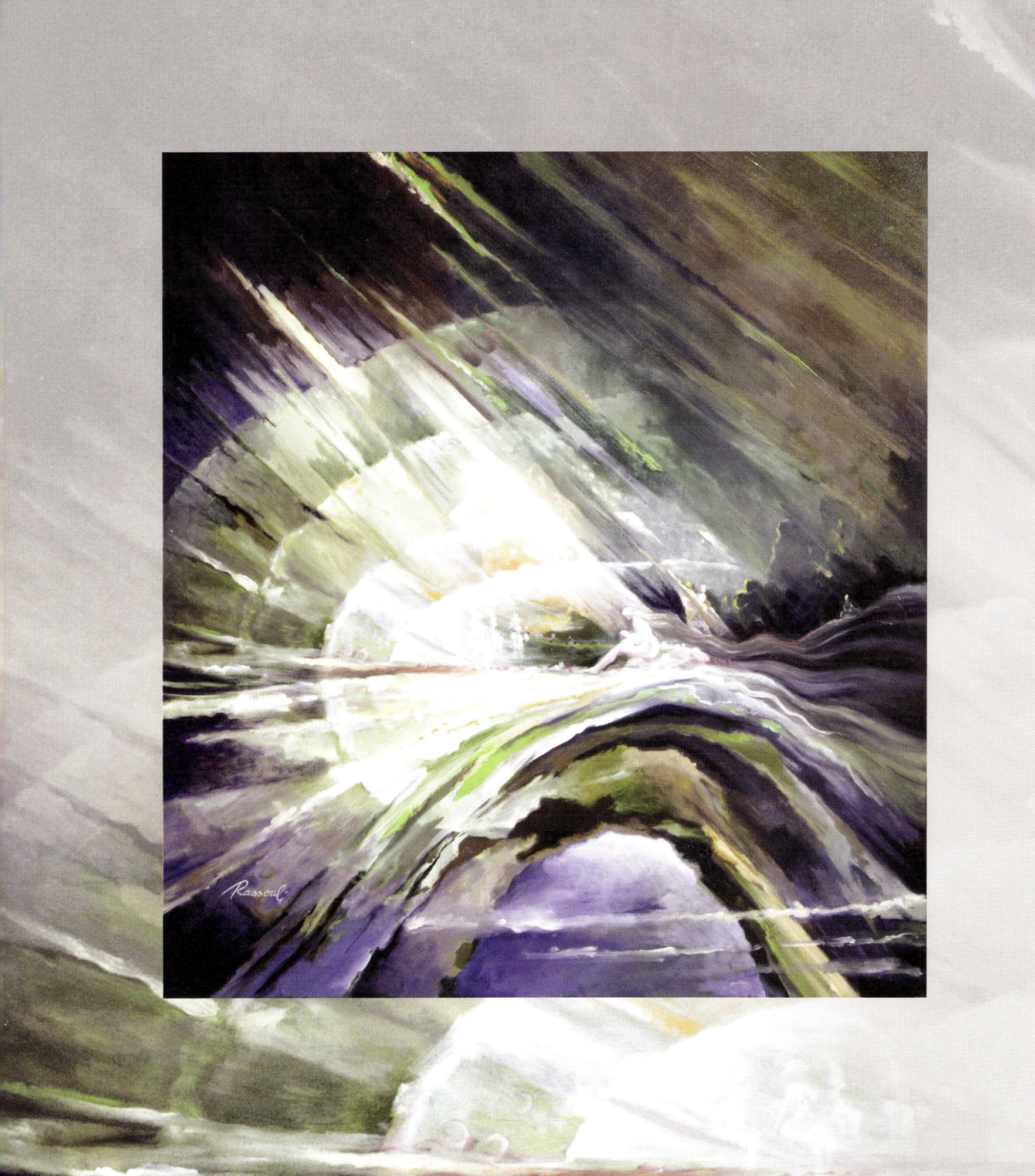

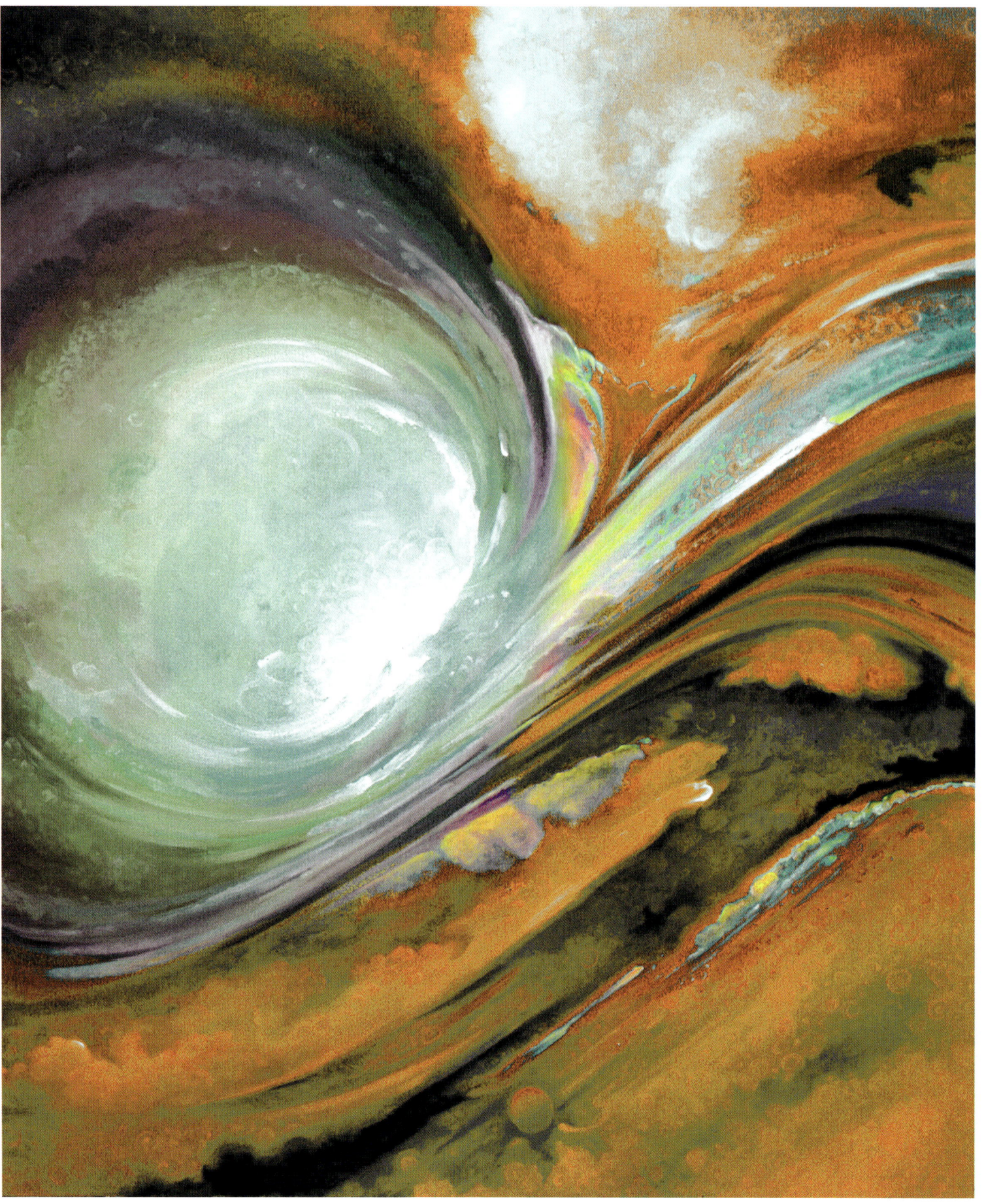

Our lives are measured in choices
we have made along the path we call living
each compass point, a possibility,
each step, an opportunity
seemingly random, each decision
moves us inexorably in a direction
both unknown and yet somehow familiar
for upon reflection, the strength we find
in choosing,
or the surrender of letting all unfold
leads us to the place we started from
when we made that first choice
to be here again

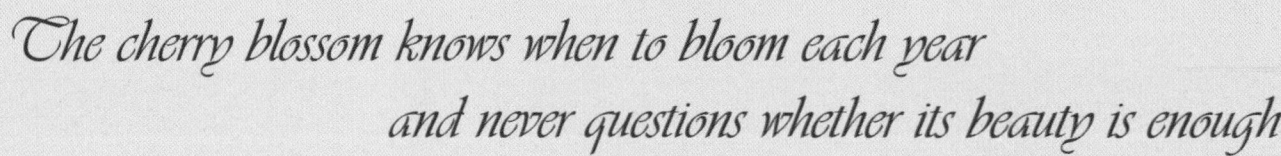

The cherry blossom knows when to bloom each year
                and never questions whether its beauty is enough

There is peace in knowing you always bloom well
                yet man spends a lifetime in wonder.

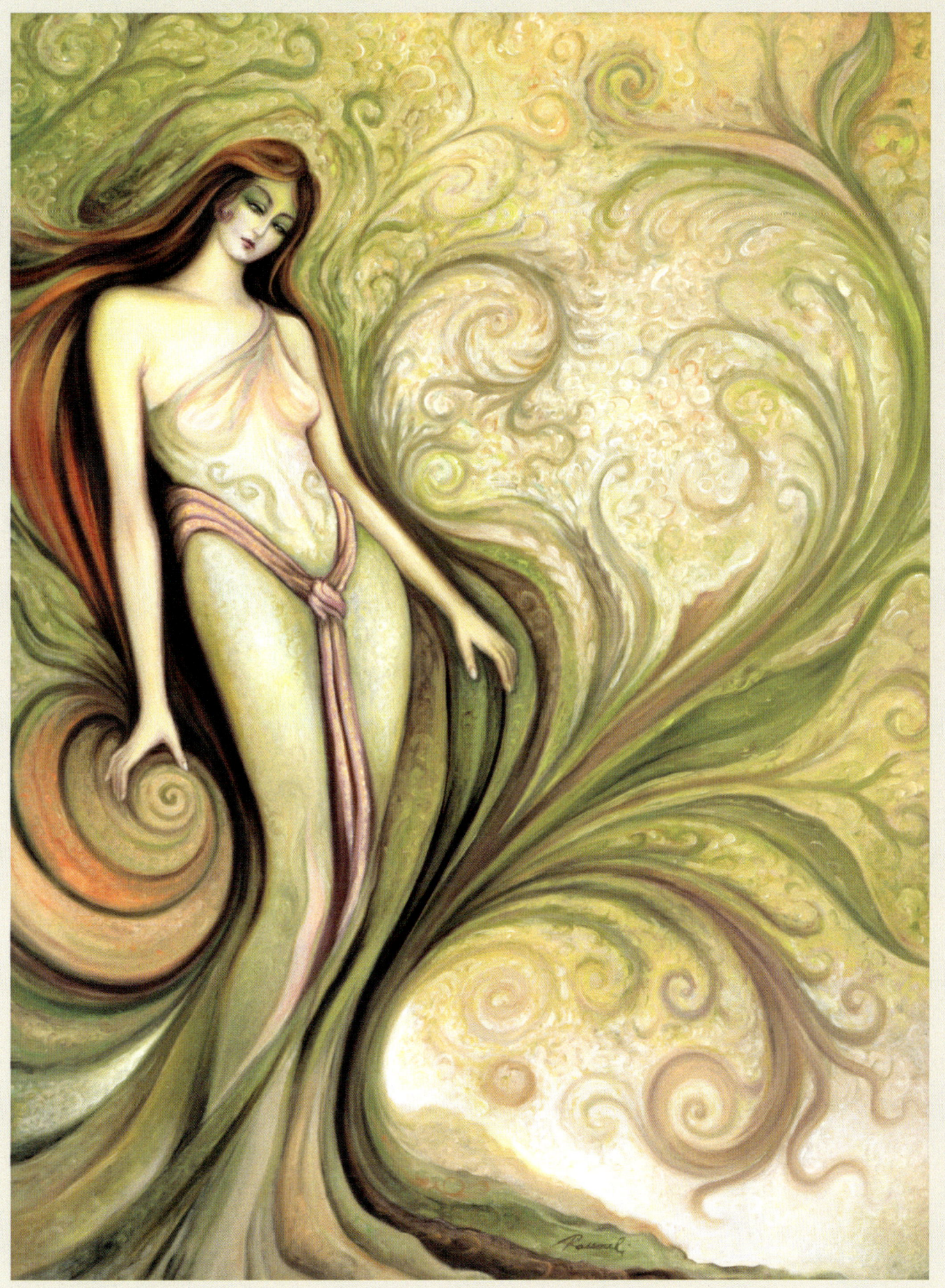

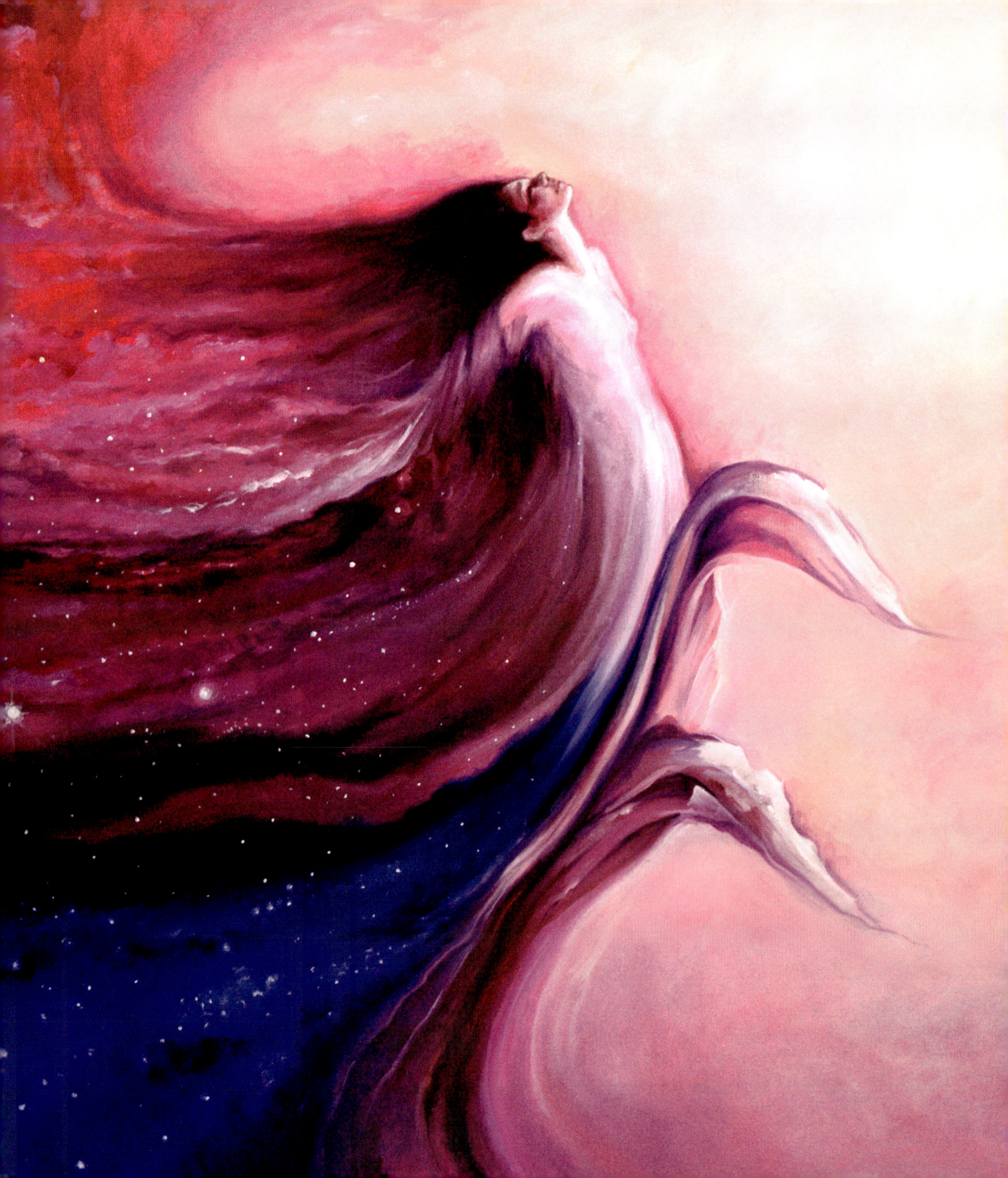

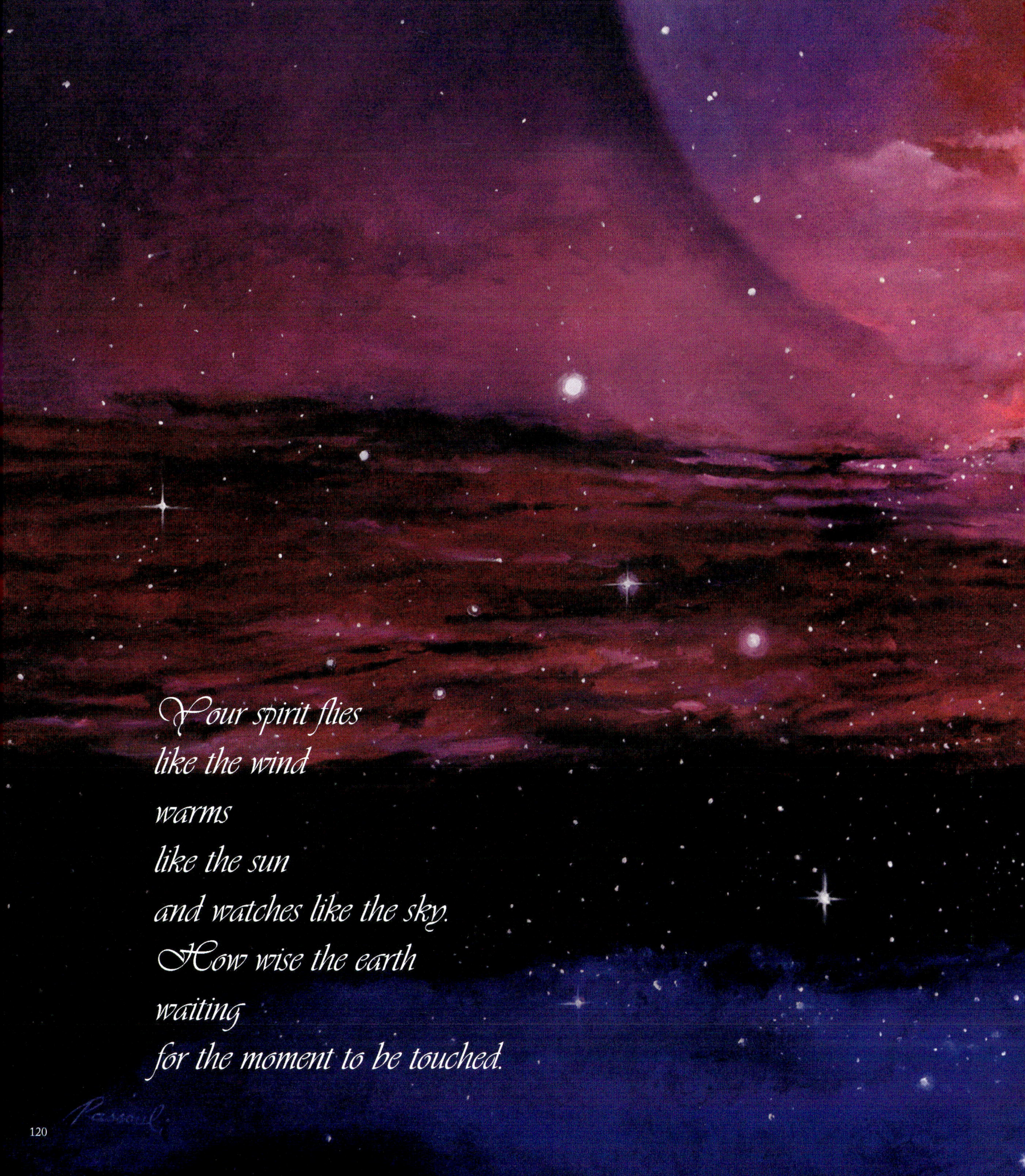

*Your spirit flies
like the wind
warms
like the sun
and watches like the sky.
How wise the earth
waiting
for the moment to be touched.*

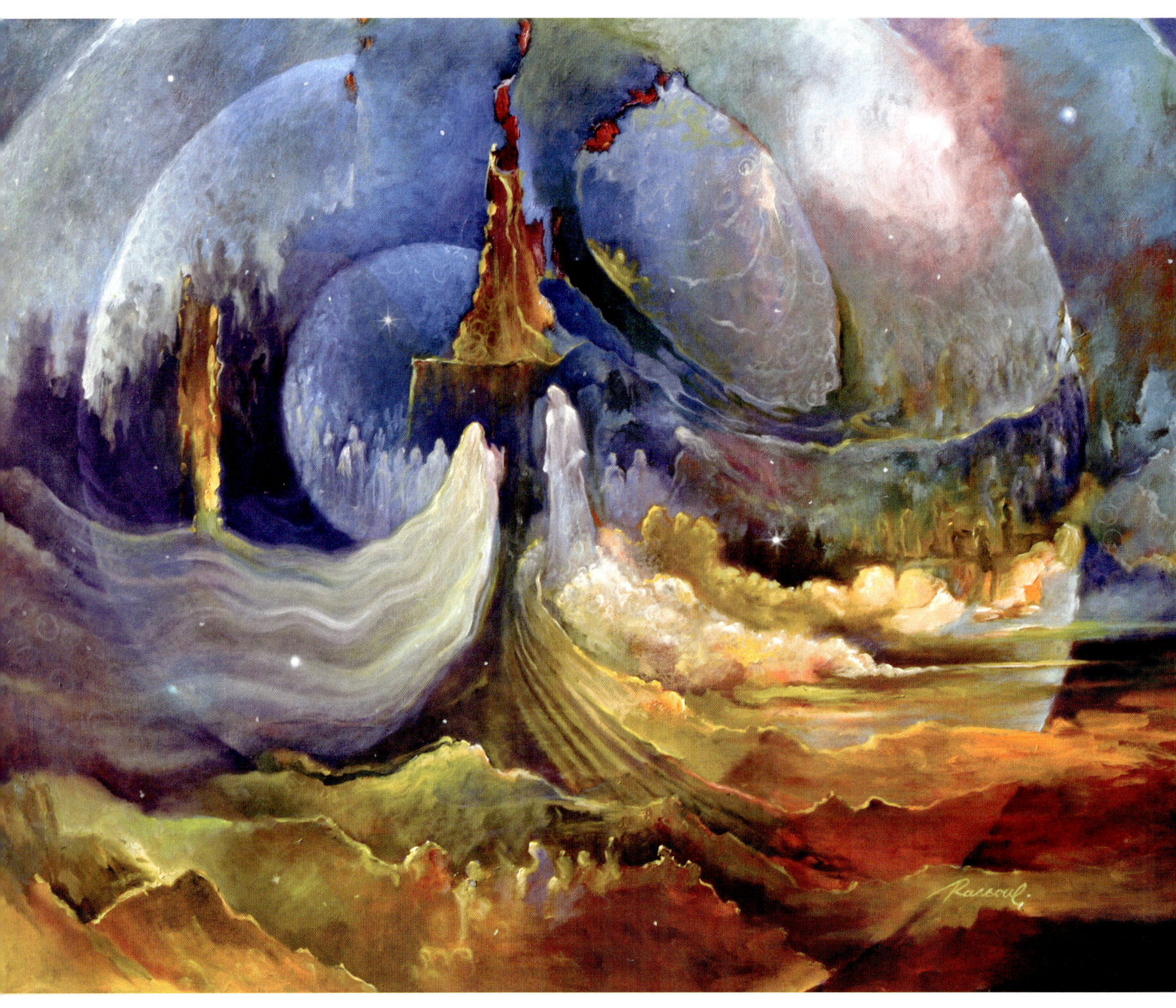

Love should be given as it is received.
On this day I grant you the love
of a thousand mountain streams
and the pleasure of a hundred bleats
from a new-born baby fawn
for I too cry for love
and like the fawn
I cry with the hunger of being alive
and on this day
I cry for the happiness of giving
and the softness of your gentle touch

It is moments like these when I smile
for the someone who
will always care.

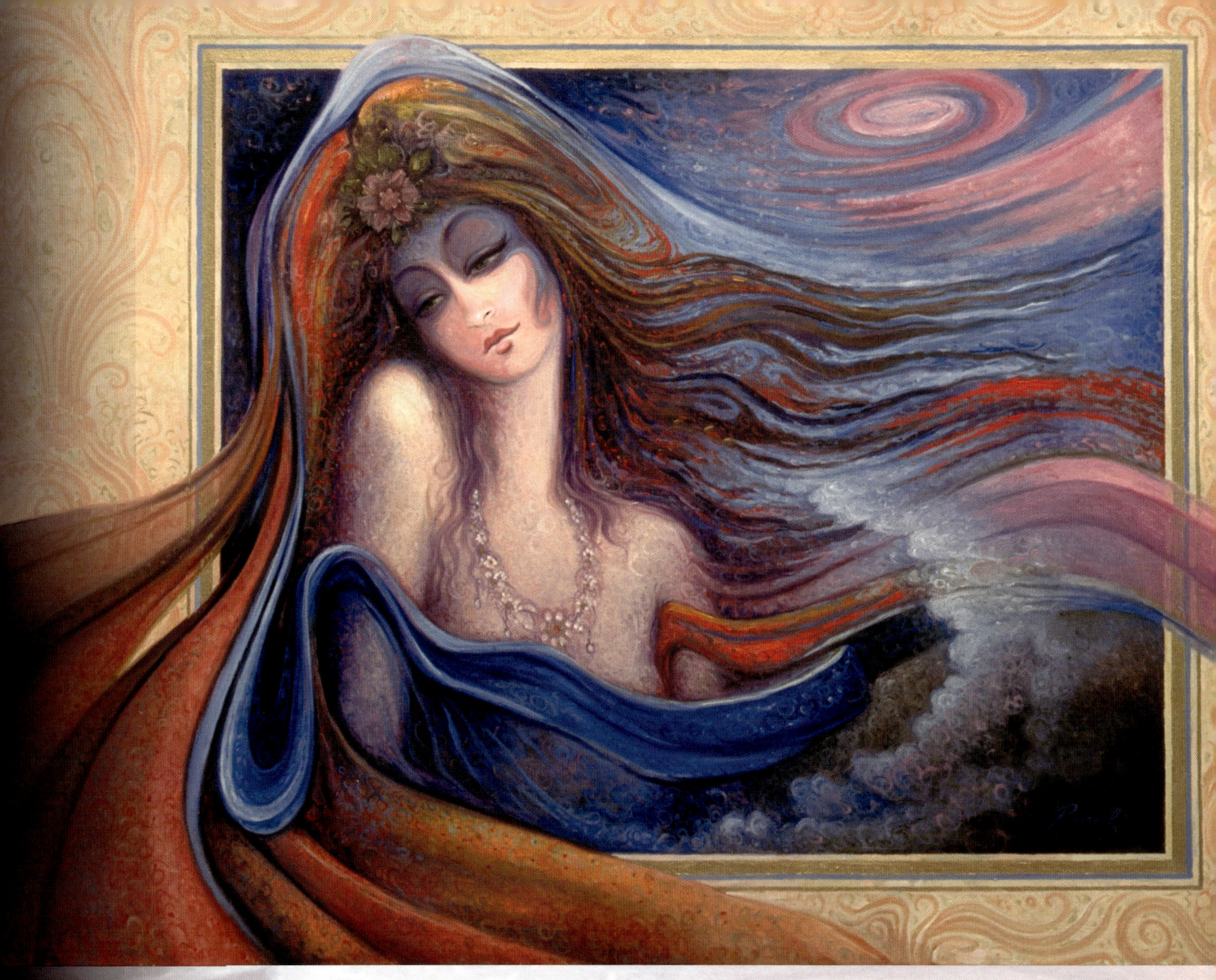

How many times
I've looked in your eyes
     and sailed away
          beyond my dreams
     to a sheltered thought on a quiet beach
  where the sand is soft as flour
You may never know this place
     and someday
          when you look in my eyes
               I will tell you.

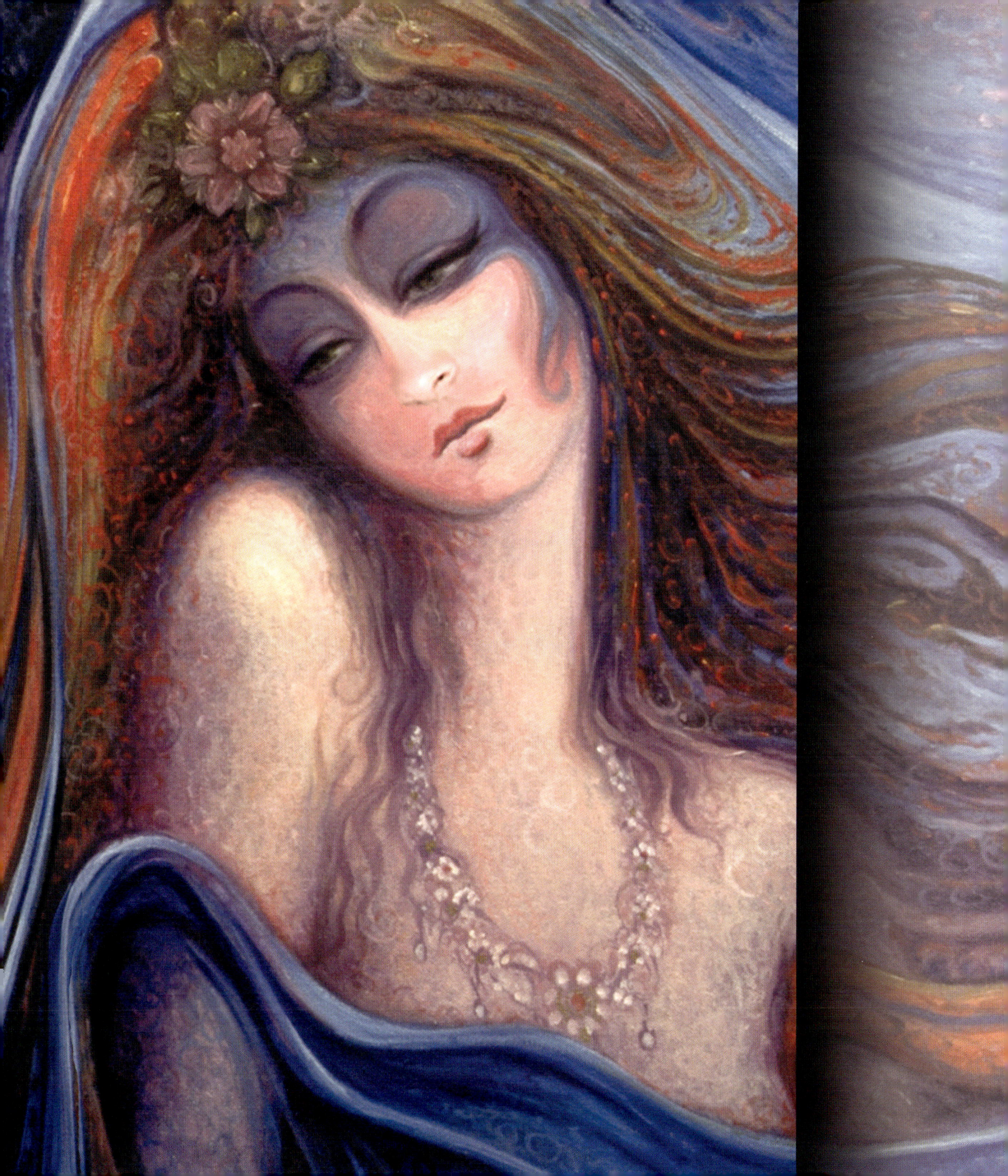

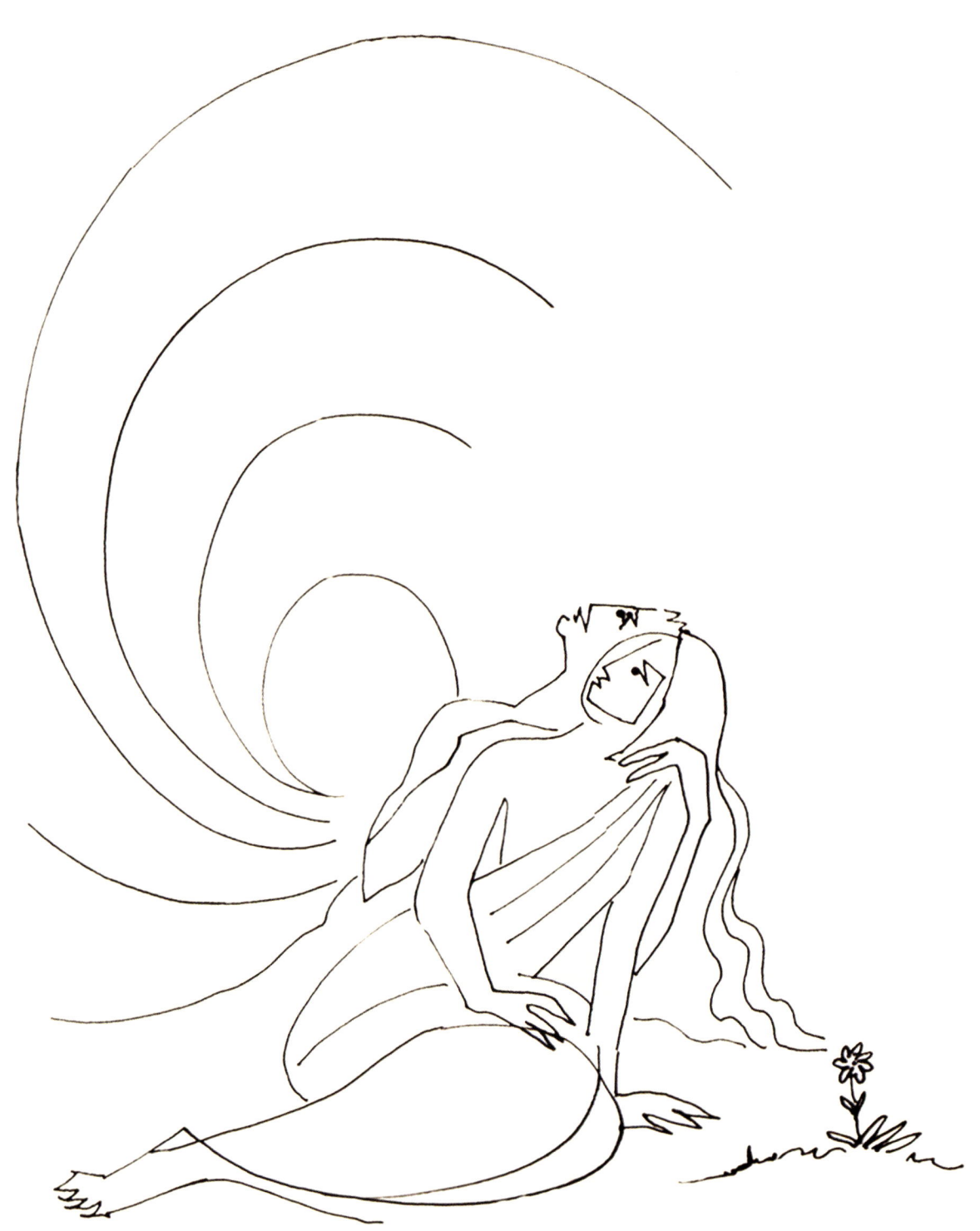

Love is a magic,
a word that holds the Universe together.
It is both an emotion
and something ephemeral that lives a fire's glow
or the pink light on the clouds
after the sun has set.

It is alive and yet, indefinable.
It causes the heart to beat rapidly,
feelings to show
and young people to write, sing, dance
and become totally immersed in its hold.

Love can beckon coyly,
or flaunt itself with wanton abandon.
Love can live and grow seemingly forever,
or vanish in a fleeting moment
when we least suspect.

And in the twilight of our years
reflecting on the life we have lived
it is love which colors
every turn and twist of our memory.

And when we pass this earthly plane
it will be love
that will light our soul
on its journey home.

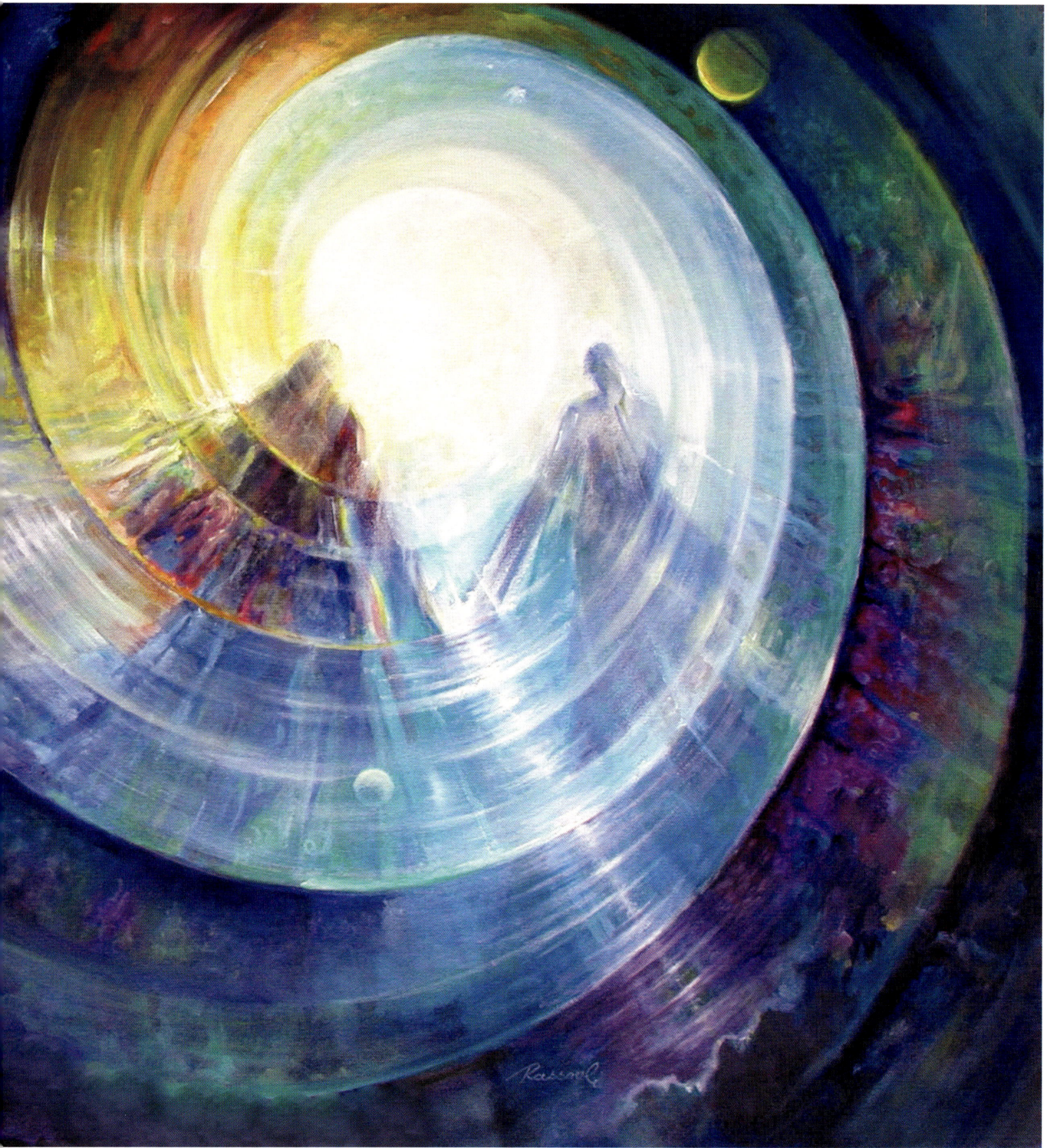

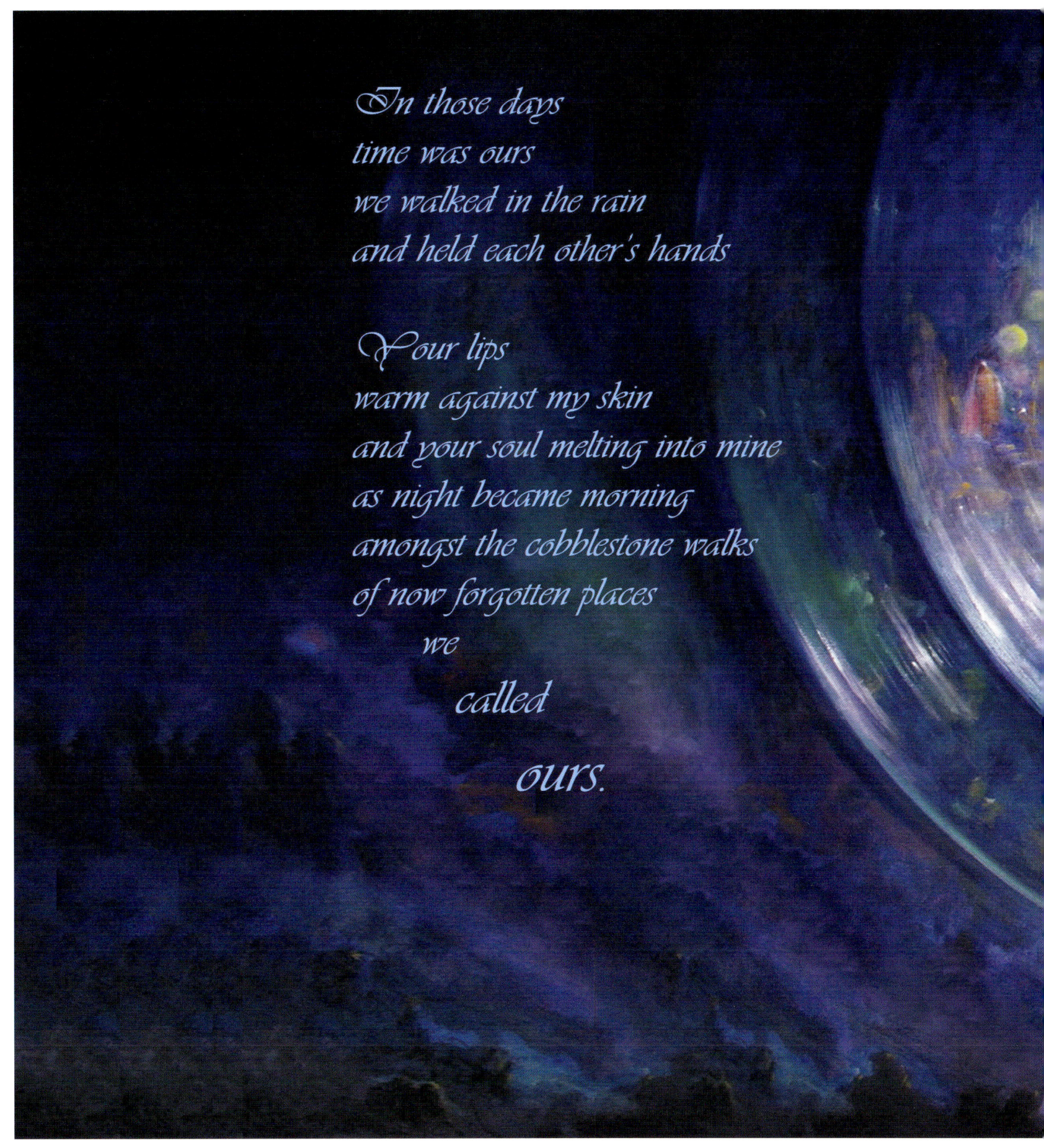

In those days
time was ours
we walked in the rain
and held each other's hands

Your lips
warm against my skin
and your soul melting into mine
as night became morning
amongst the cobblestone walks
of now forgotten places
    we

        called

            ours.

Shall we find
> some sunshine
> amongst the cloudy days
> a gentle touch
> that softly warms
> and leads us on our way
> > past stately oaks
> > and candles glow
> > and places we've never been
> > a friend to share the memories
> > before it's home again

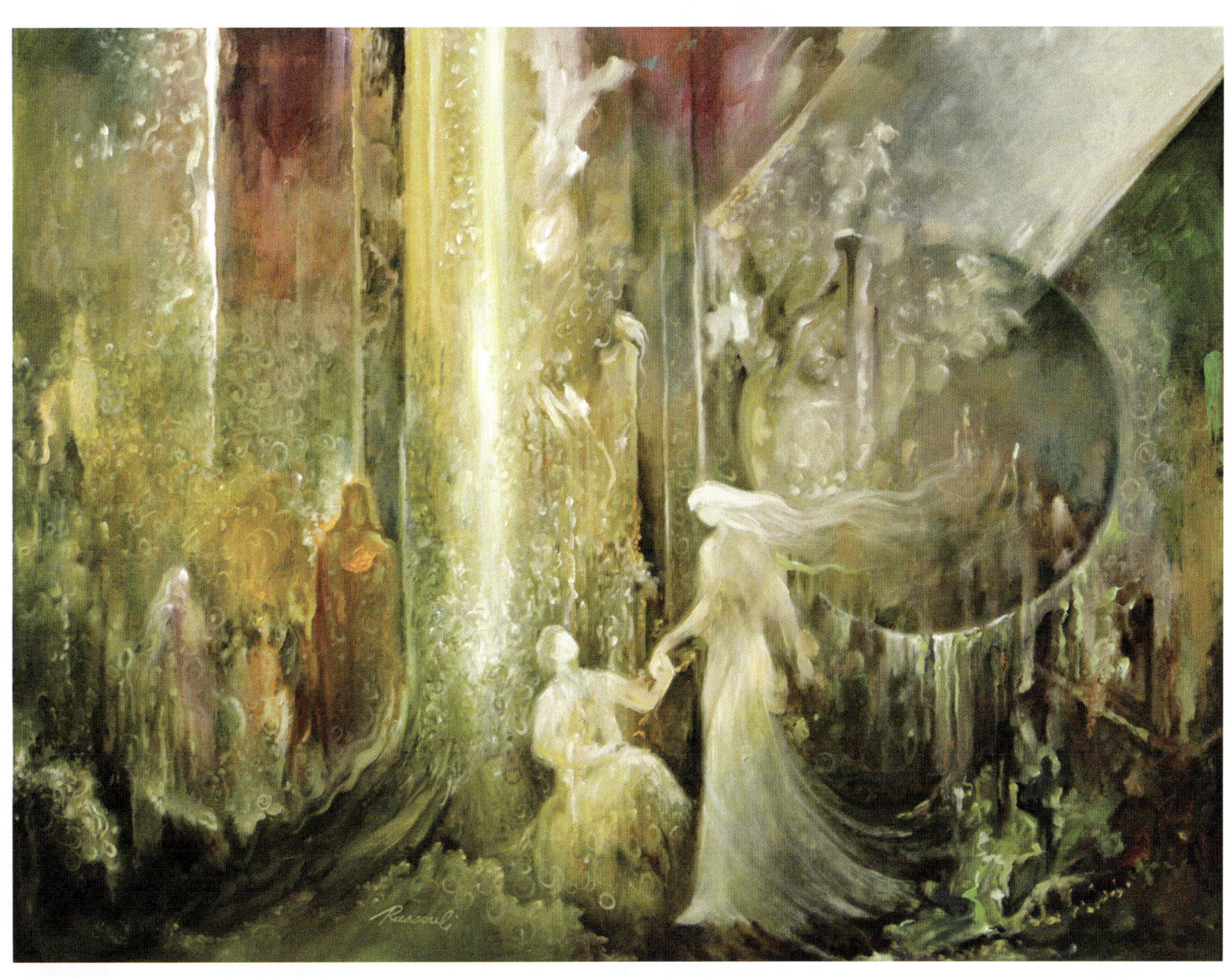

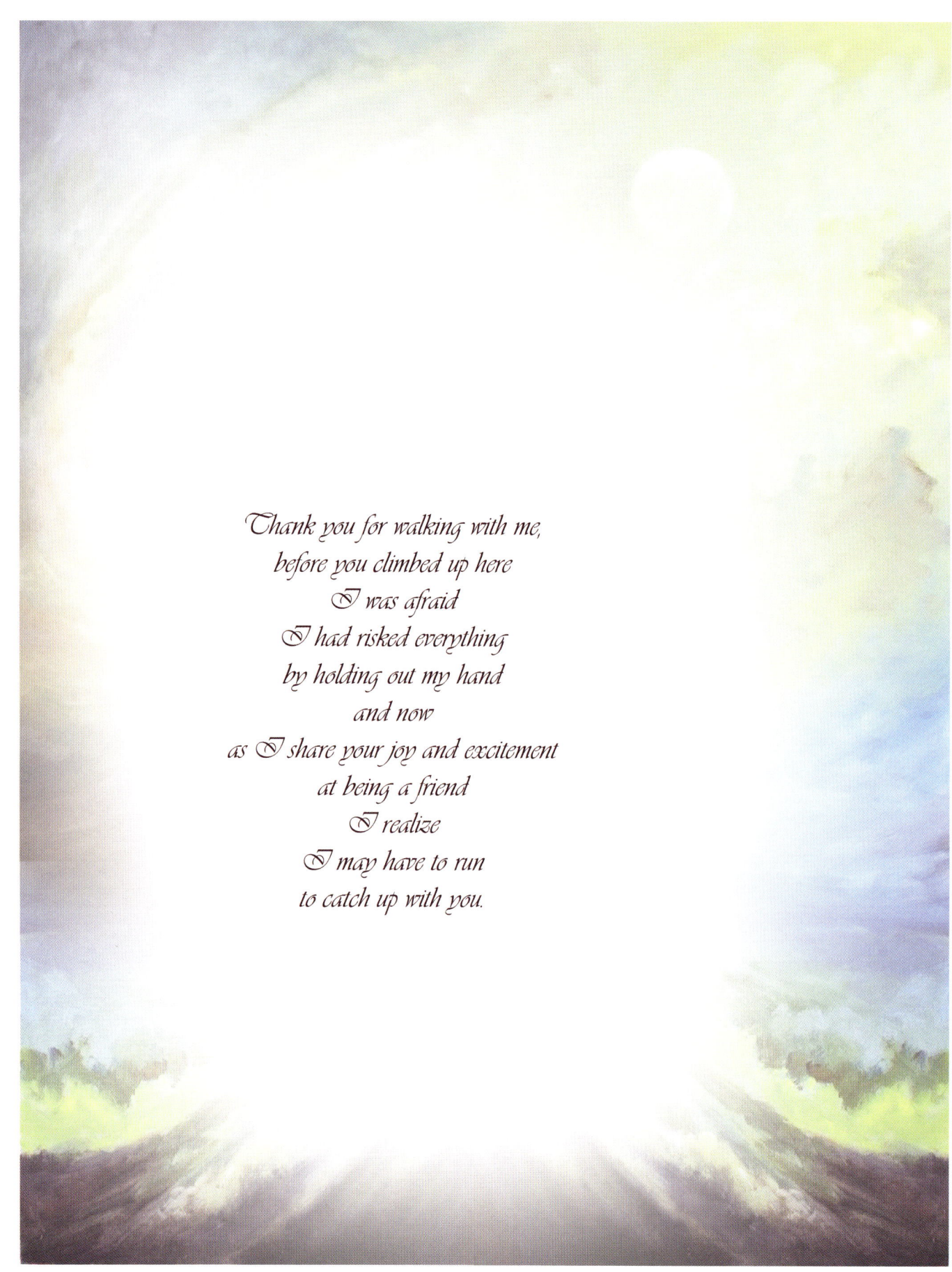

Thank you for walking with me,
before you climbed up here
I was afraid
I had risked everything
by holding out my hand
and now
as I share your joy and excitement
at being a friend
I realize
I may have to run
to catch up with you.

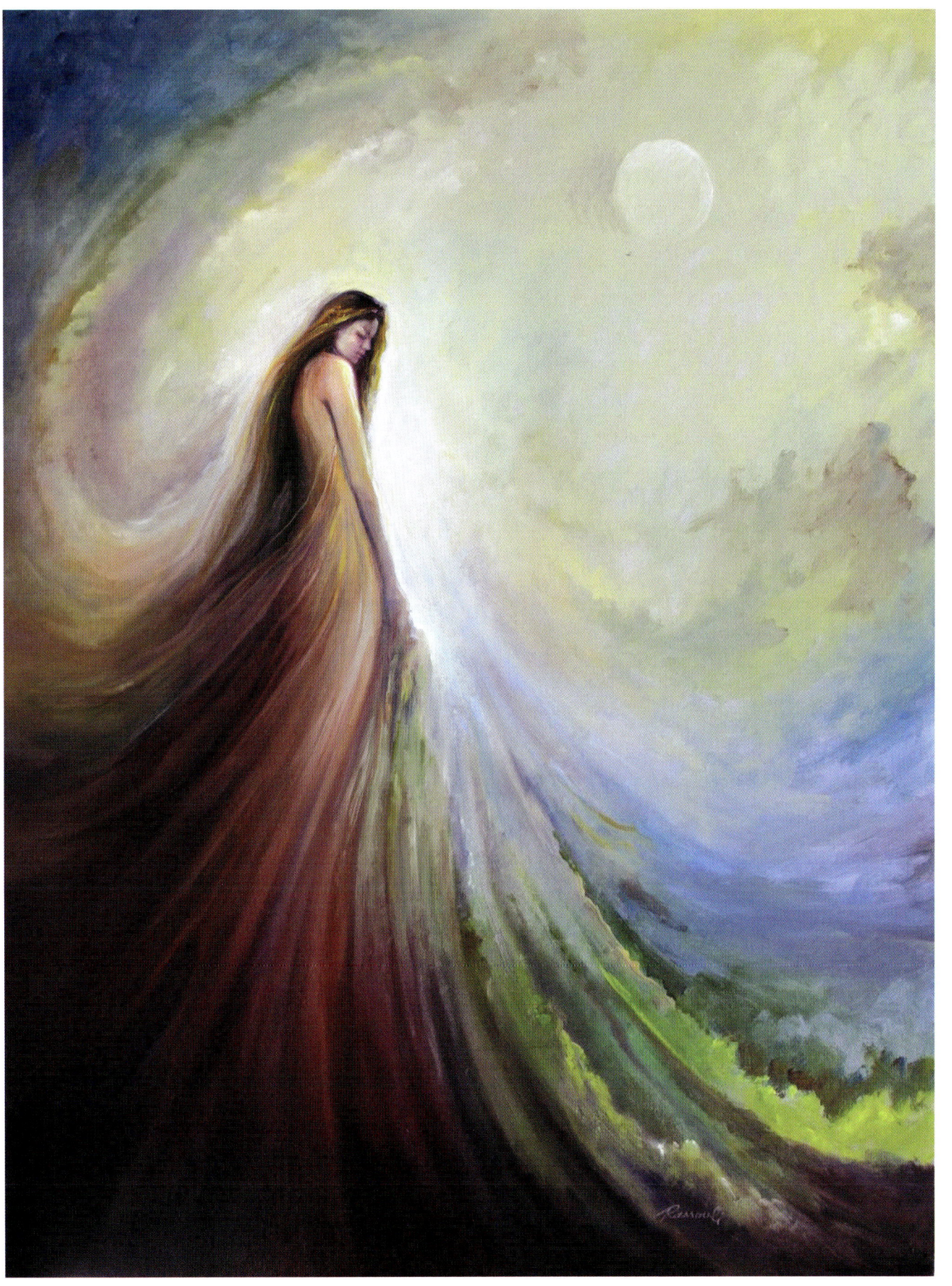

I measure time
in years
in memories
and good friends.

Thanks
for helping me
to see
I can count
the special ones
on my hand
that I can count
on you!

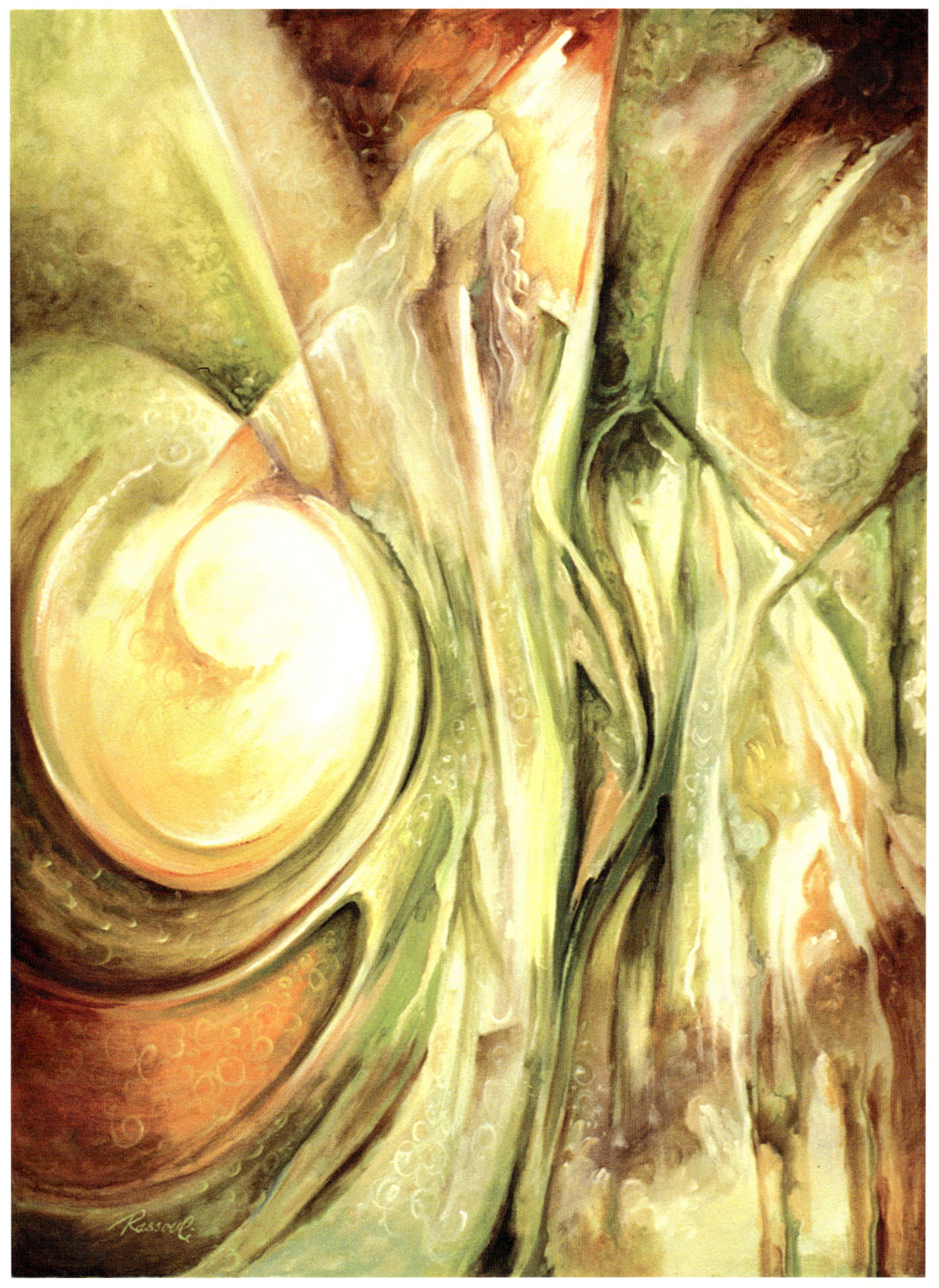

*Here's wishing you
some sunshine
the day after rain*

*Here's a hug
of understanding
when life
seems filled with pain*

*Here's knowing that emotion
like wind
blows many ways*

*and our course
will seem more certain
with the dawn
of each new day*

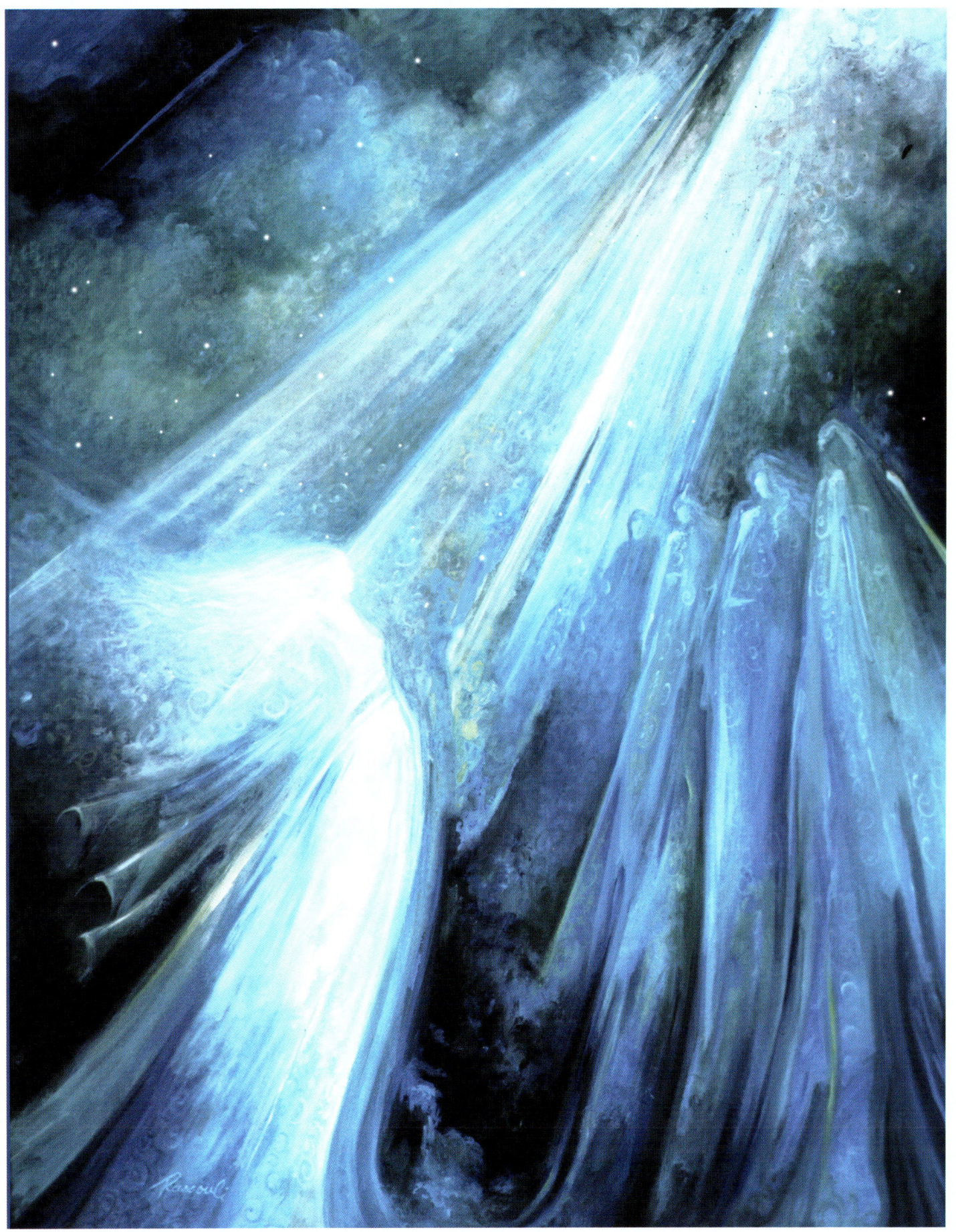

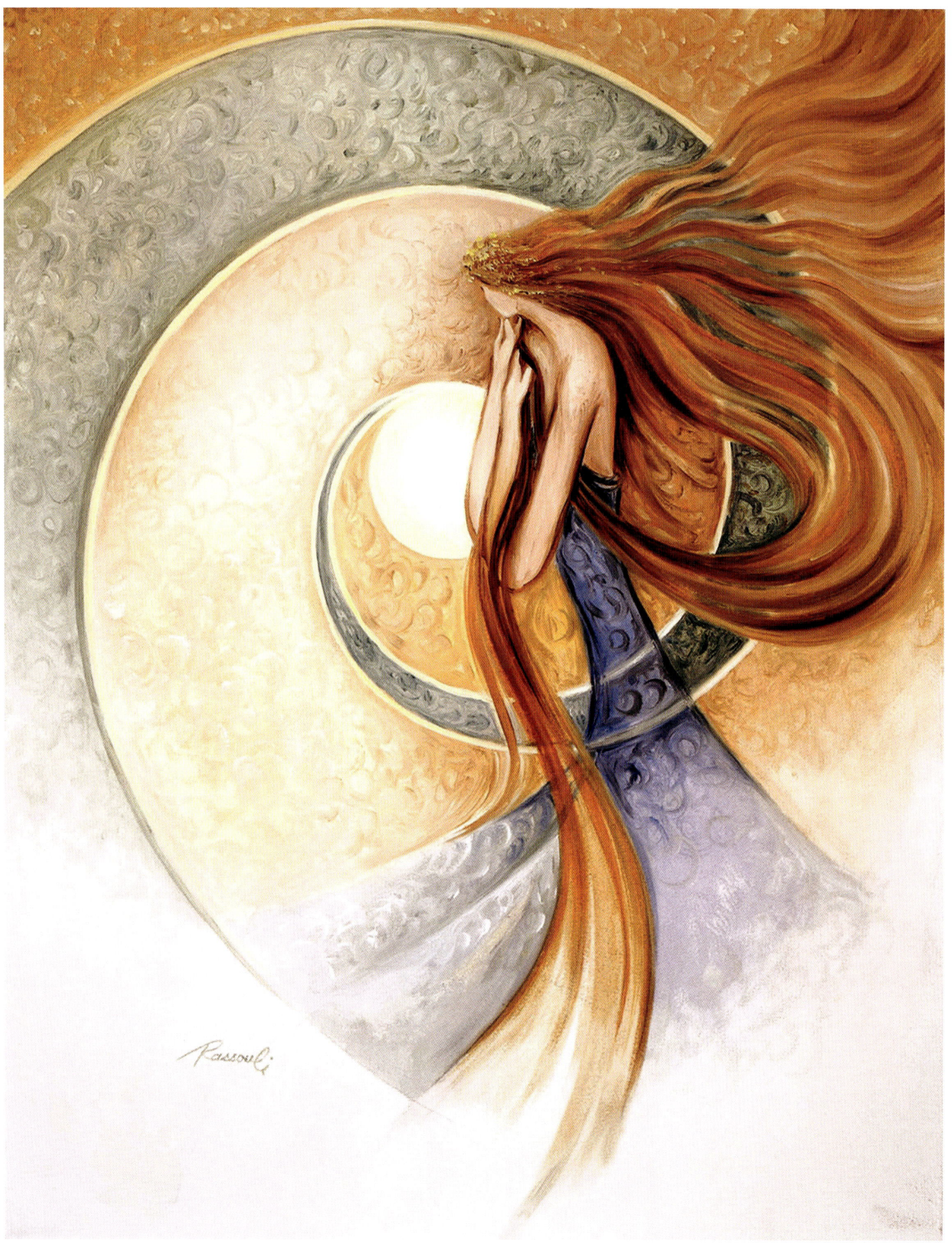

From unexpected meetings
we walked and shared our lifetime
a gentle peaceful quiet time
reflected in our smile.

We winged our way to distant places
and walked among remembered faces
of lives we knew
we lived some time before.

and like a bud about to flower
having reached its appointed hour
we watch ourselves begin to open
in the warm touch of spring.

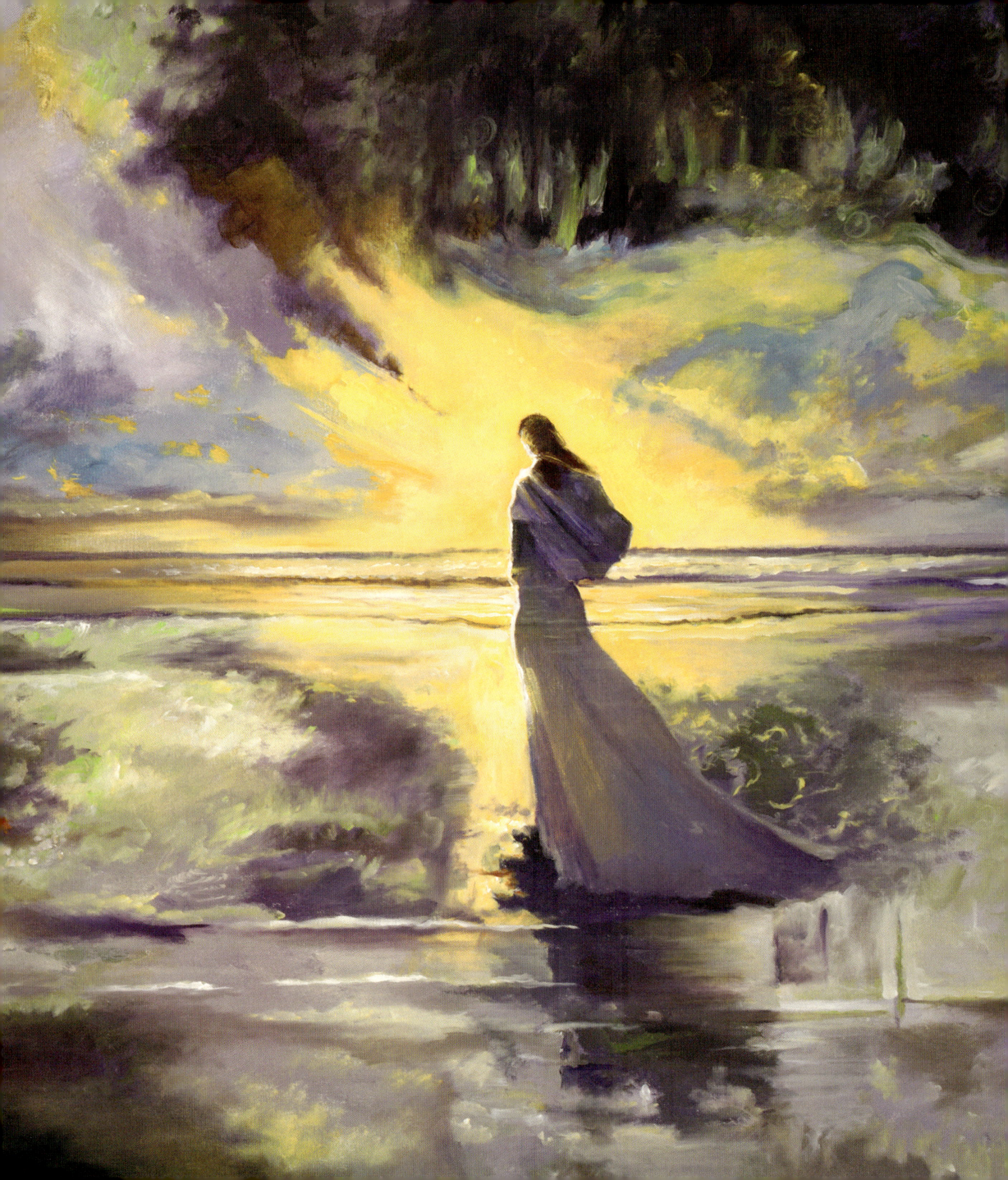

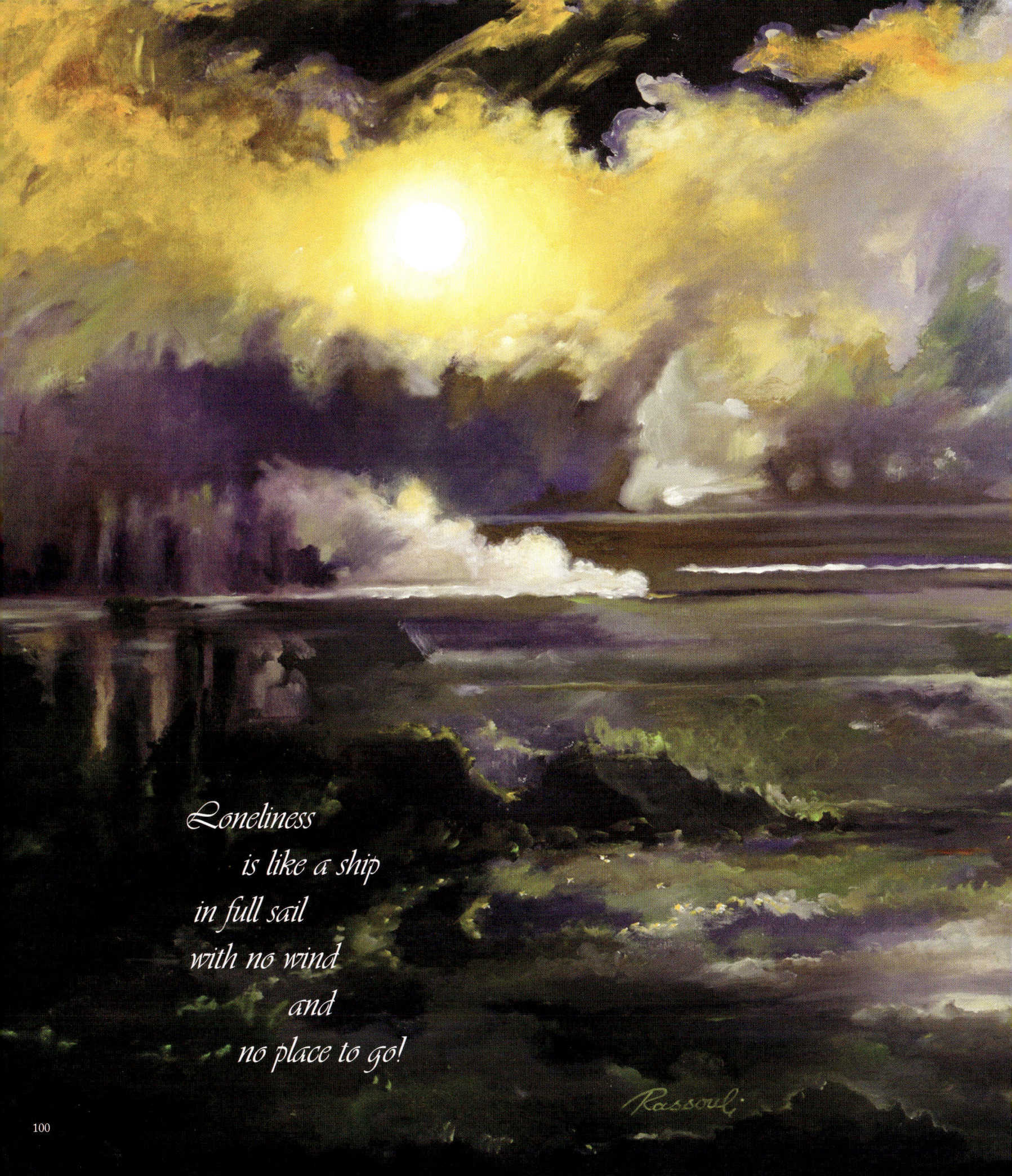

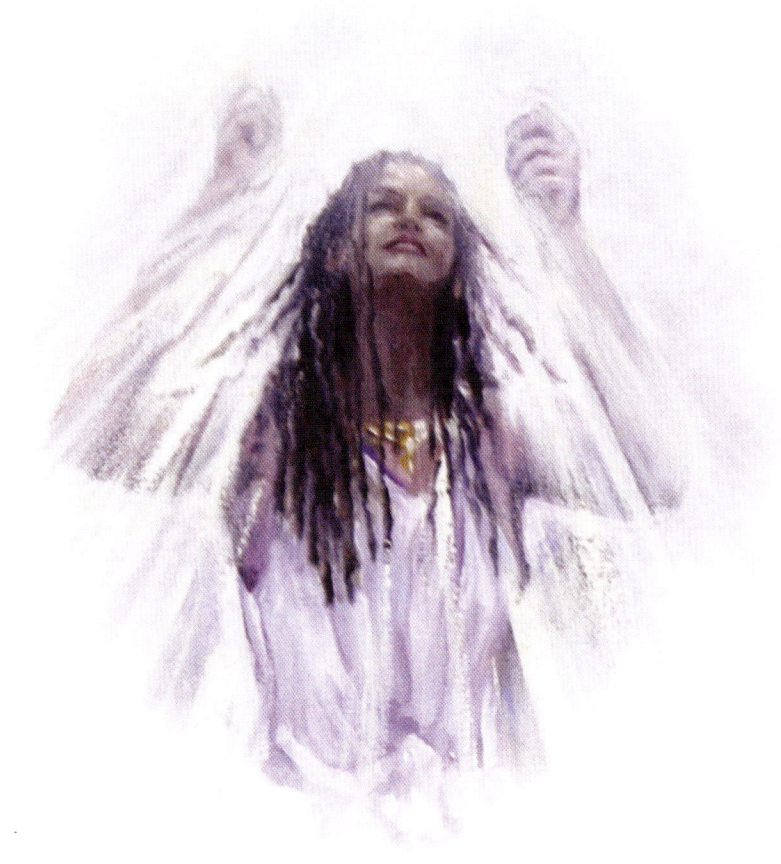

*I asked God for a deepening of my love
without realizing that the deeper I was willing to go
the more it involved letting go of any part of myself
that wanted to love and still be safe.
In the surrender to the possible
lay the greatest potential for love
at levels before unknown
like a cistern that holds the nectar of life
and gives its precious liquid
only to be filled again with nature's flow.
Such knowingness is a gift
for if you can embrace the blessing
you can love without question
releasing and replenishing with each breath, with each kiss,
always whole.*

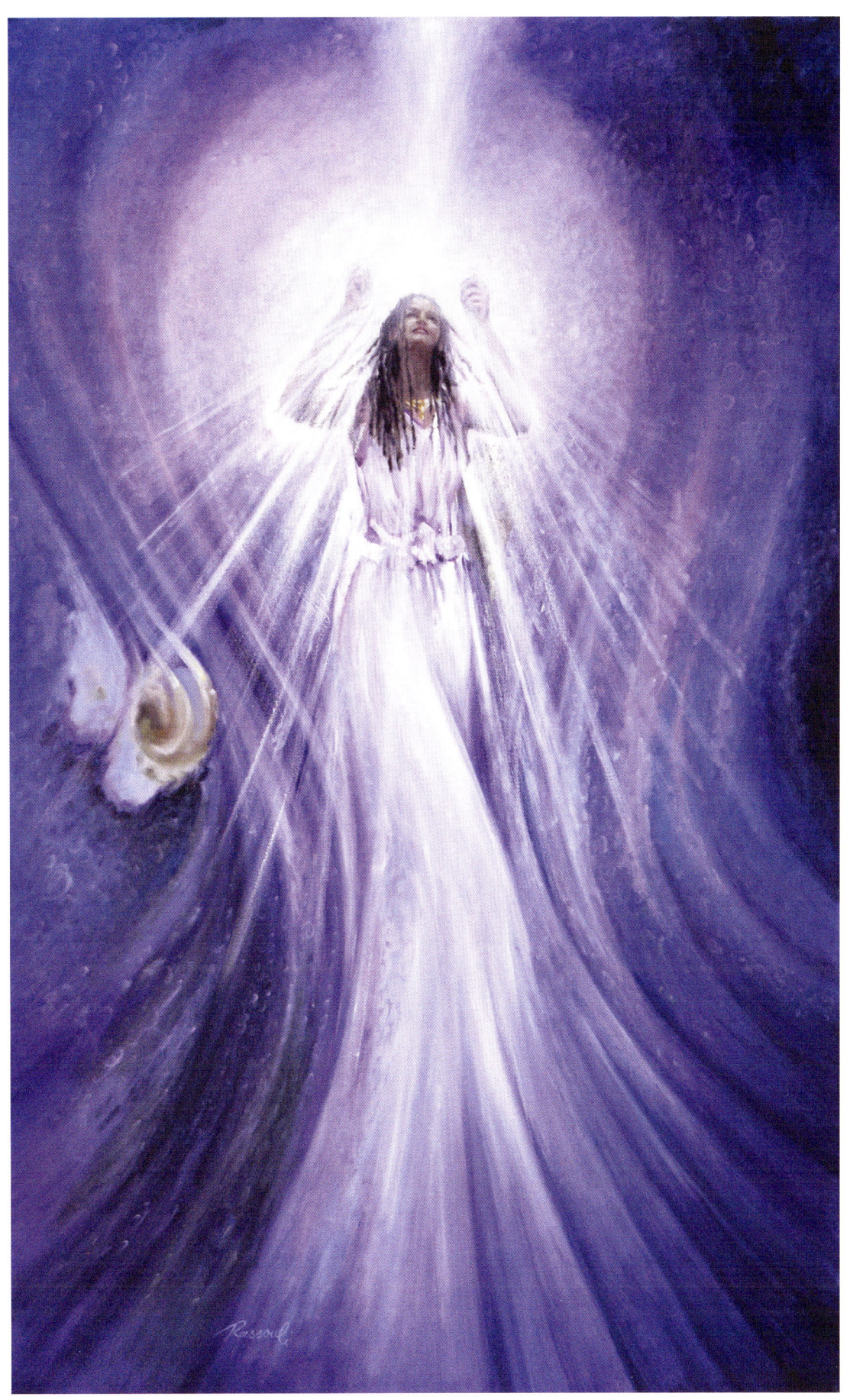

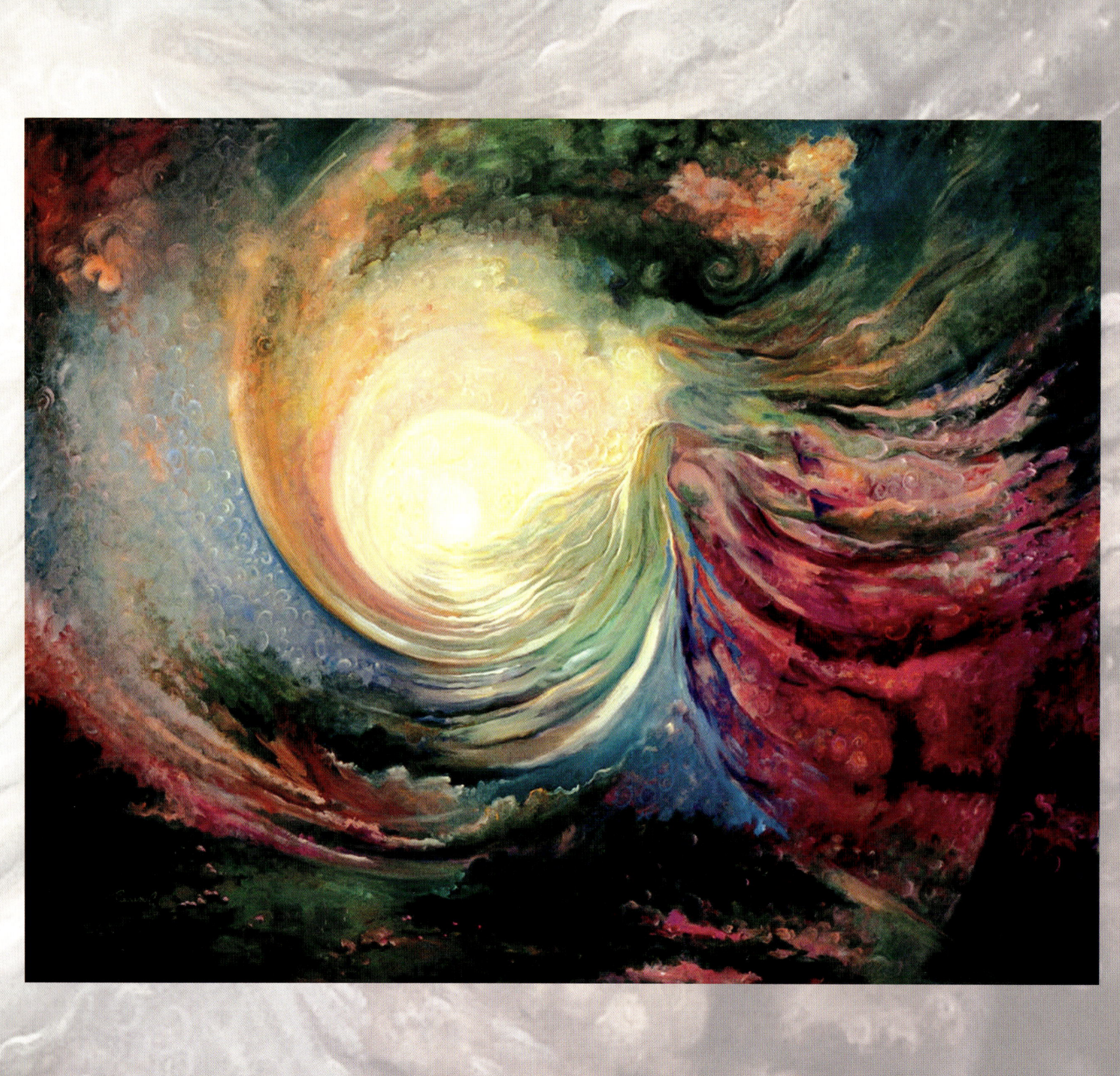

How rare to be born with a name of love
what challenges await that I must face
or voice to listen from above
telling what I must embrace

Each day I walk a path unknown
with no regrets for where I've been
each experience is mine to own
no choices call to live again

How strong I am I ask myself
the measured test unfolds each day
a blessing of enormous wealth
inside the gift will always lay

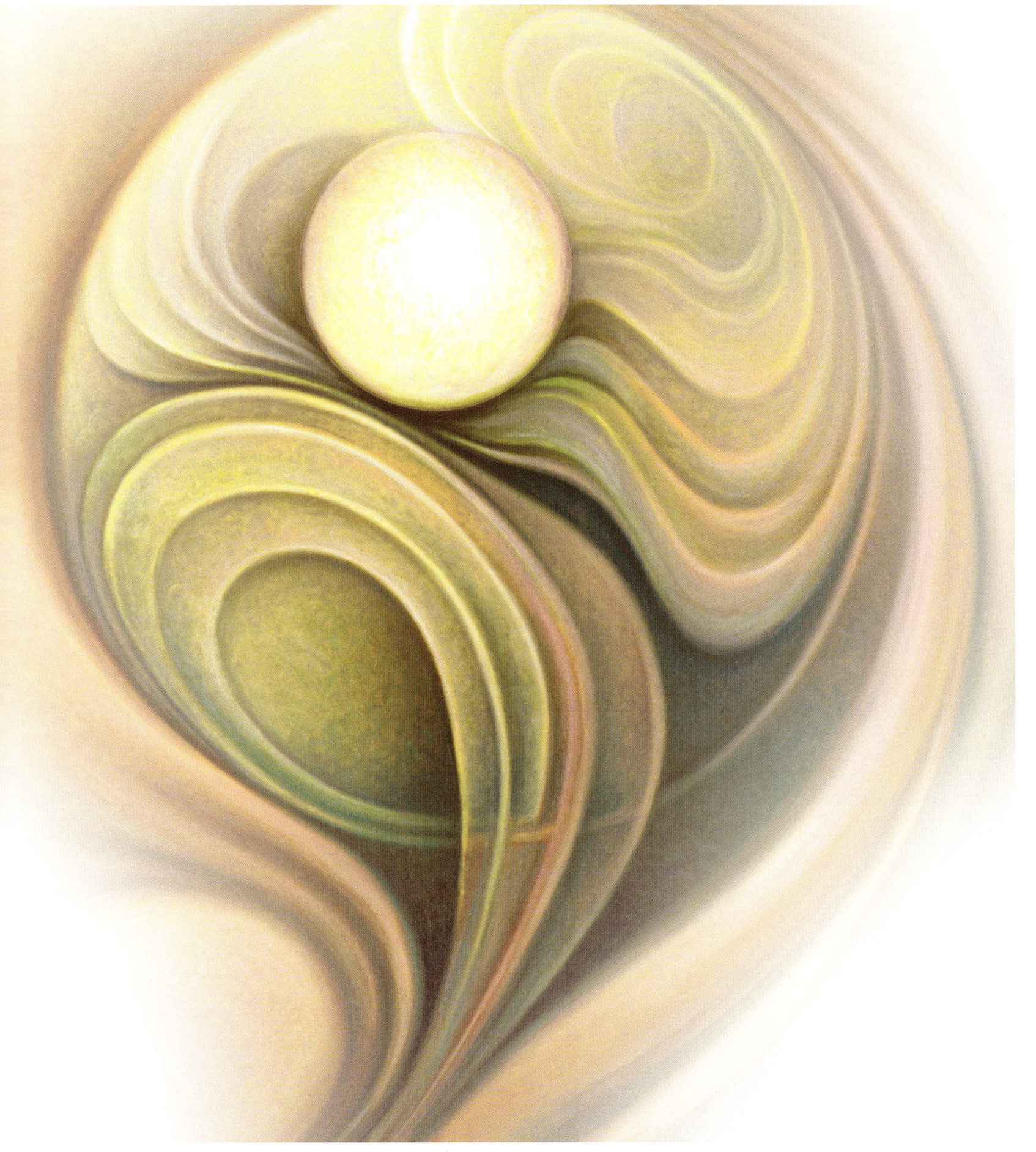

You are the softness he desires
You help to light his way
You nurture all
    that he holds dear
        though tempest clouds dismay

And in the quiet of the storm
    his gentleness comes through
        and in the shelter of his arms
            his heart is there for you.

Love is magic,
like a balmy breeze
on a winter night
it feels so good
you want it to last forever
and love is magic
because we make it so
by opening
to the pleasure of being alive
and sharing the joy we feel

and when we're not looking
the night may warm again.

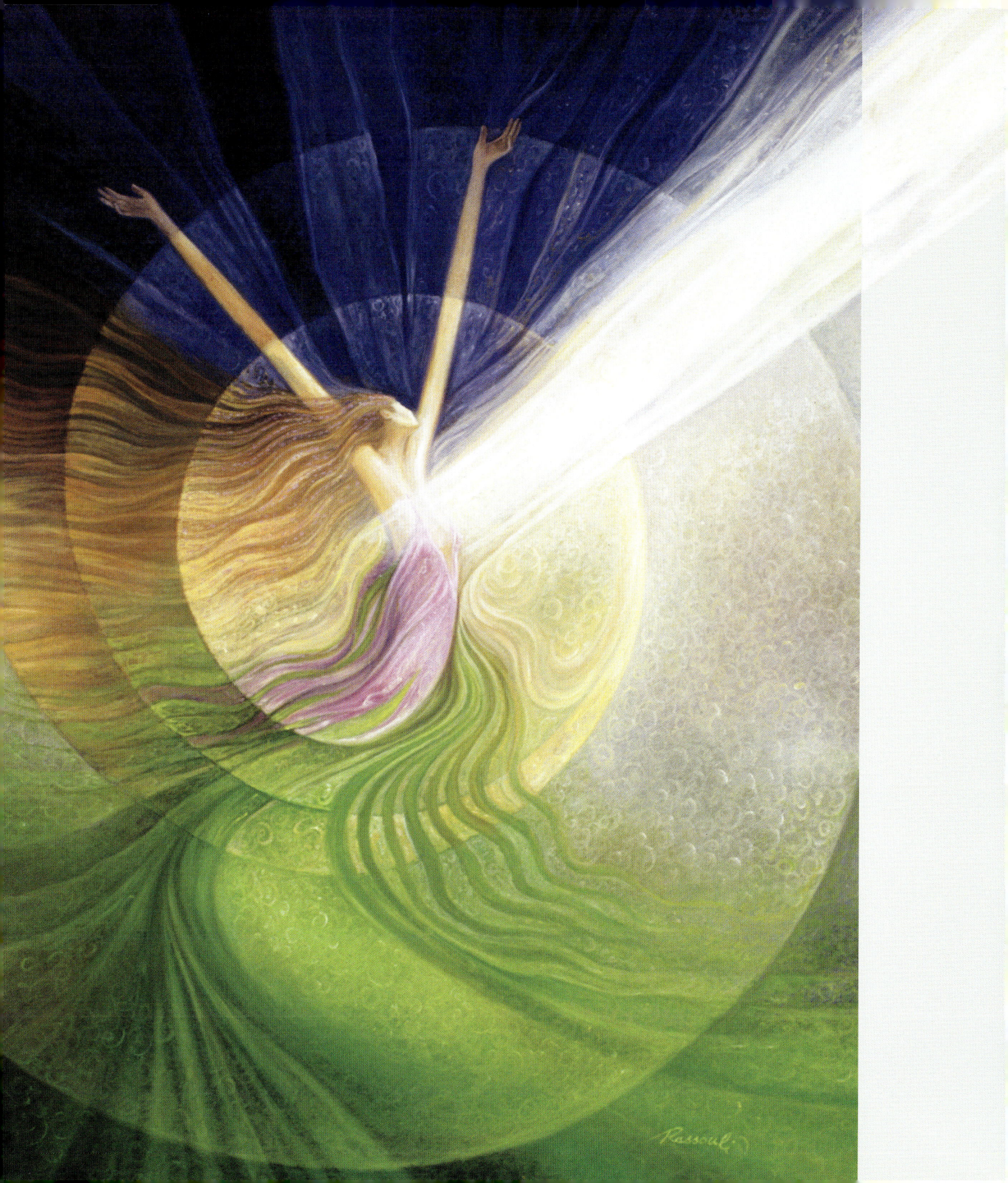

When I close my eyes at night
I see your face,
your lips,
the brush of your hair
across your brow
the down of your skin
soft against my touch

My love grows in the solitude
listening for the morning light
and you.

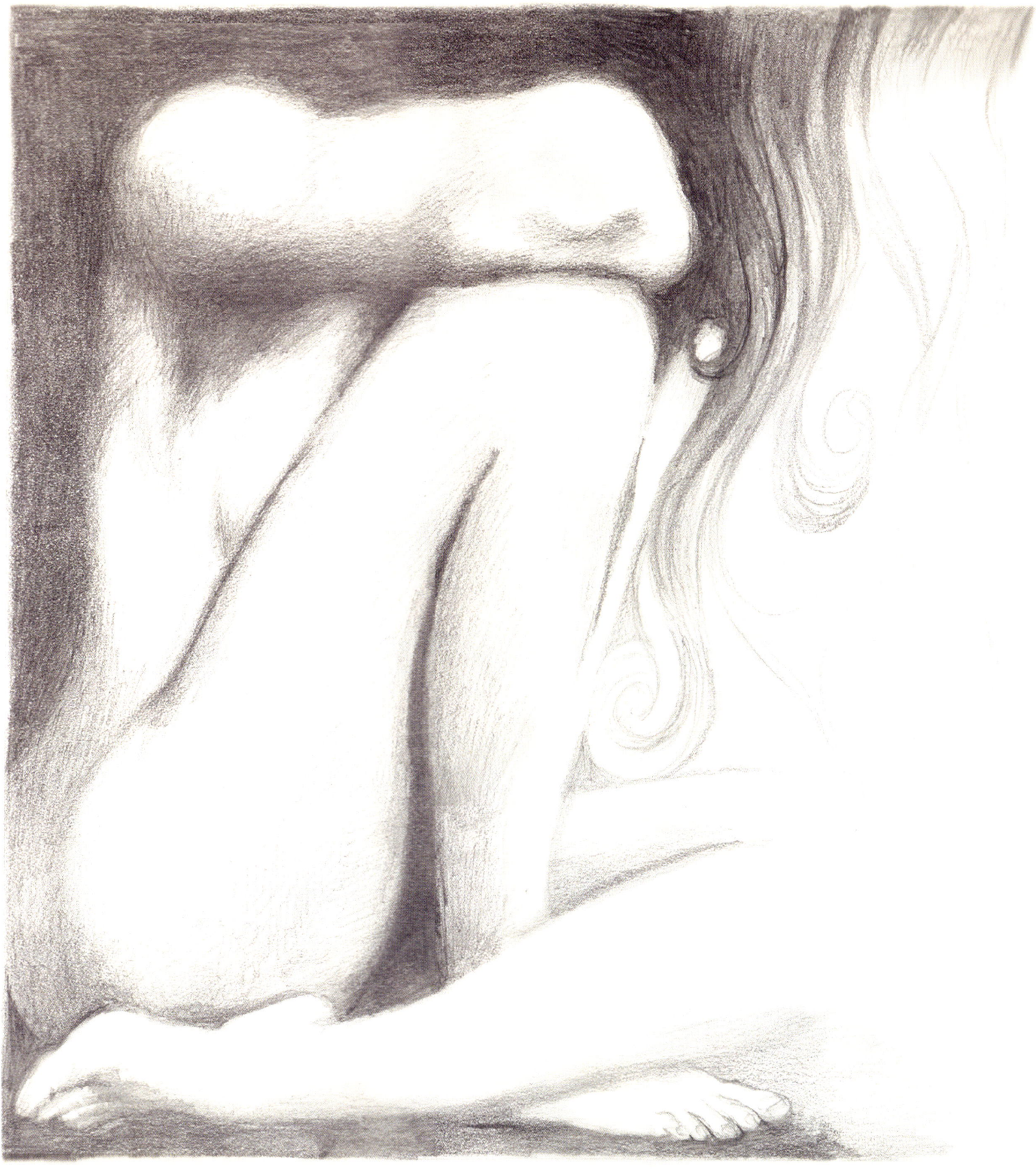

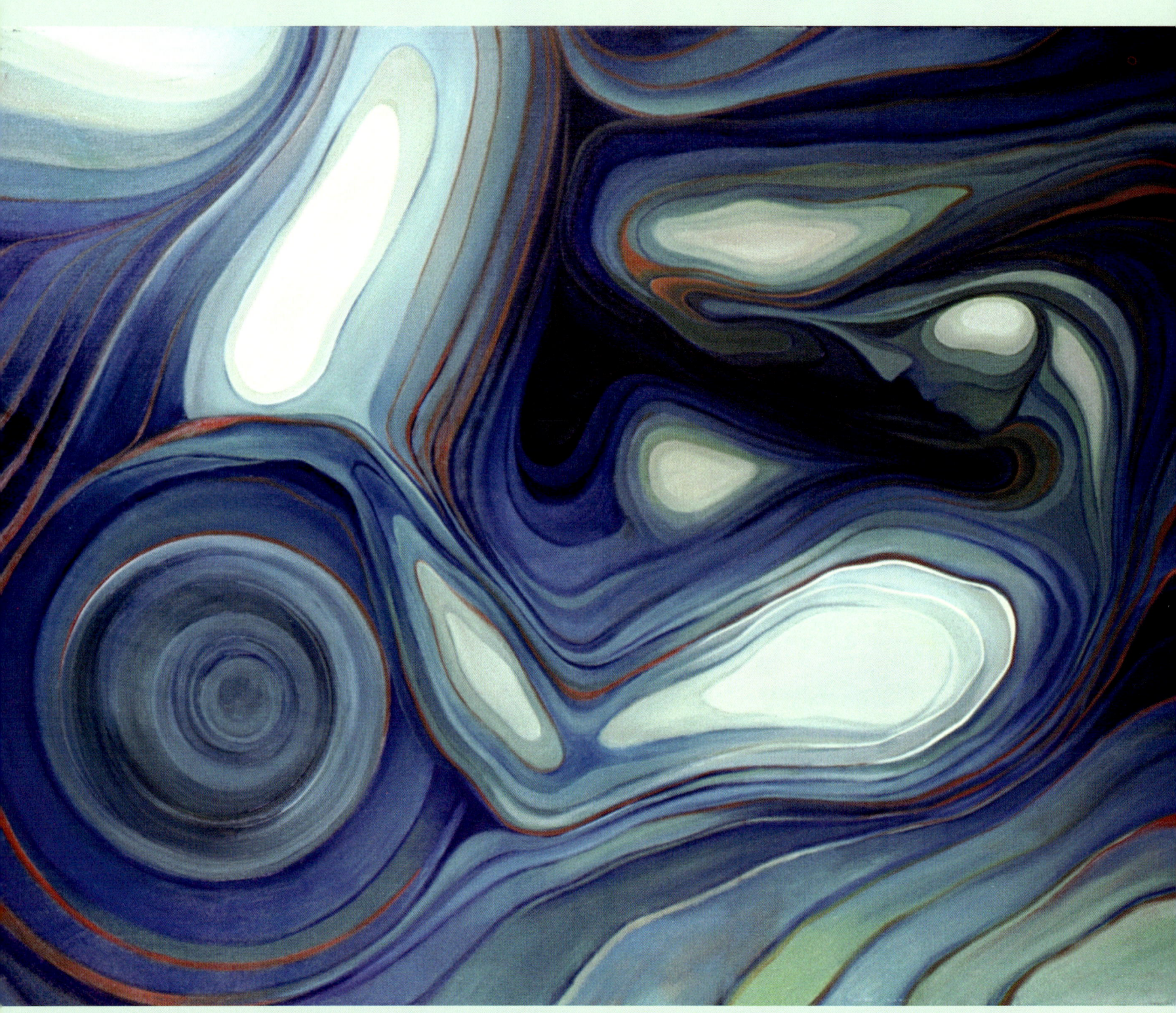

There is a beautiful silence now
as I hold your hands
and listen to your eyes
across a span of moments called time

There are no words that say as much
nor walls that can confine
the wings of our feeling
or the rhythm of our eyes.

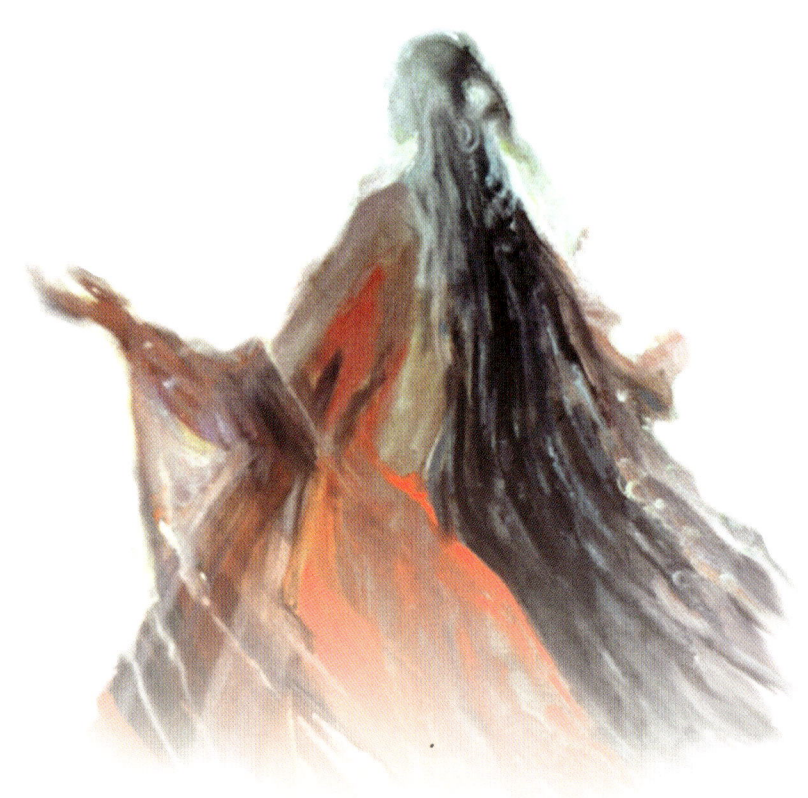

How careful we must be close
how fragile we must feel
how sad not to be
when someone is real

To say approach with caution
when we already know
that inside there's a likeness
and experience goes slow

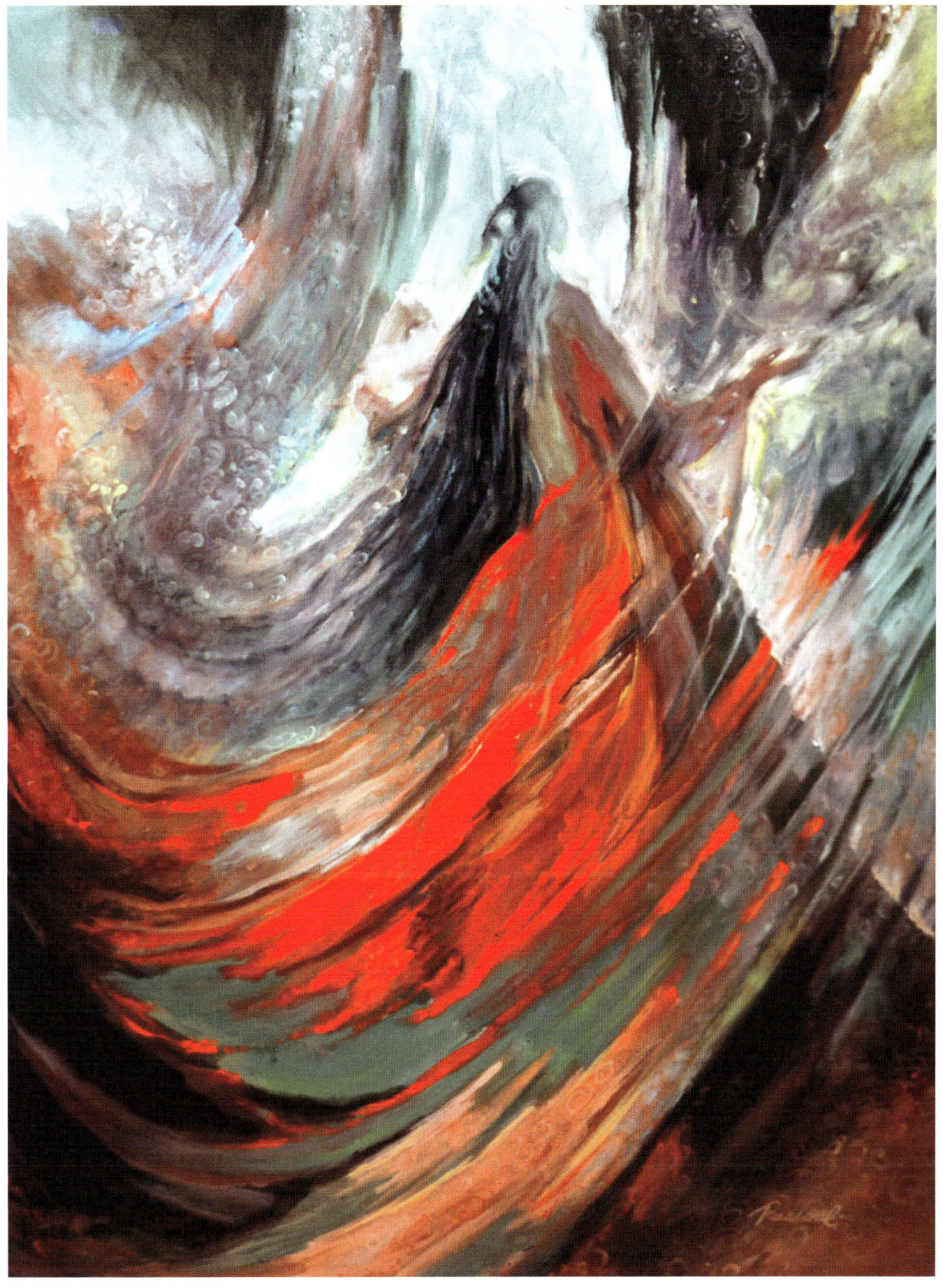

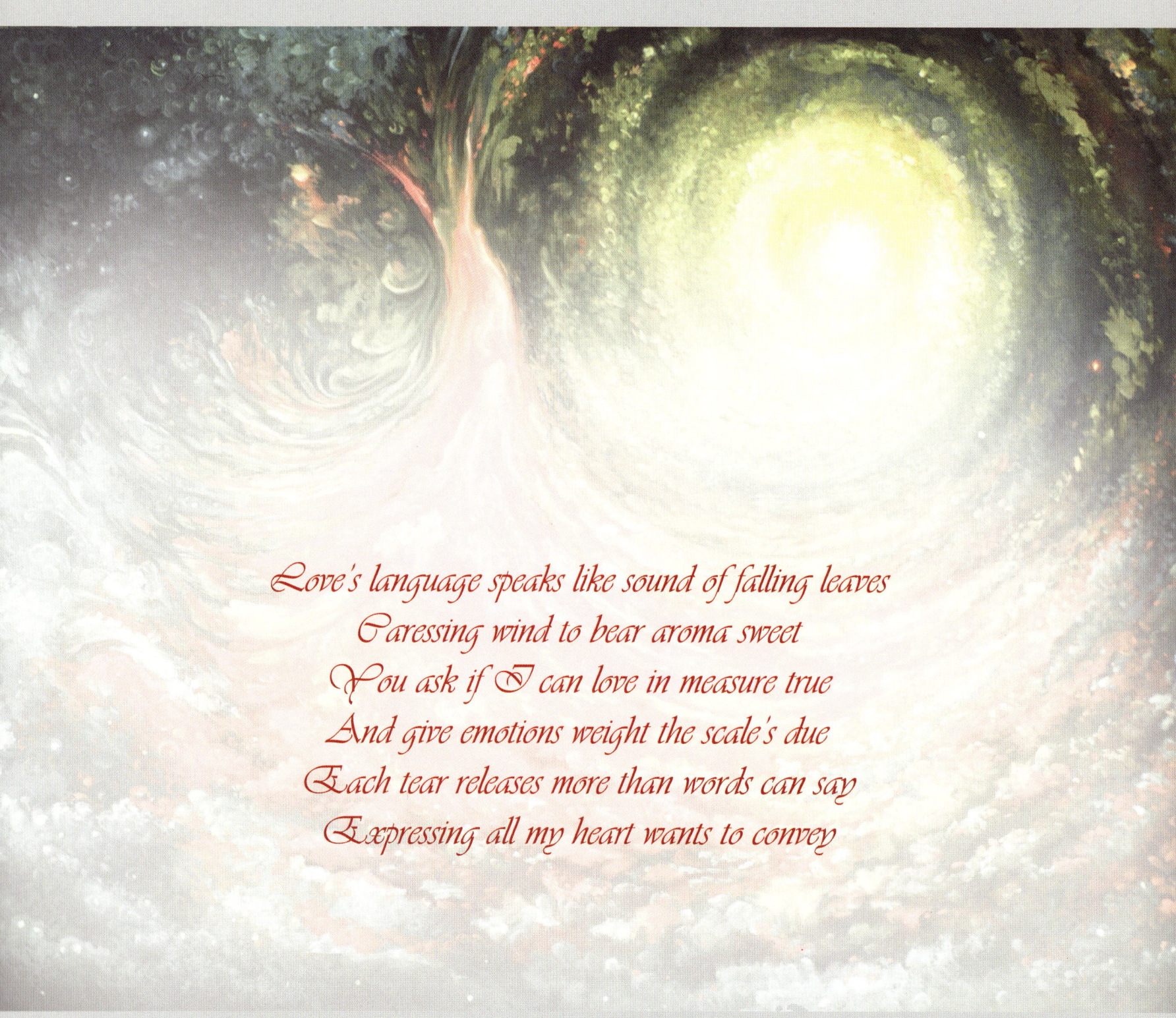

Love's language speaks like sound of falling leaves
Caressing wind to bear aroma sweet
You ask if I can love in measure true
And give emotions weight the scale's due
Each tear releases more than words can say
Expressing all my heart wants to convey

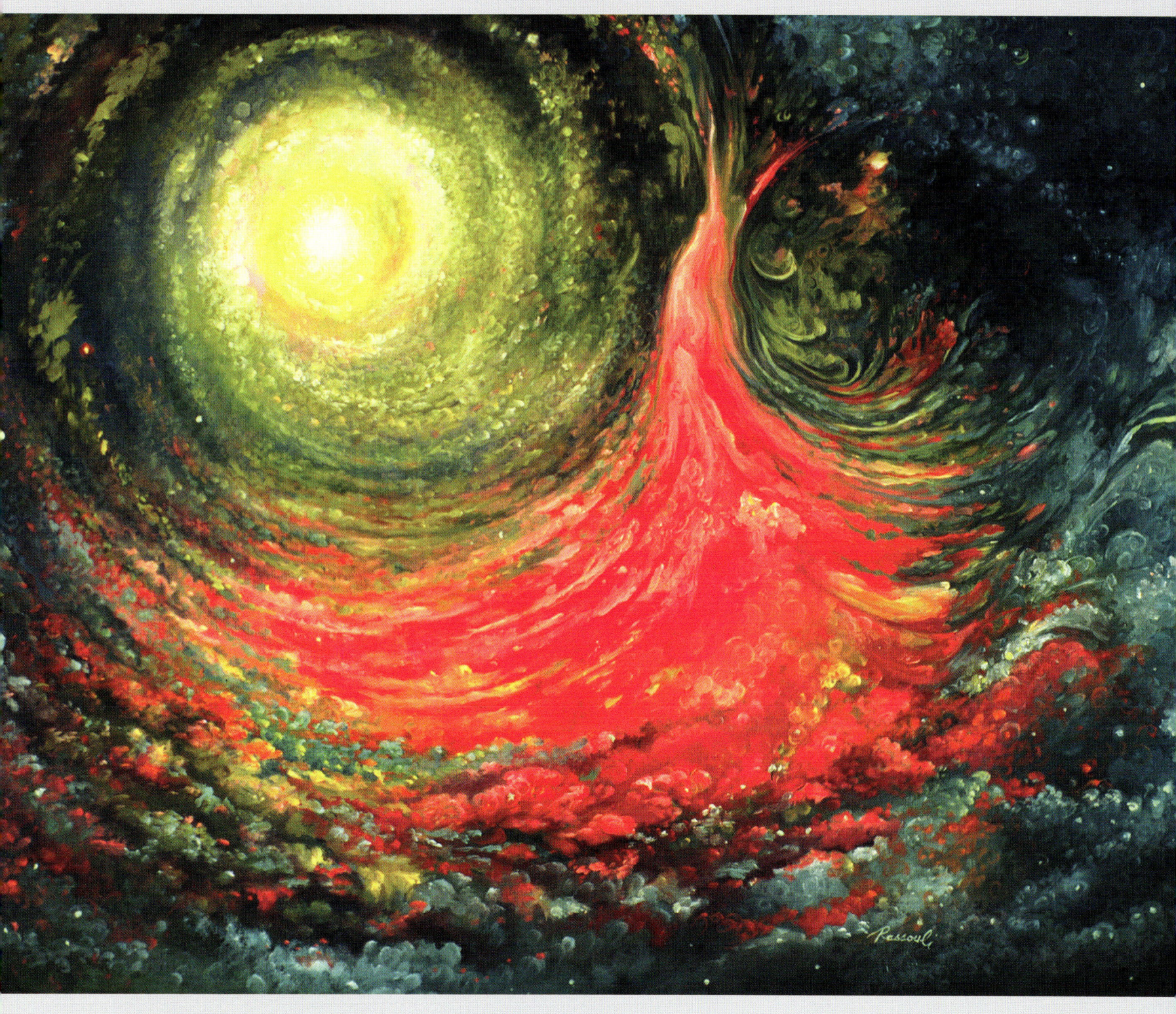

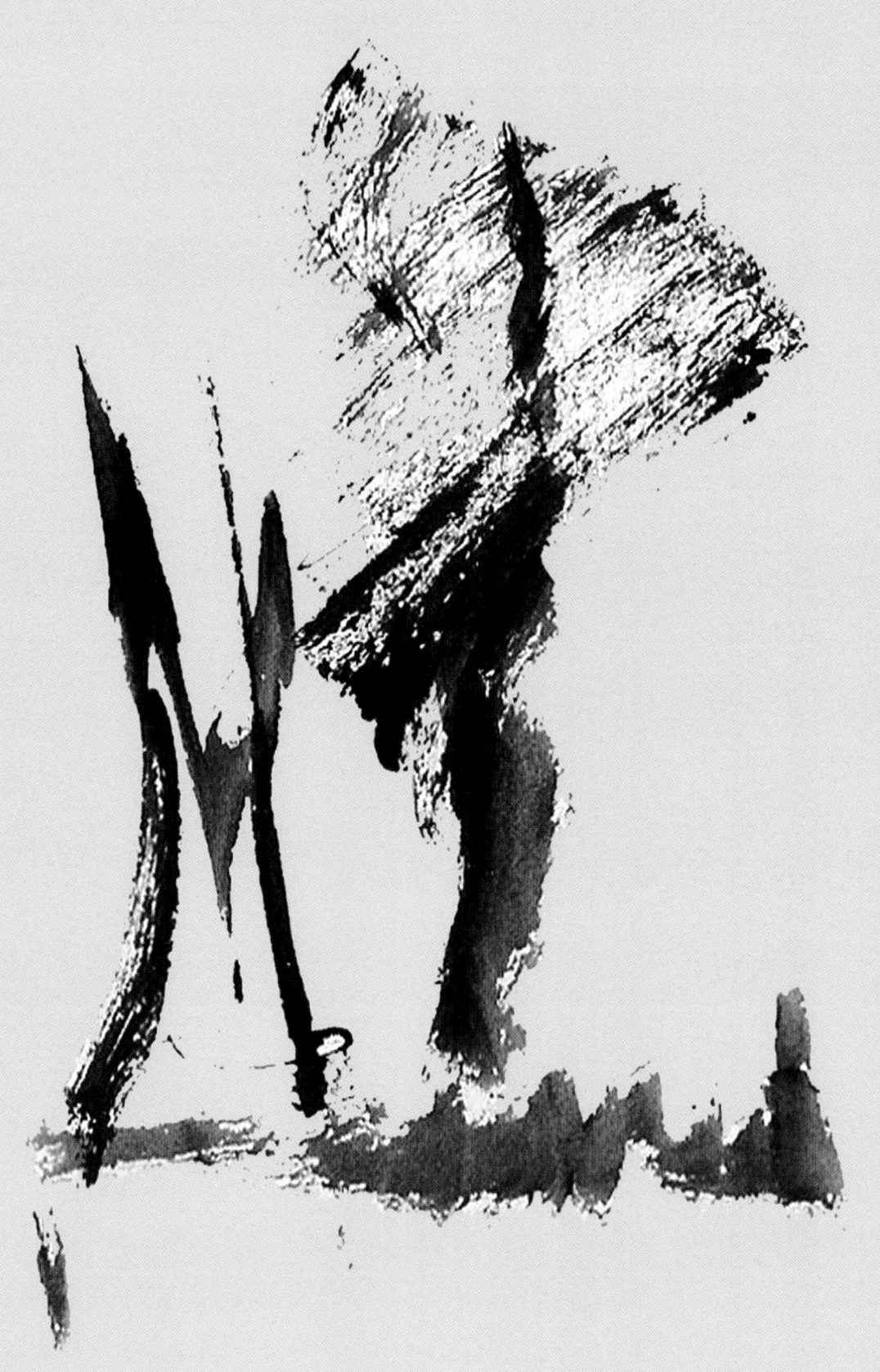

*I have been here before
aromas open the doors
I walk through knowing.*

A coming together
a blending of one
where understanding
spans the space between
and separation disappears

to form

Anew

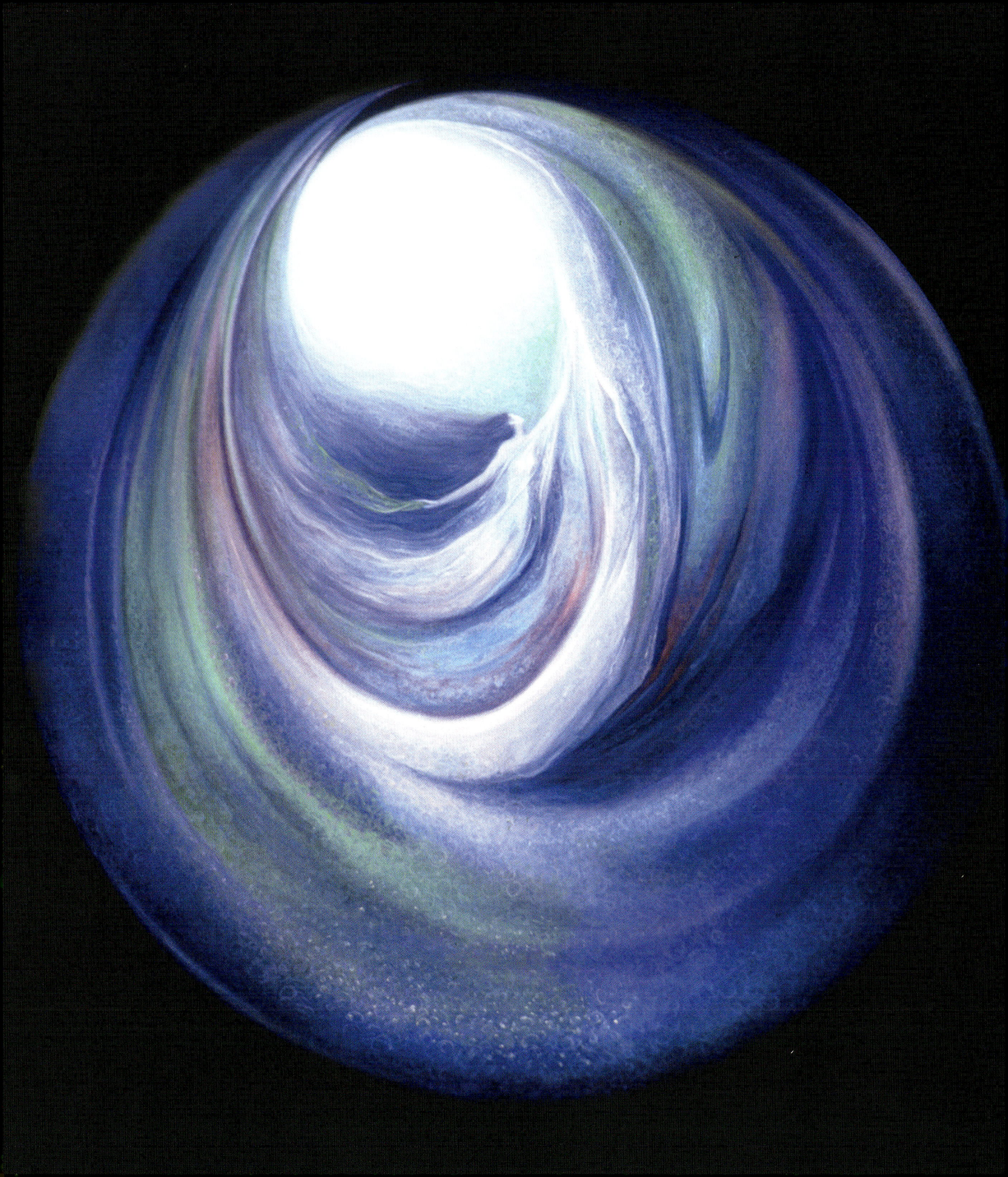

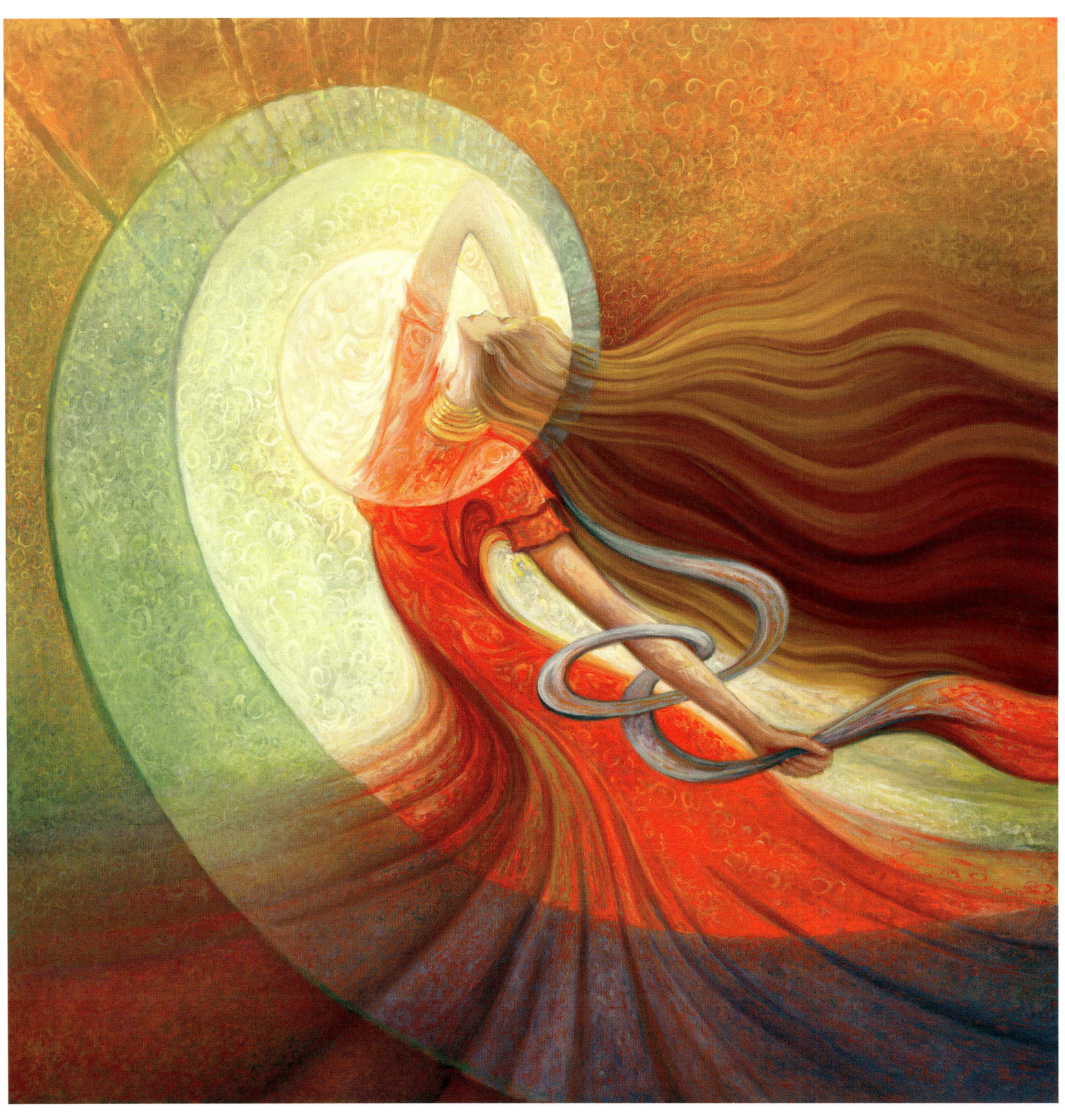

My
coming out
is the freedom to fully be who I am
and the surrender to the divine essence
expressing through and around me

My
coming out
is the marriage of twin souls with my life partner
in gratitude
in love
unfolding as more than we could ever be on our own

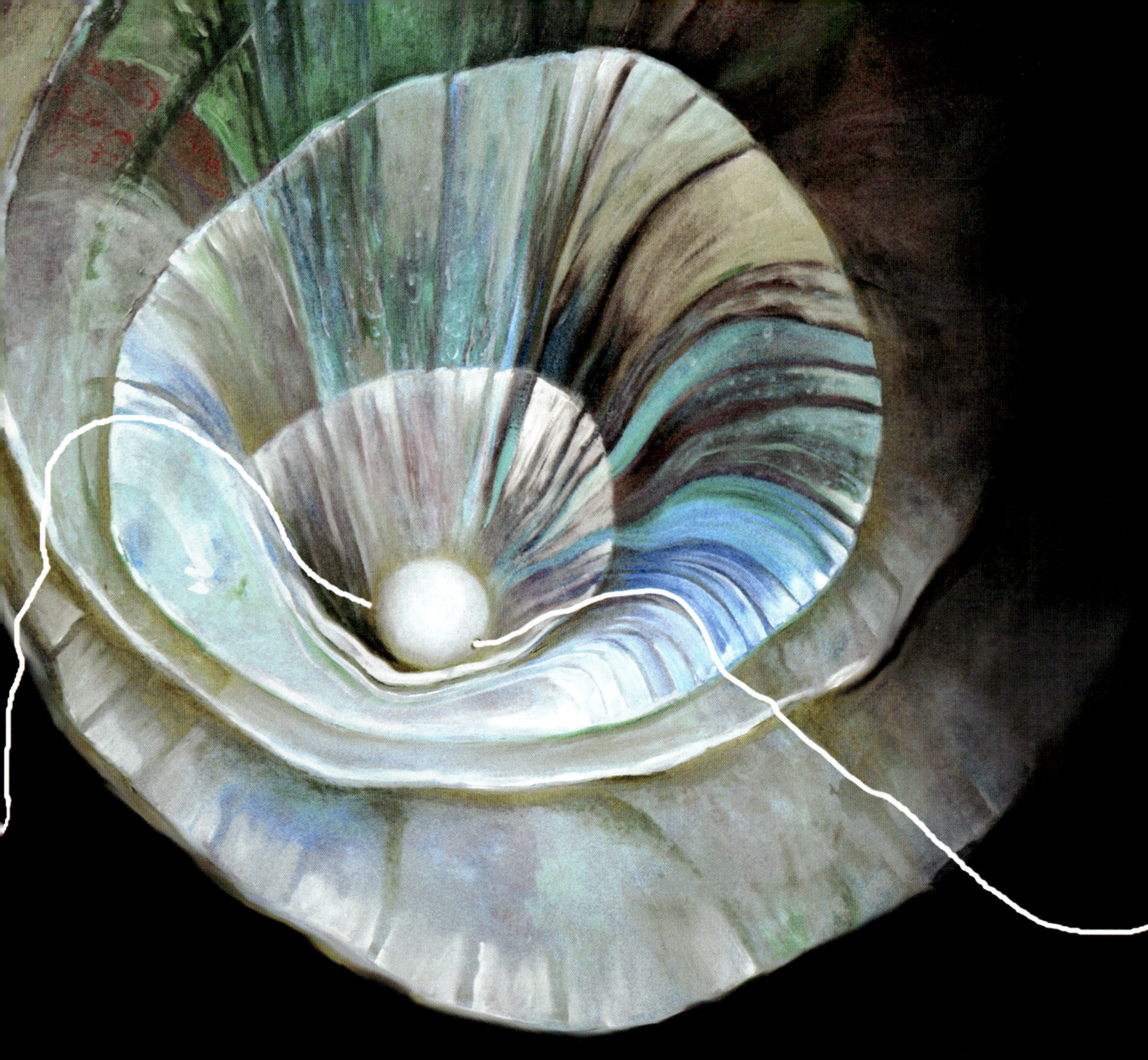

*Hearts apart remember love
and time stands still.....*

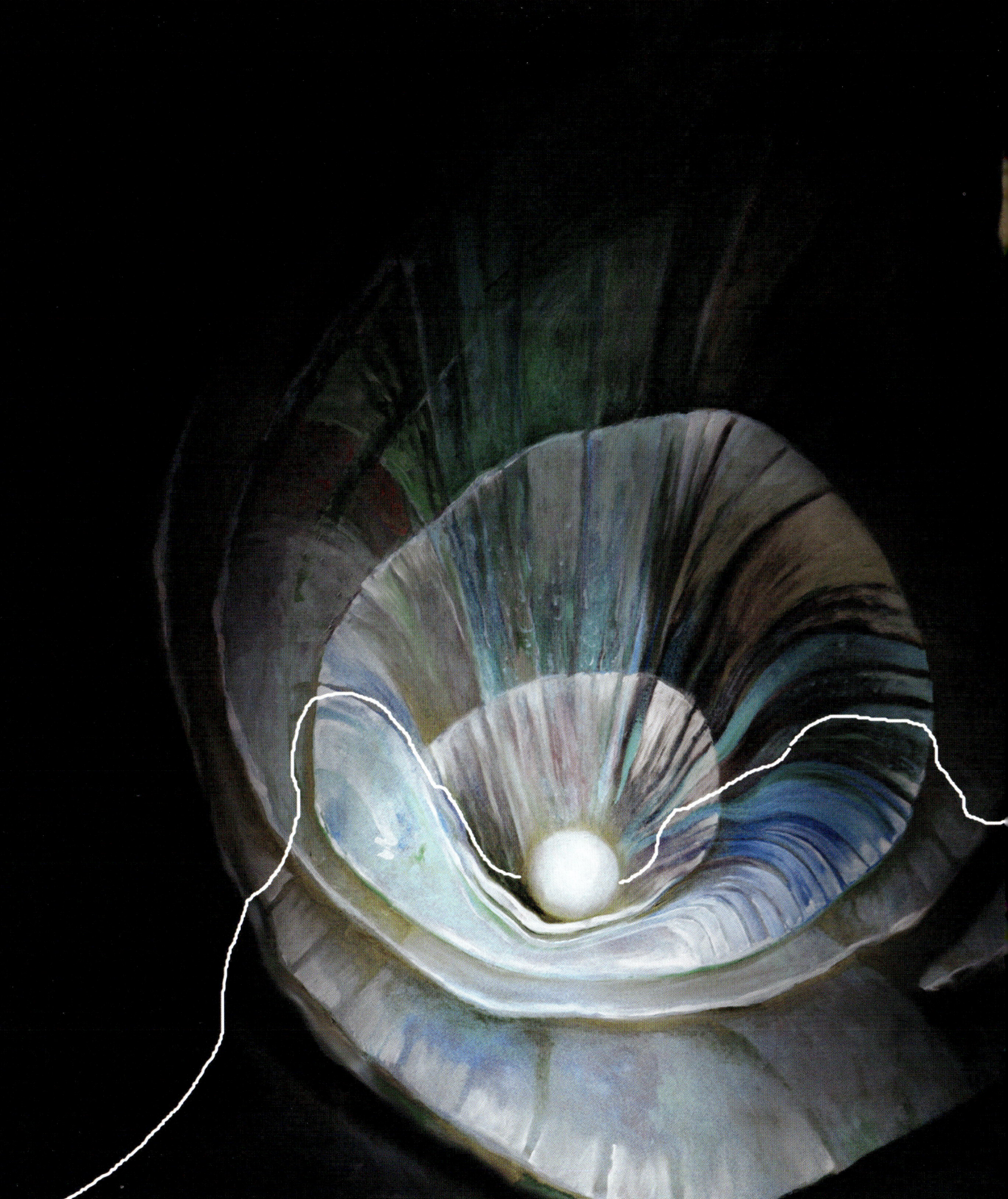

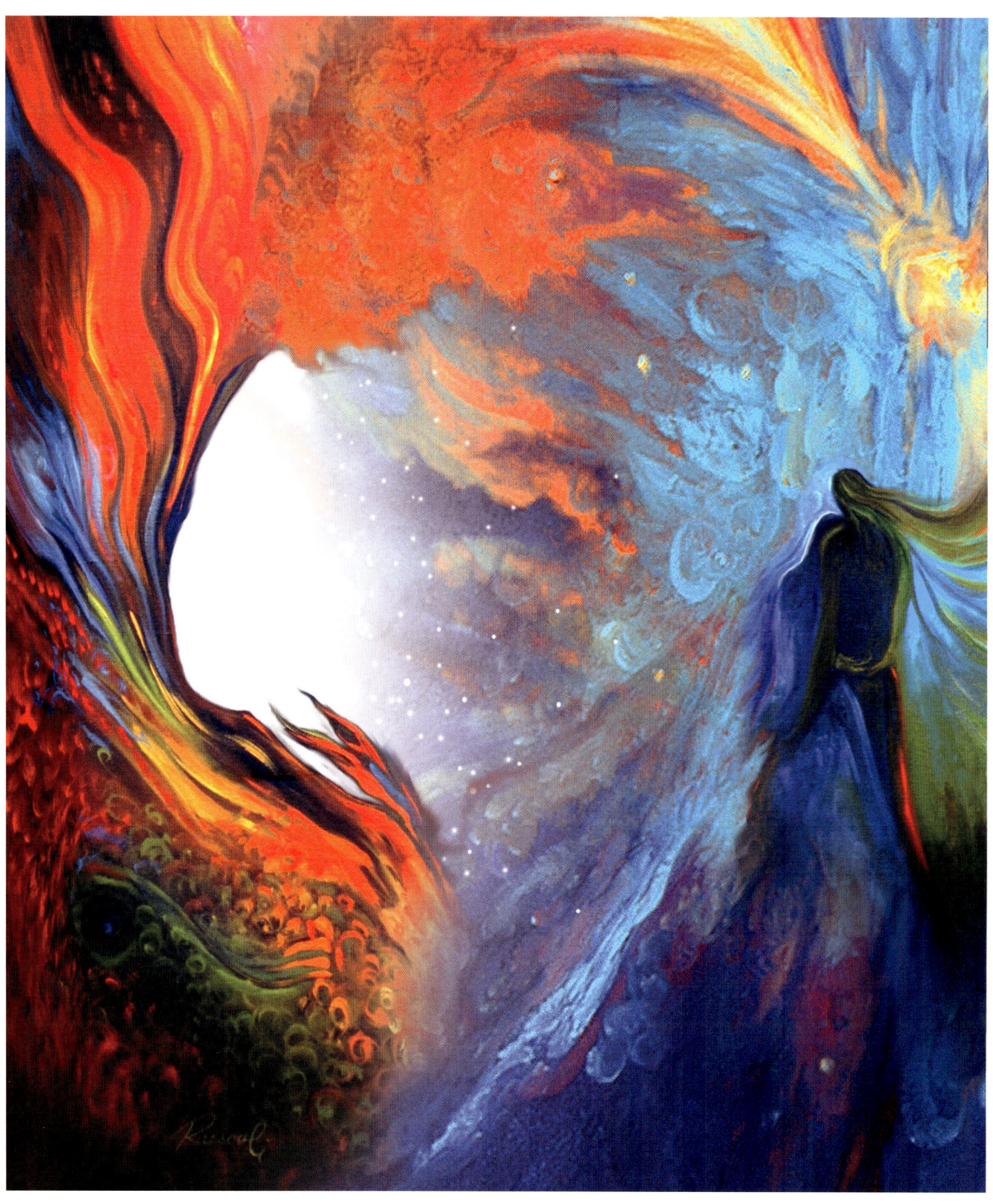

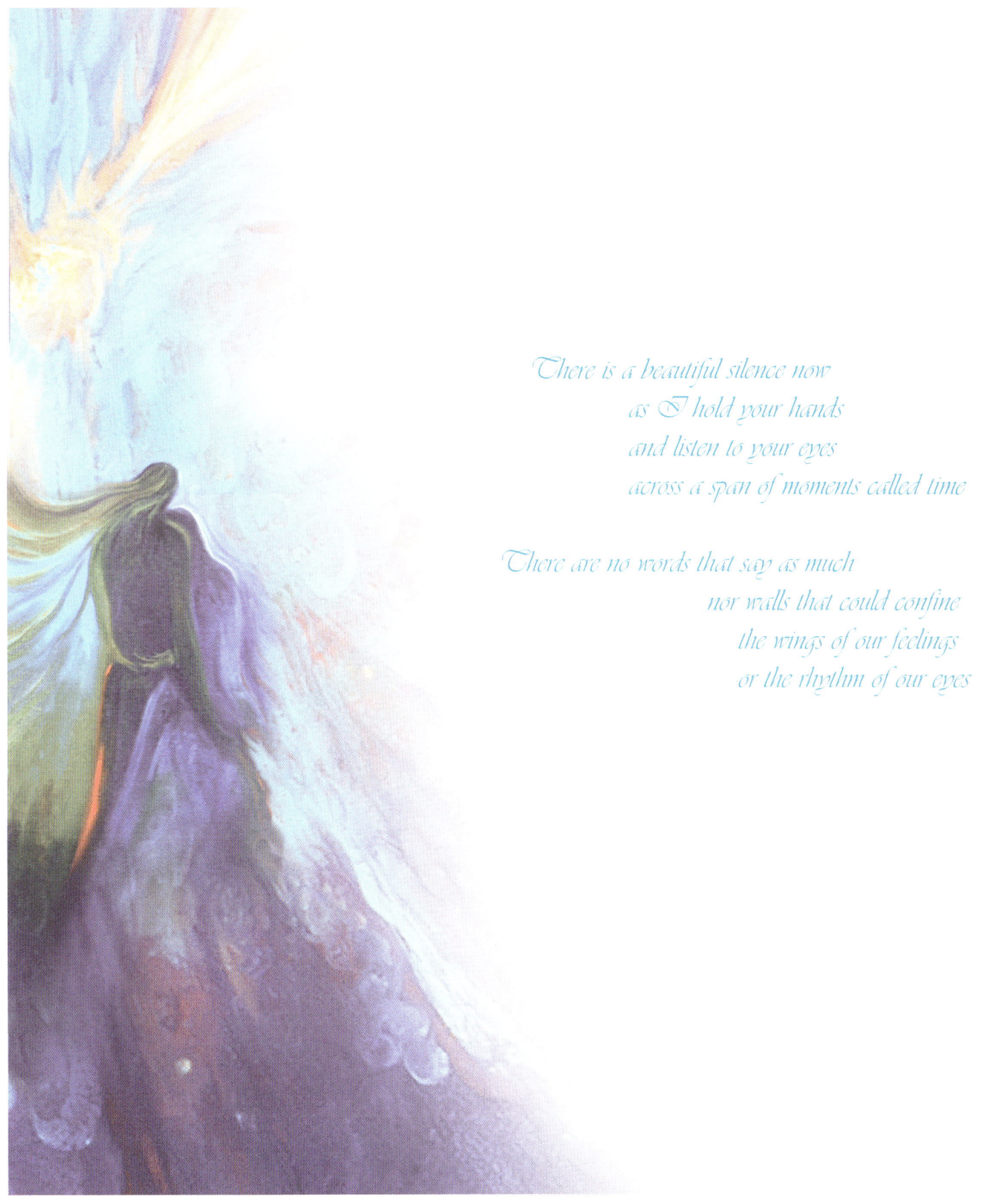

There is a beautiful silence now
    as I hold your hands
    and listen to your eyes
    across a span of moments called time

There are no words that say as much
    nor walls that could confine
    the wings of our feelings
    or the rhythm of our eyes

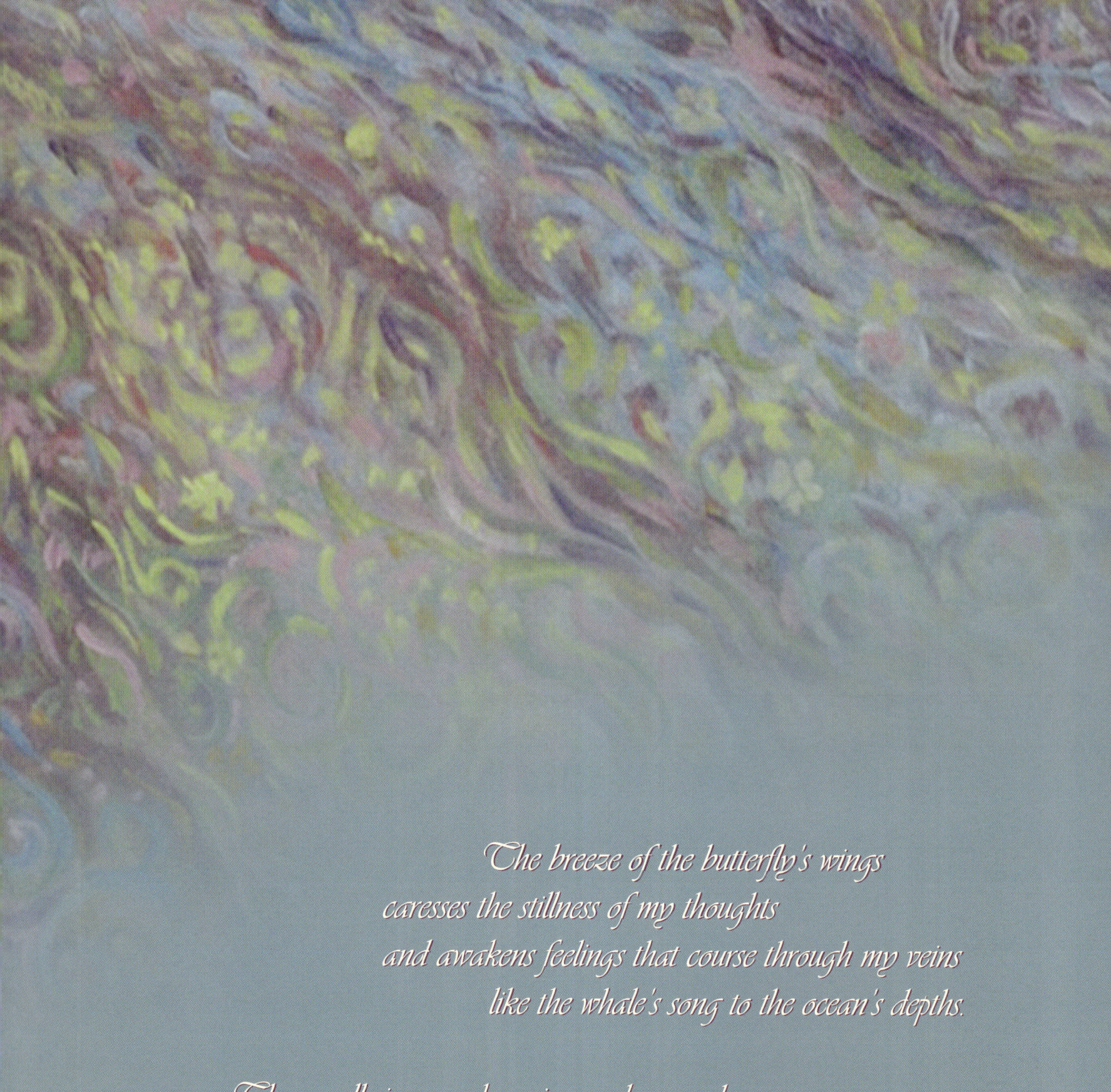

The breeze of the butterfly's wings
caresses the stillness of my thoughts
and awakens feelings that course through my veins
like the whale's song to the ocean's depths.

There wells in me a knowing and a wonder
for what is yet to be.

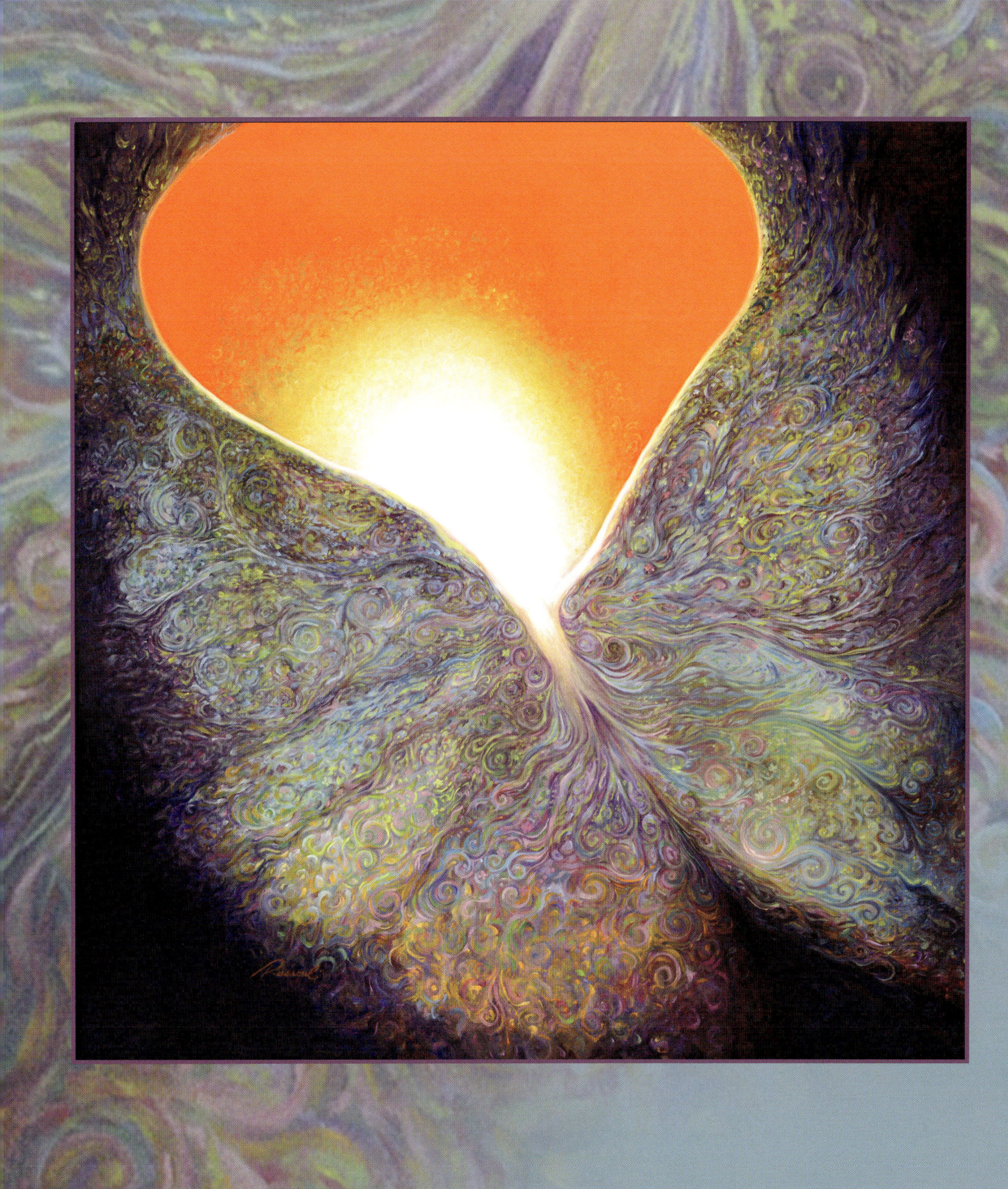

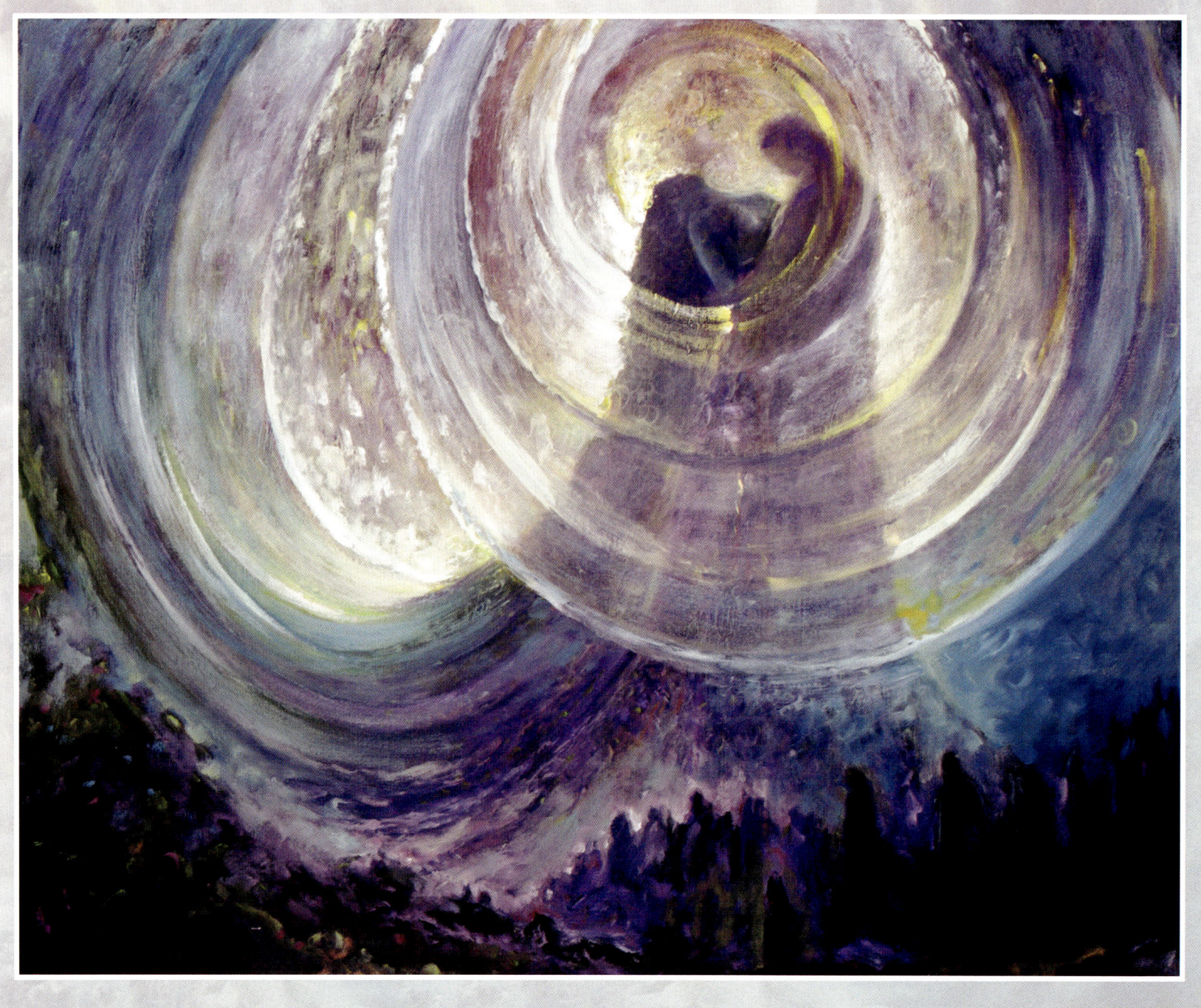

intimacy intimacy intimacy intimacy intimacy intimacy intimacy intimacy intimacy intimacy

Becoming one
      allowing all that is
    both within and without
              to blend
         like a wave meeting the shore
each aspect of who we are
      is part of a grander whole
      and in truth, yet greater still

To know myself is to know you
      whether I look in your eyes,
          or touch lips,
         or hold hands,
          or bathe
        in the warmth
           of our embrace

Intimacy intimacy intimacy intimacy intimacy intimacy intimacy intimacy intimacy intimac

Take heed my friend for time is ticking fast
illusion grand in hopes this dream will last
such memories we keep for days to come
a looking glass that only shows what's done

It would be sad to think there is nothing more
a well-worn path reflecting what's in store
God's gift was not that days would be the same
each dawn's first light would sing a fresh refrain

of light and cloud to bathe the earth's surprise
with change afoot to stop would be unwise
a pallet rich awaits the artist's brush
creating life at one with God's soft touch

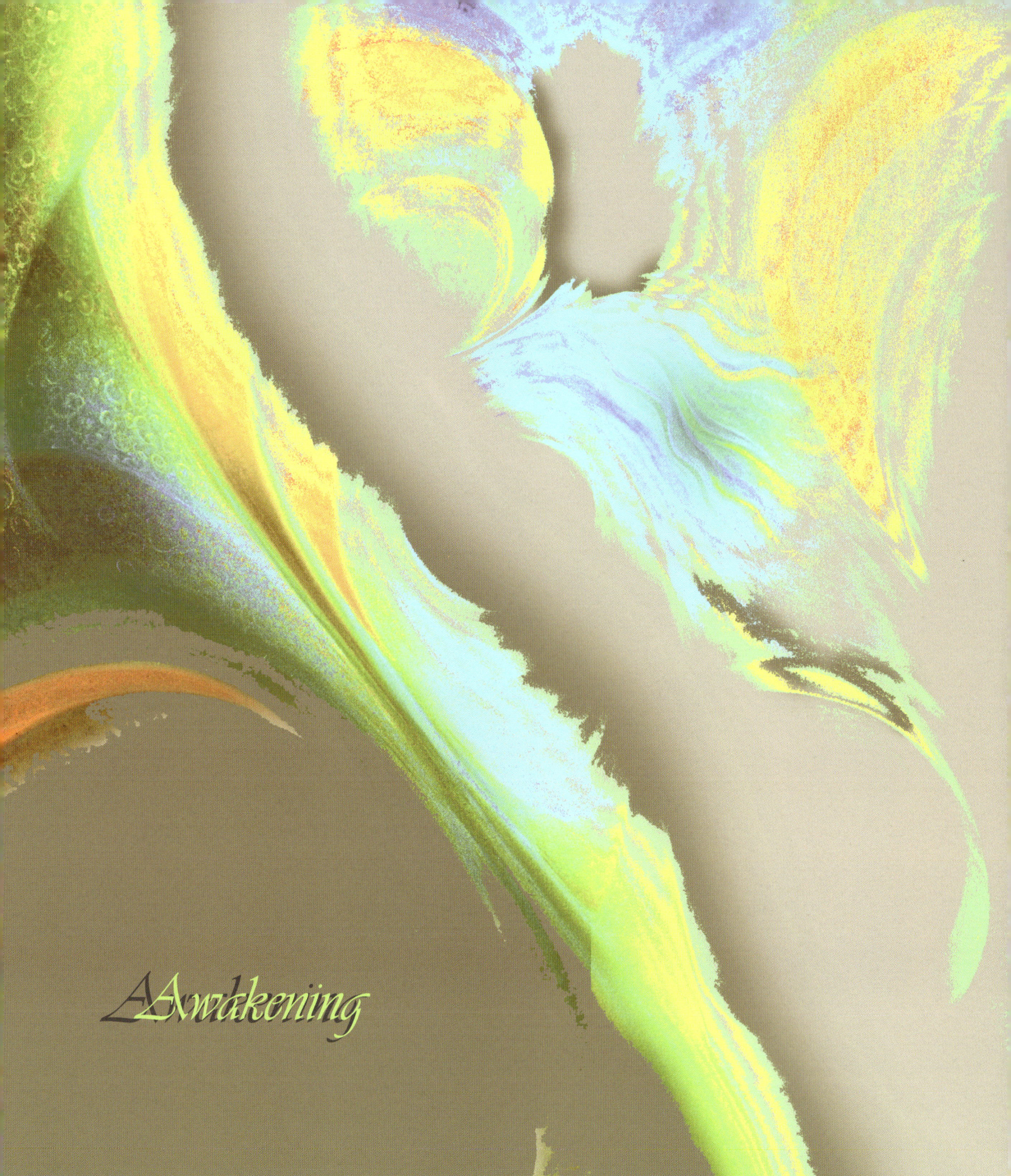

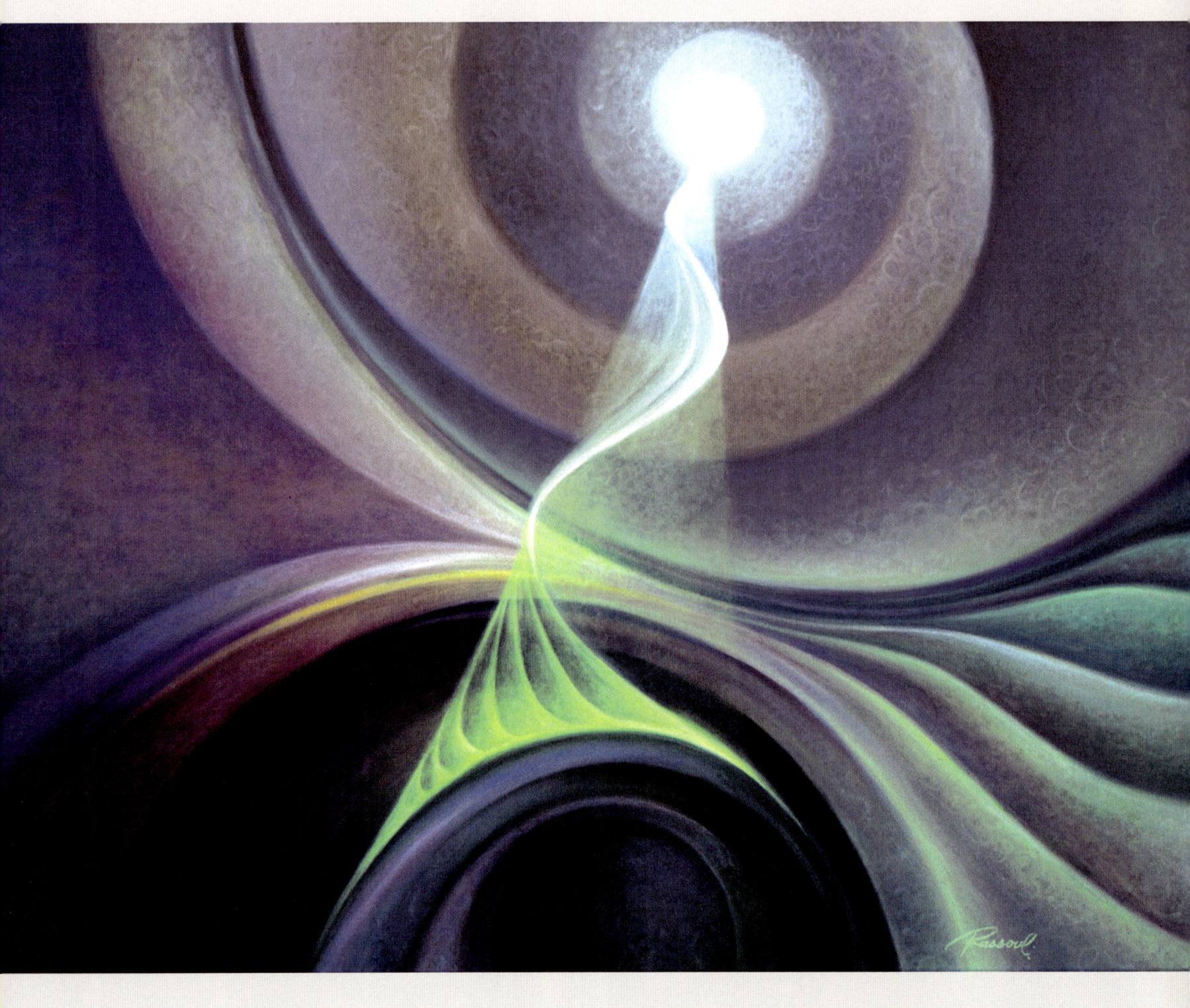

When the first sound was born
the air was filled with fantasy
like the flower's sweet perfume
alive in the moment
there was nothing else
only the energy coursing through my body
and the tears on my cheeks.
I was carried away on the strings
Each note striking a chord within
and answering with the emotions of my soul.
How priceless the surprise
how powerful the memory
to be with the violin when it sings.

*A flower is a poem
that tells you
the truth of a thought
in the fragrance of a dream
as fleeting as a heartbeat
as lasting as a memory.*

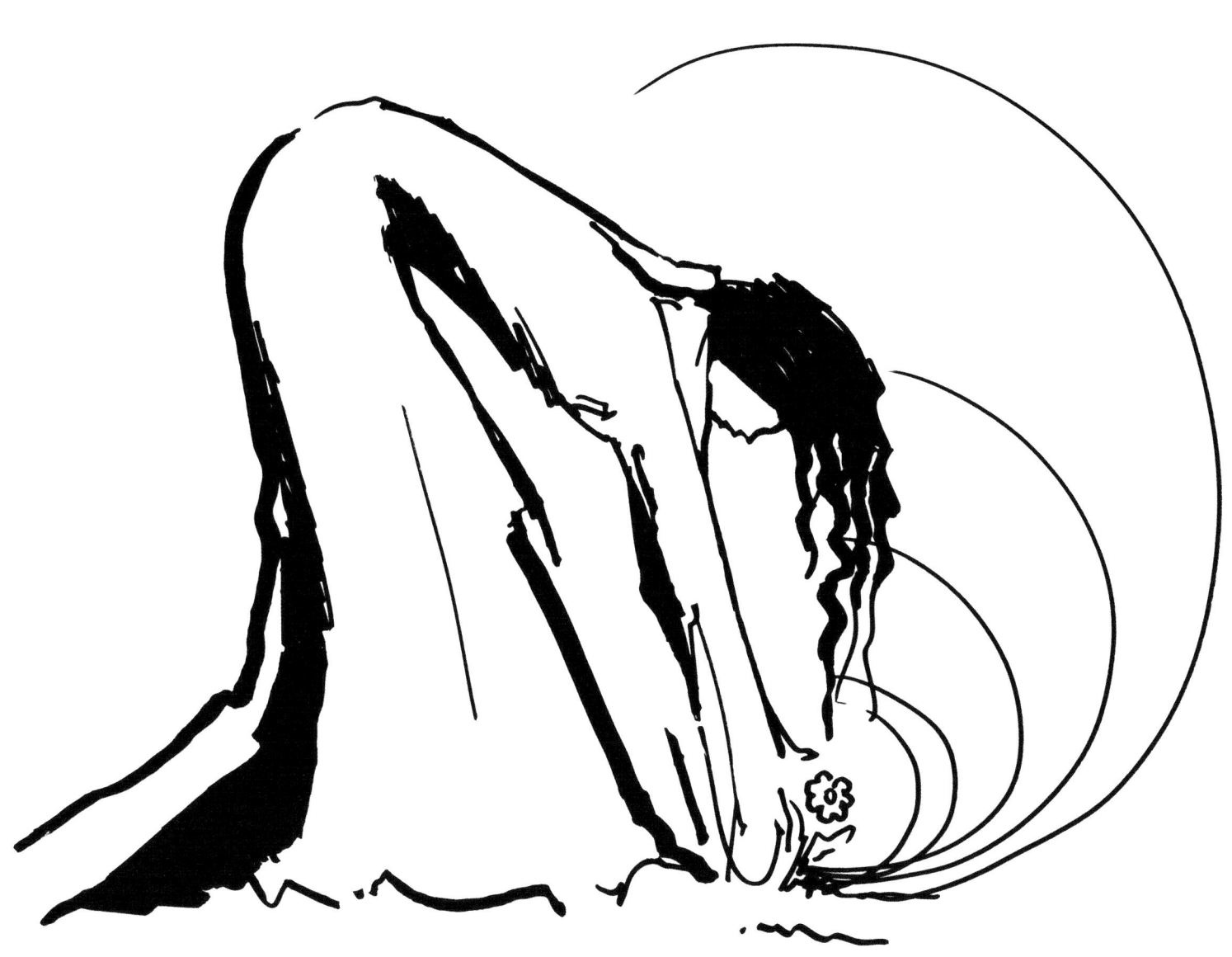

Love

is more than words can define
It is a feeling that wells up inside
and longs for release.

It is a smile which starts in my heart
and spreads across my face like a silly grin.

It is a knowing so deep in my being
that every cell speaks in a language
only lovers know.

And most of all it is the beginning,
the birth,
the possibility,
the promise of tomorrow,
the hope that grows into something
we can only imagine,
when hearts combine
and love becomes more.

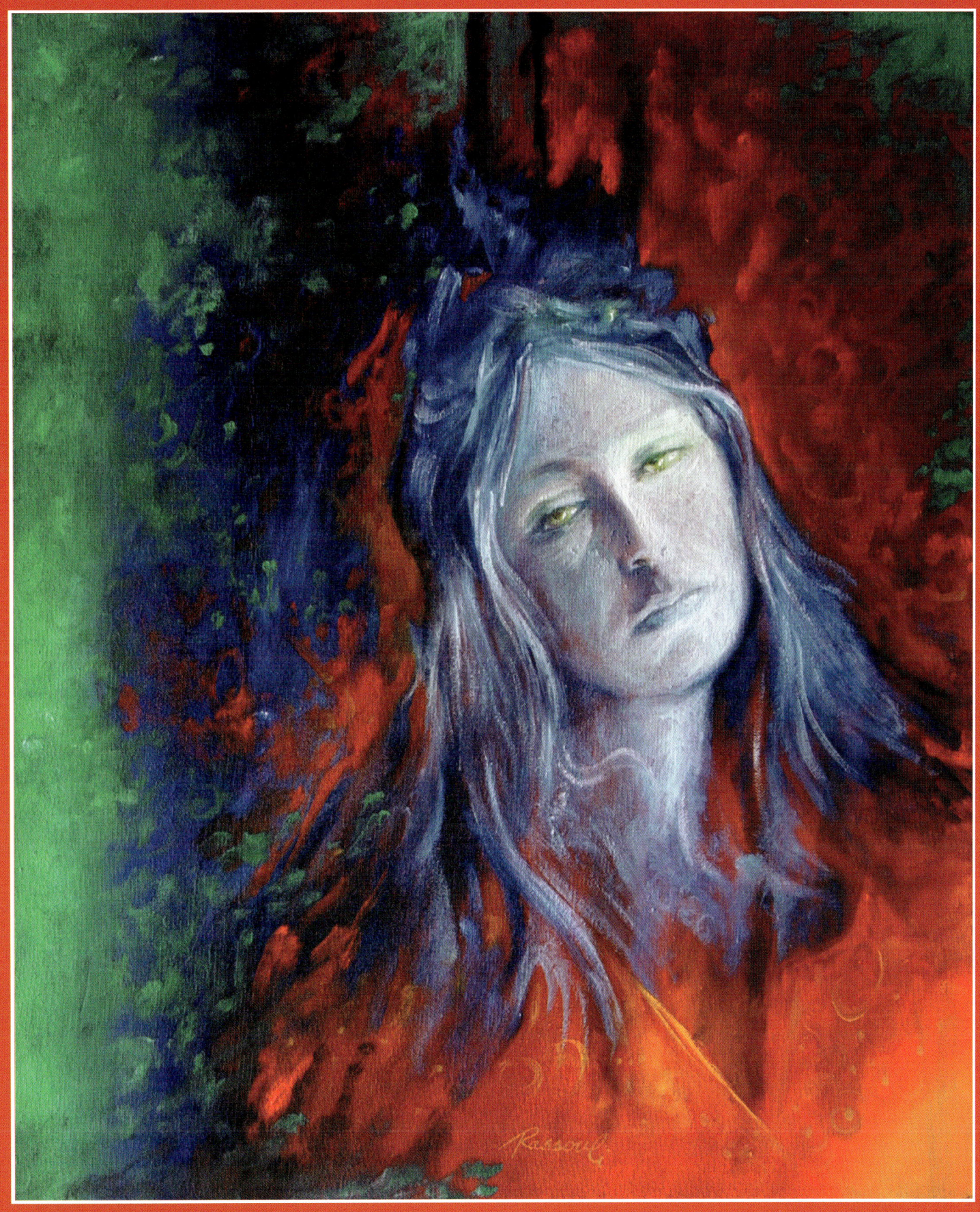

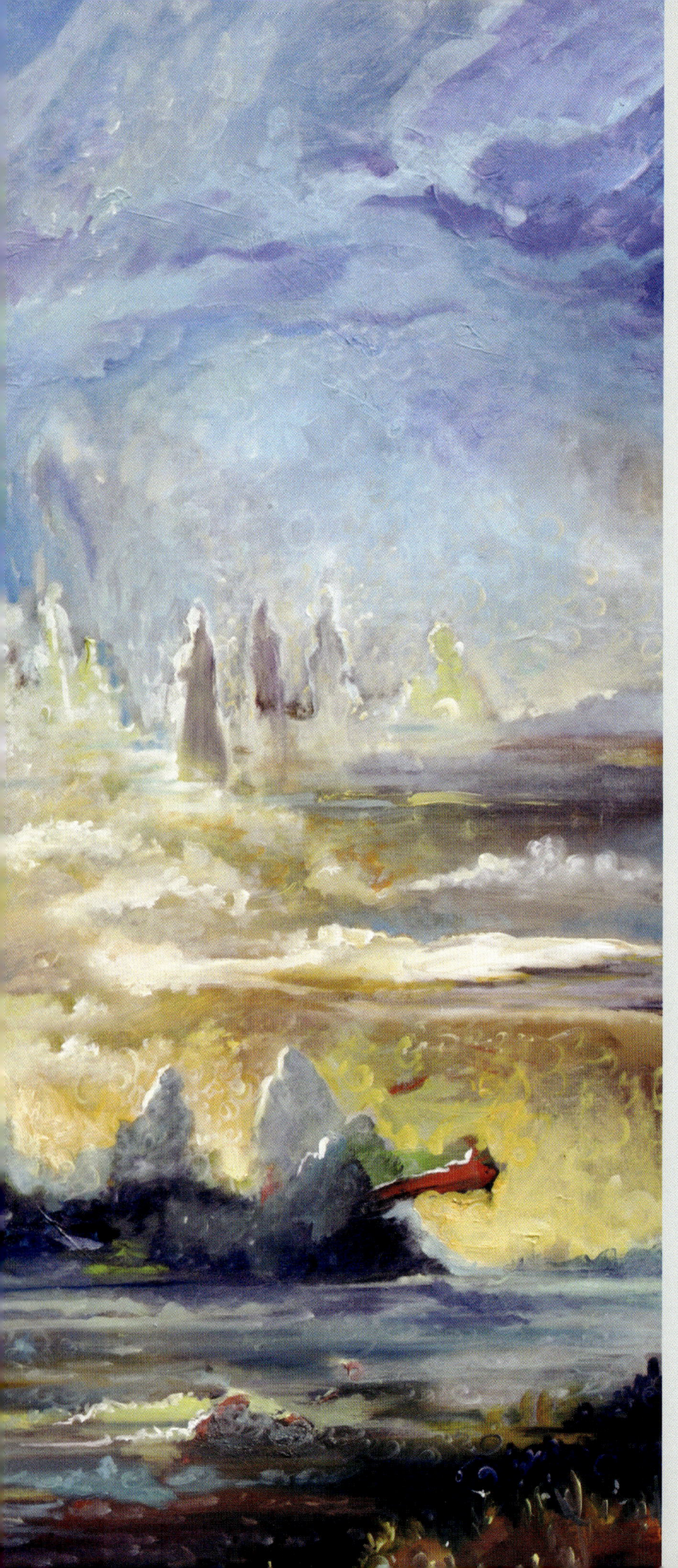

*Mighty sentinels
connecting heaven and earth,

wisdom of the ancients
waiting for those who listen,
in the quiet.*

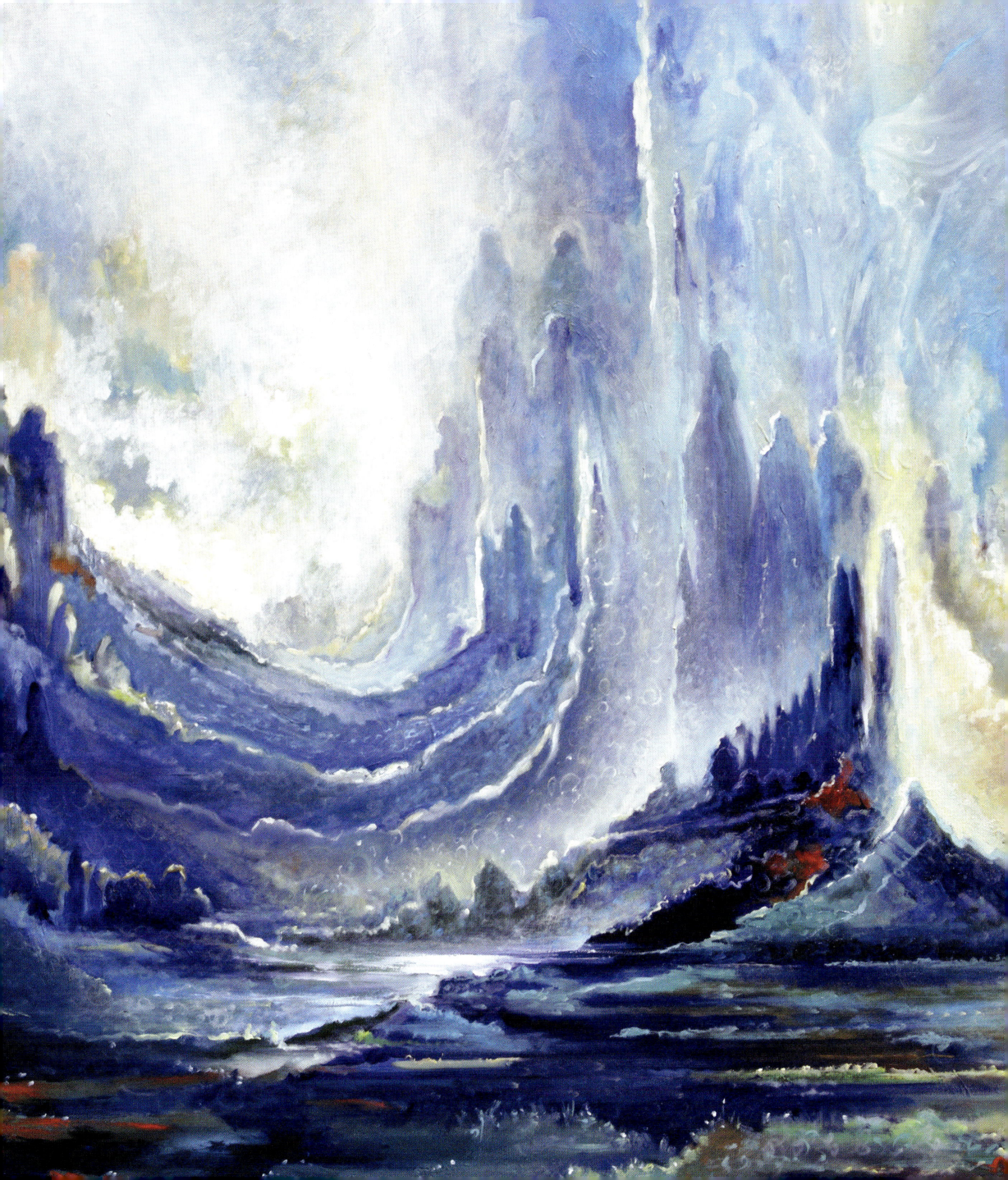

The inner movement
in expressive flow
an outward breath of dance and light
becoming one
becoming free

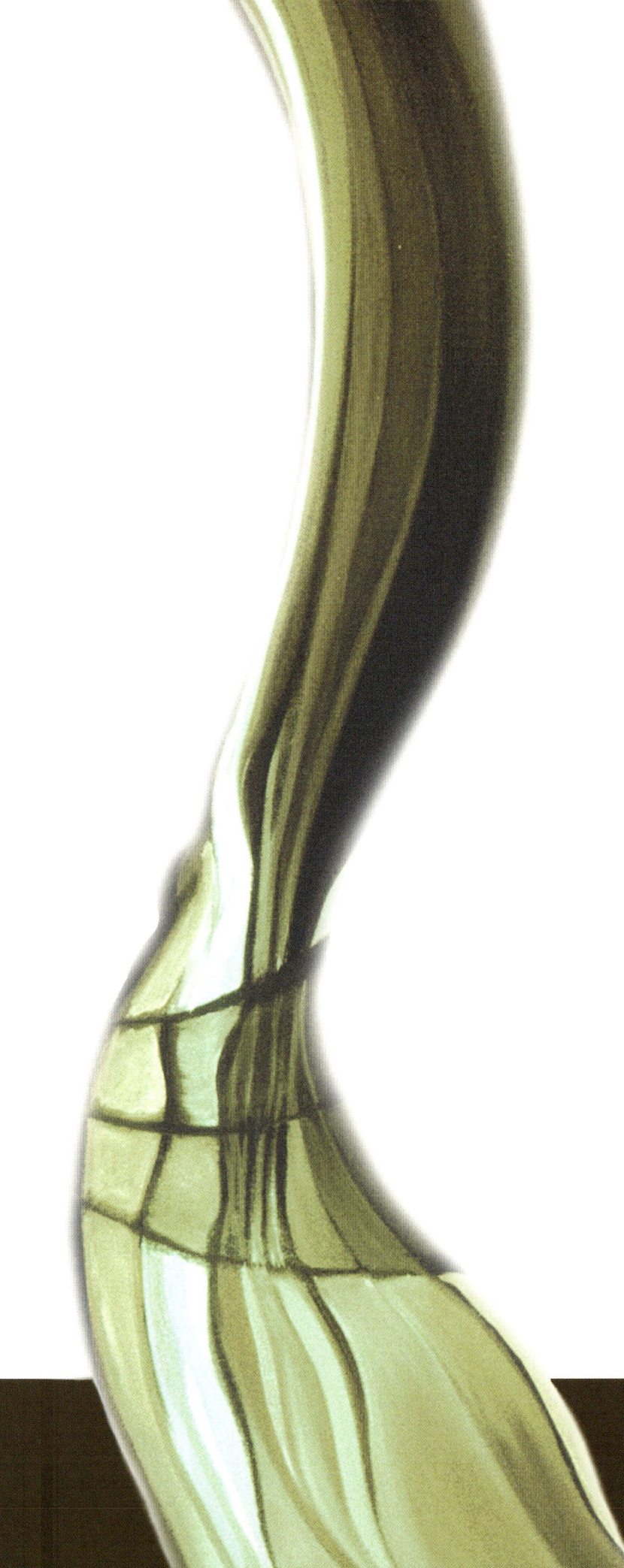

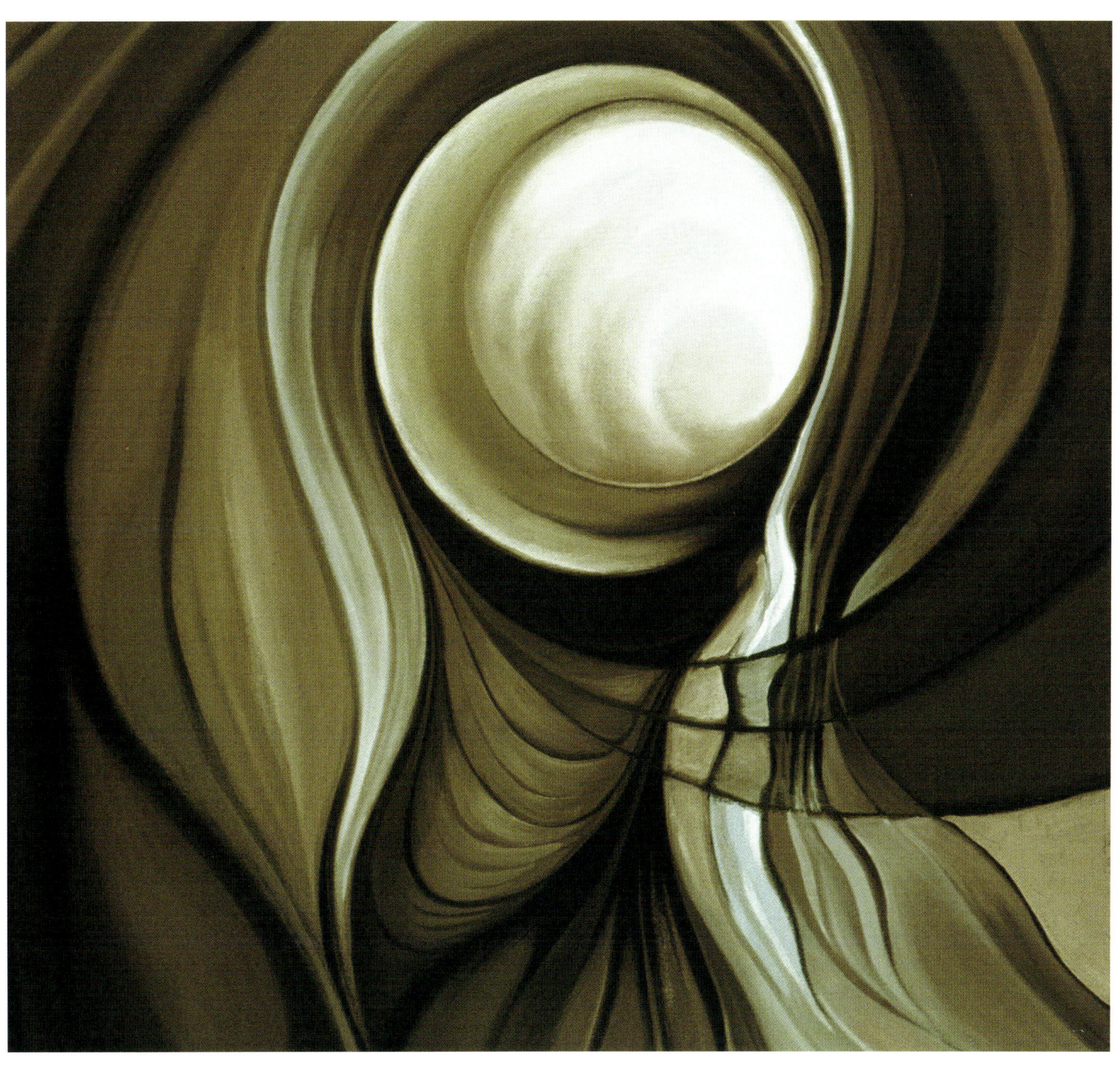

From the white foam on a surface of blue
to the mystery beneath the waves,
wherever your travels may lead,
May the artist's touch inspire us to explore
the ocean realm and celebrate the beauty
as land gives way to water
and water to the unknown.

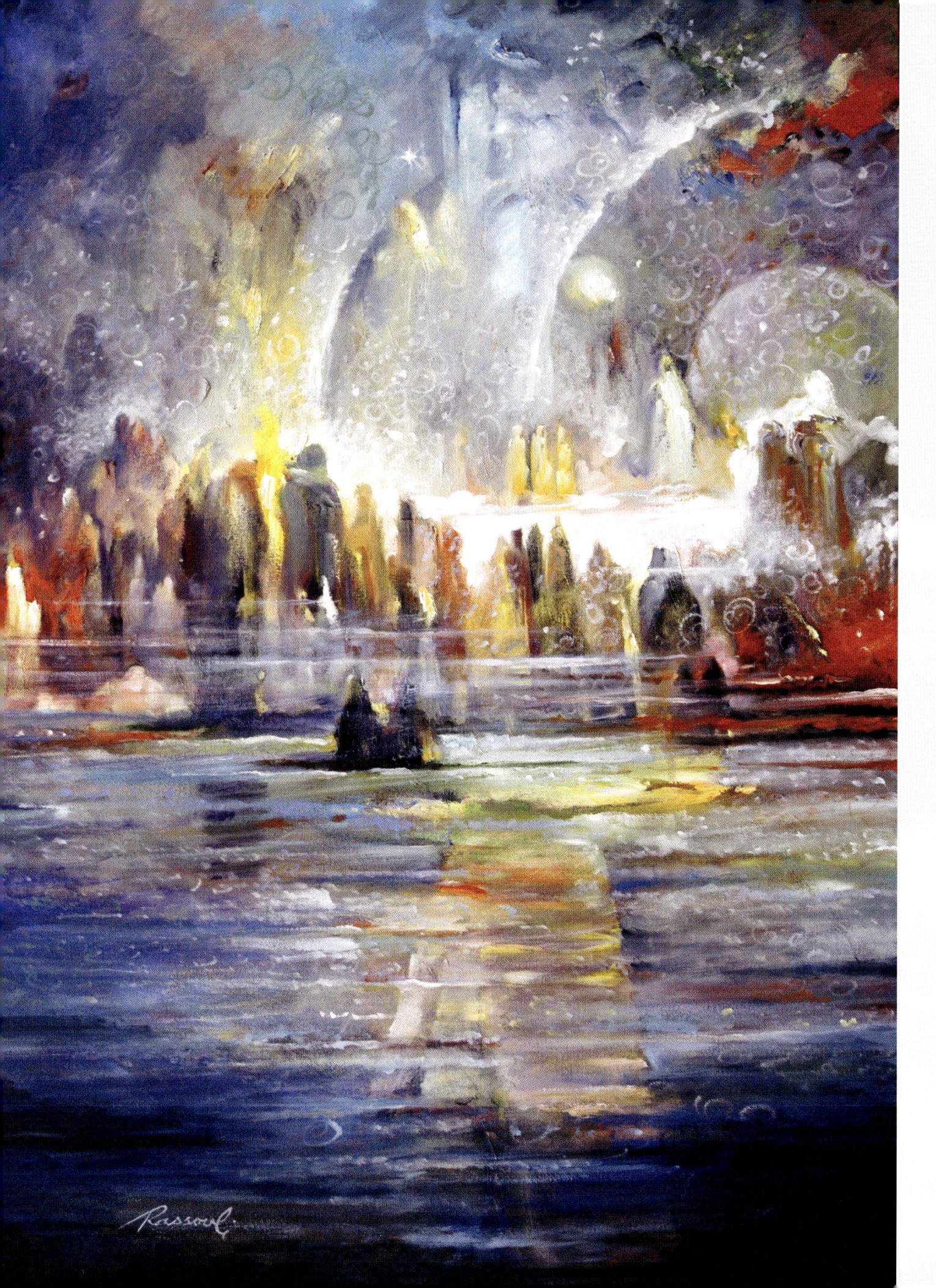

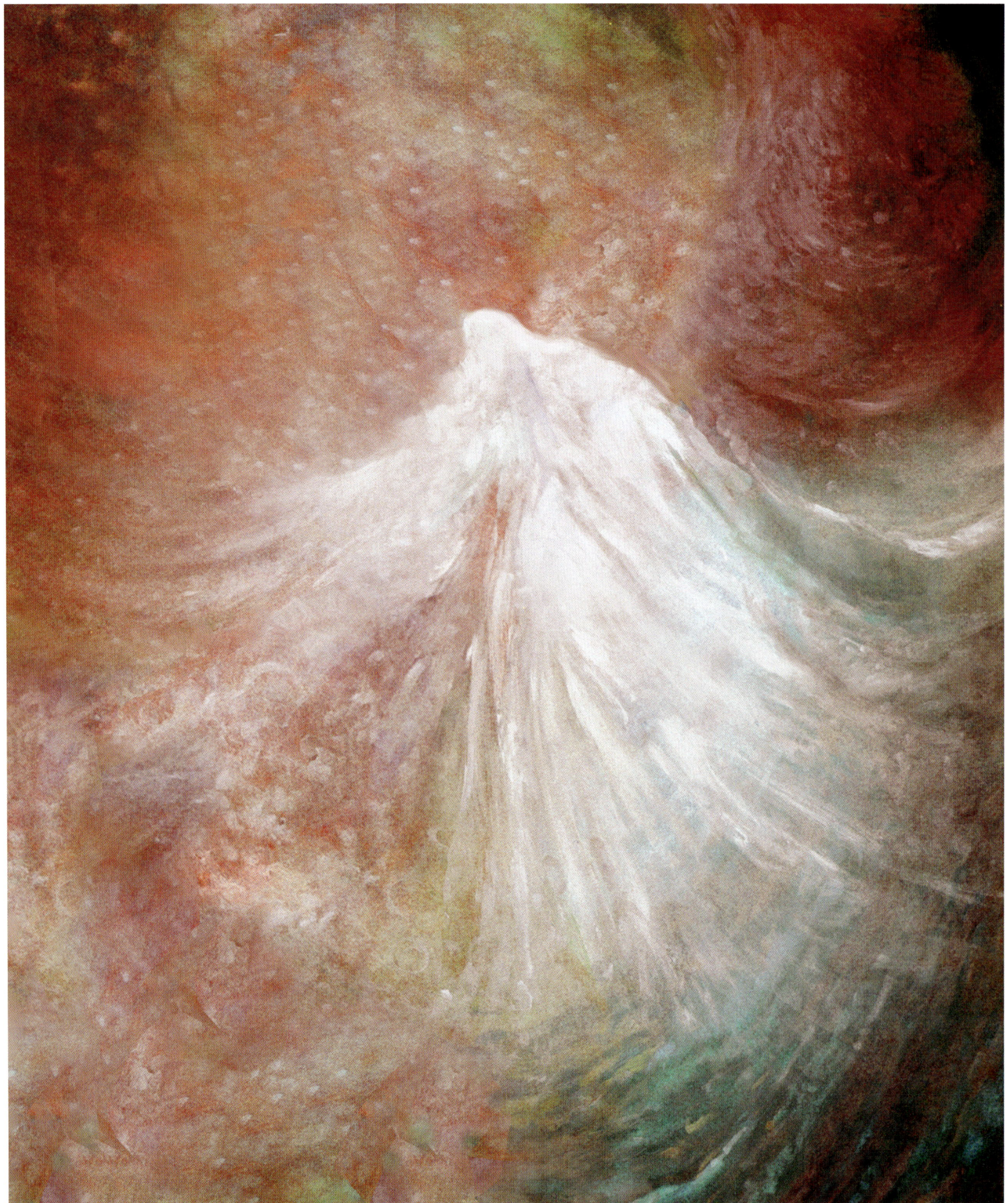

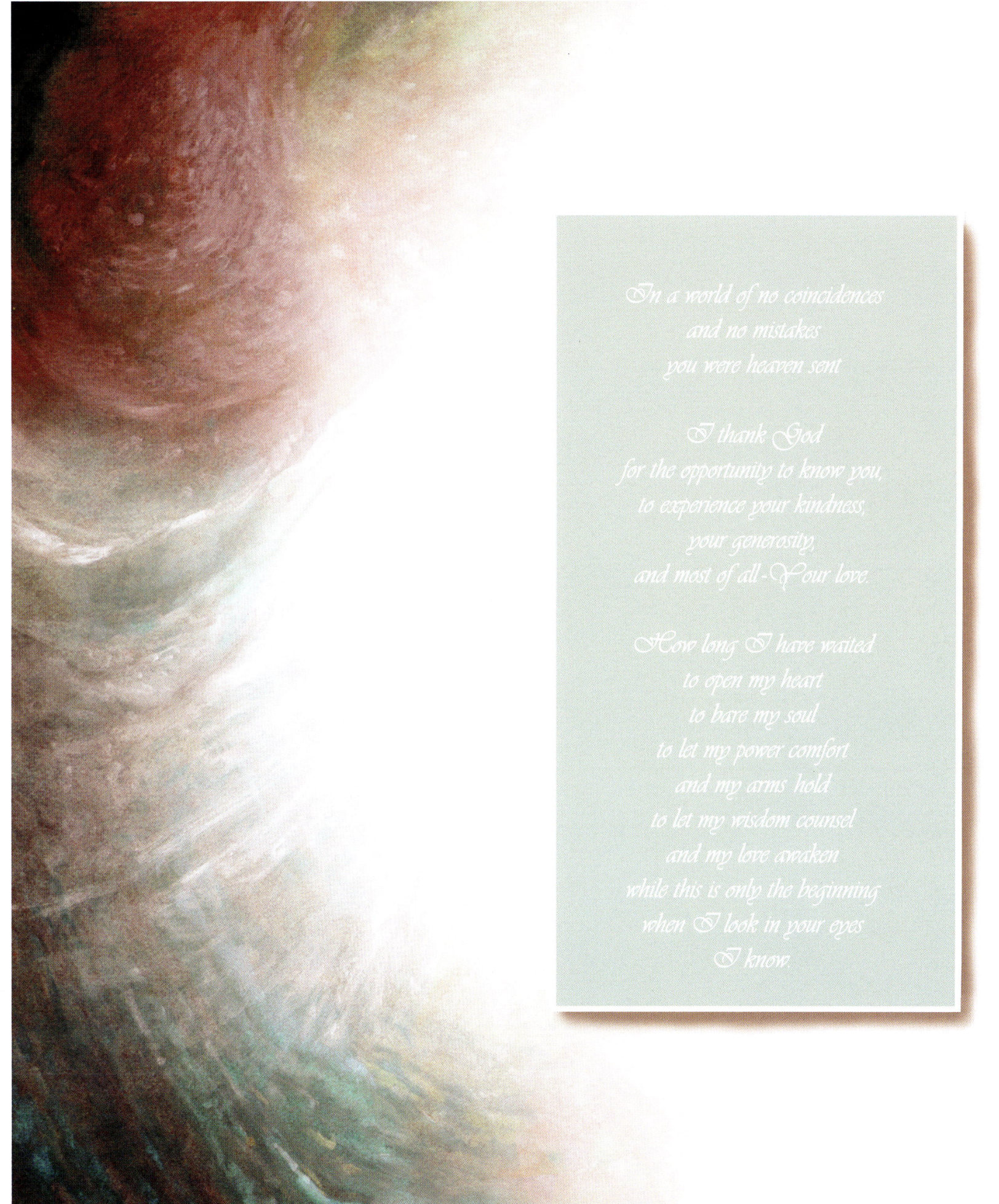

In a world of no coincidences
and no mistakes
you were heaven sent

I thank God
for the opportunity to know you,
to experience your kindness,
your generosity,
and most of all - Your love.

How long I have waited
to open my heart
to bare my soul
to let my power comfort
and my arms hold
to let my wisdom counsel
and my love awaken
while this is only the beginning
when I look in your eyes
I know.

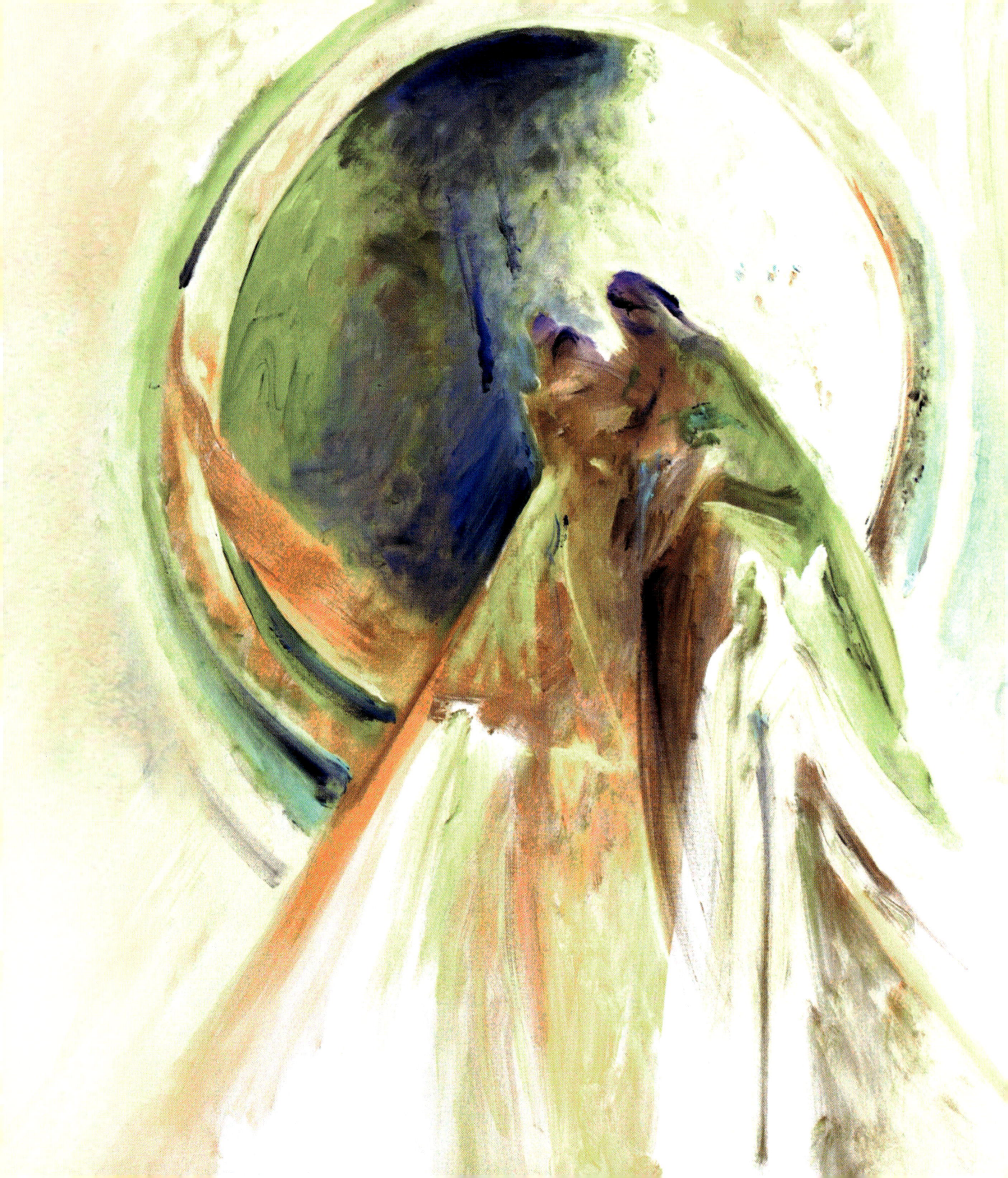

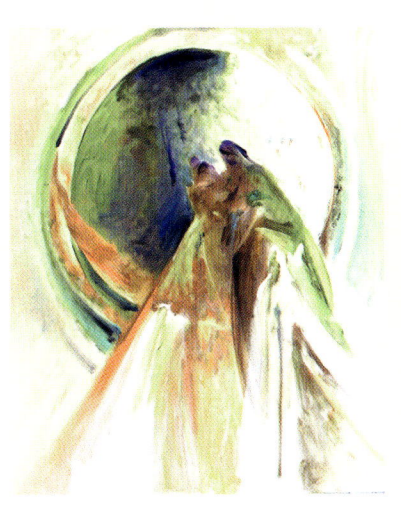

When I open my heart
        you cover me
            with a blanket of love
            and warm the silence
                with your caress

Words unspoken say it all
        as we become more
            than we are alone

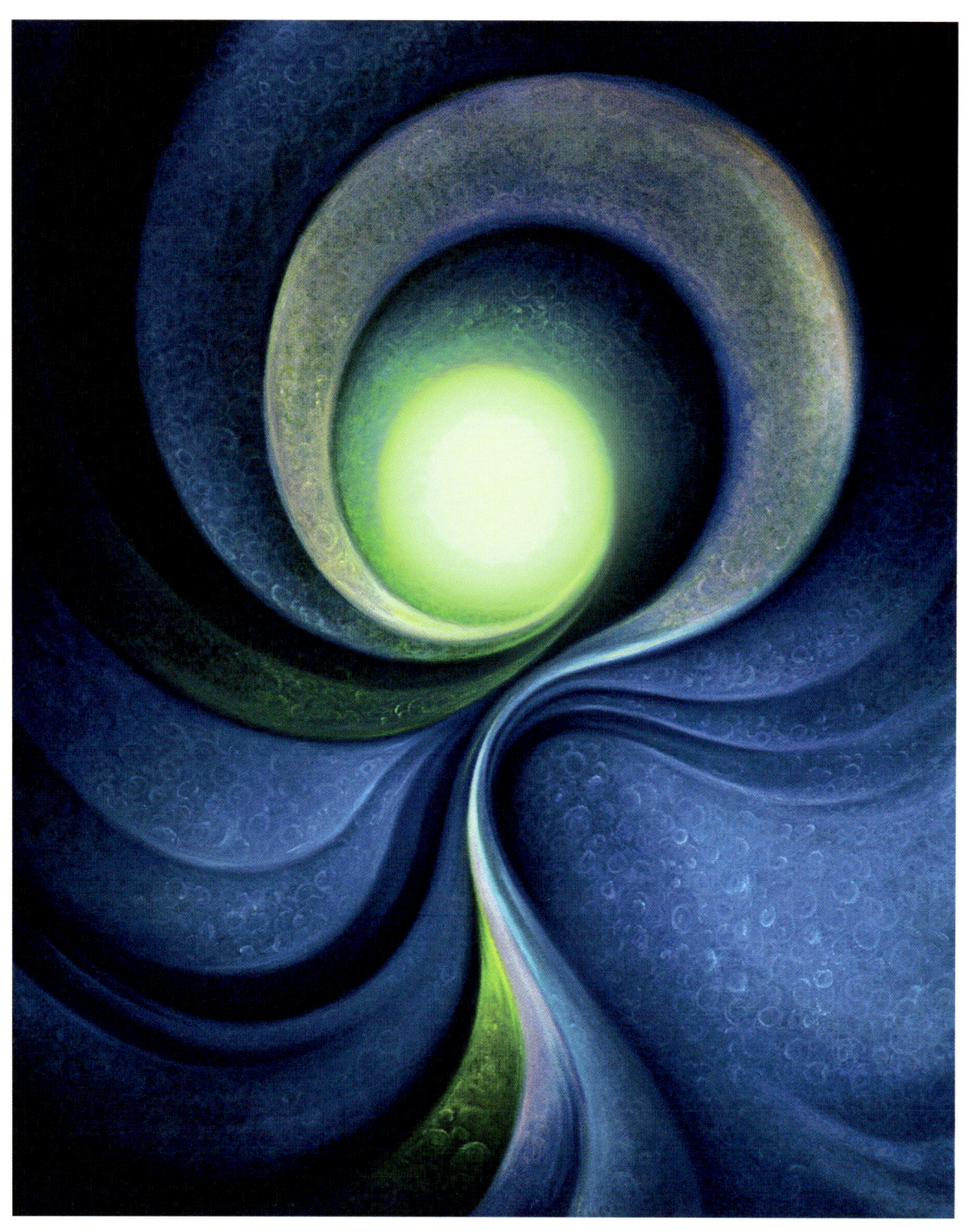

When sky can imagine
    the dark awake
        in awe, light pervades
    and bares the vast tranquil mystery
        softly caressing the blue bold birth

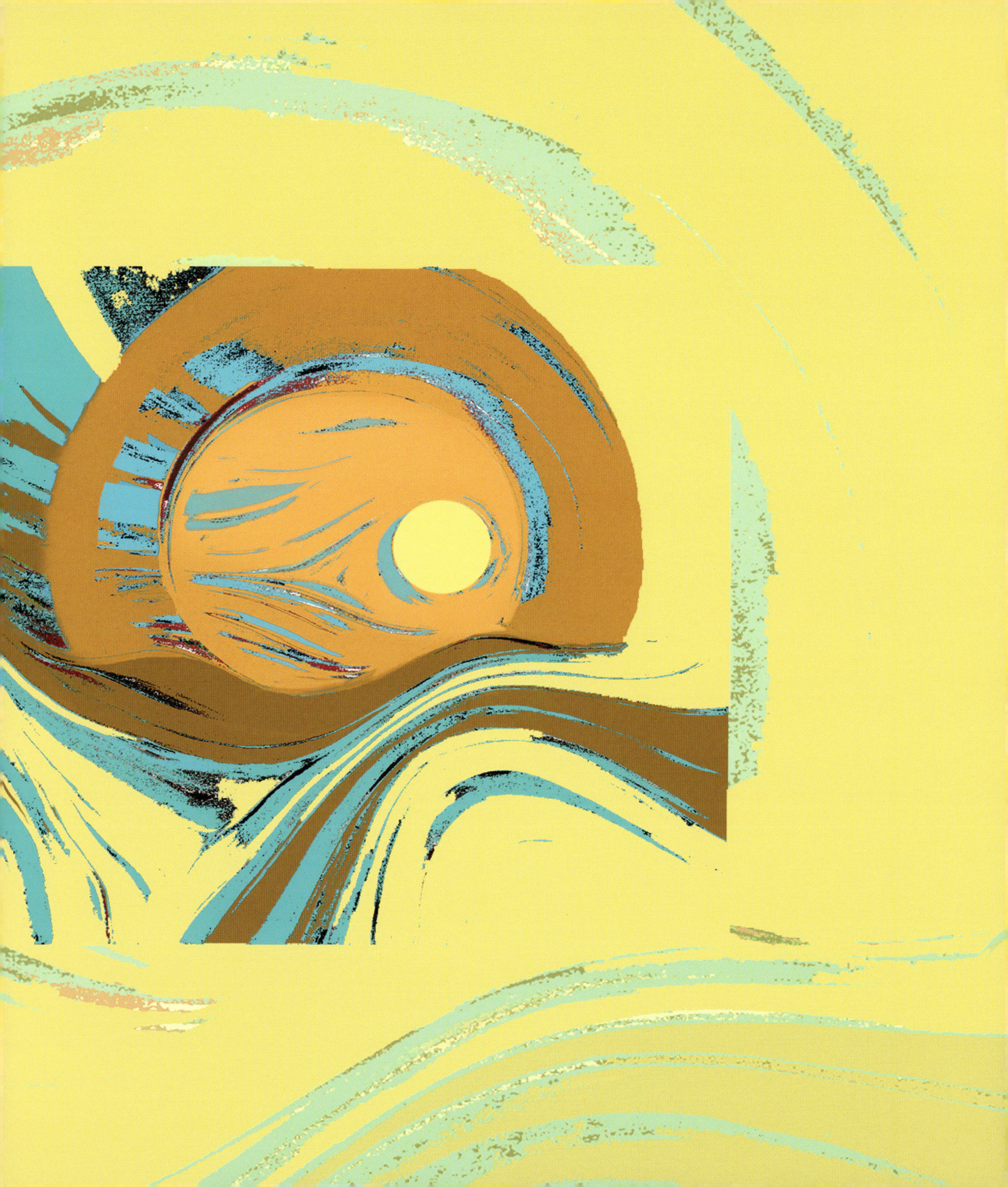

Day Birth

The Eastern rise of time
   on new born wings
bursts out across the lifeless crowd
and sings its climb to heights unknown
of beauty warmth and power upon its throne
      to fade again in Western sky
   and only for a moment lie
before it takes its course again
    to breathe once more in heart of man

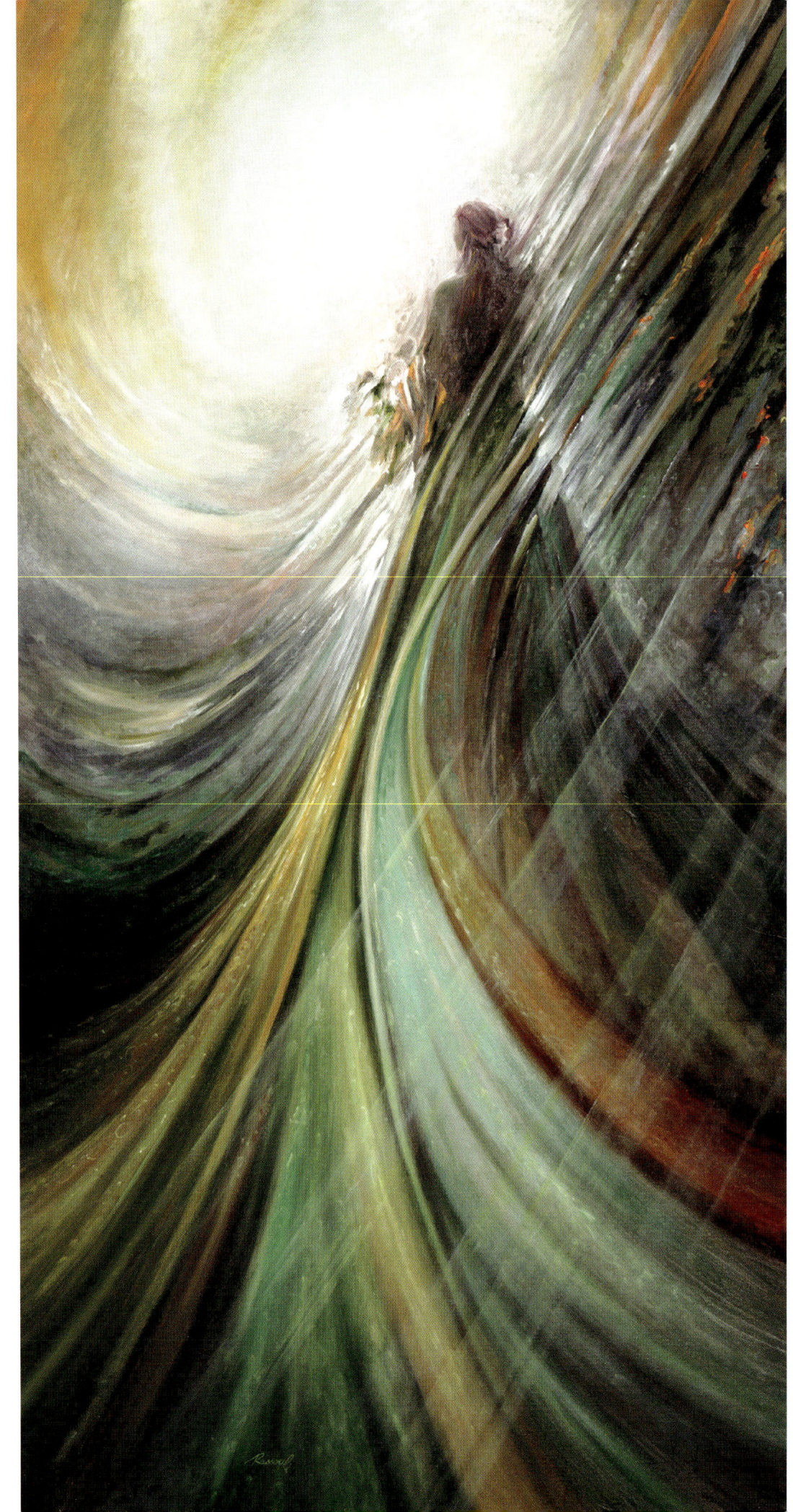

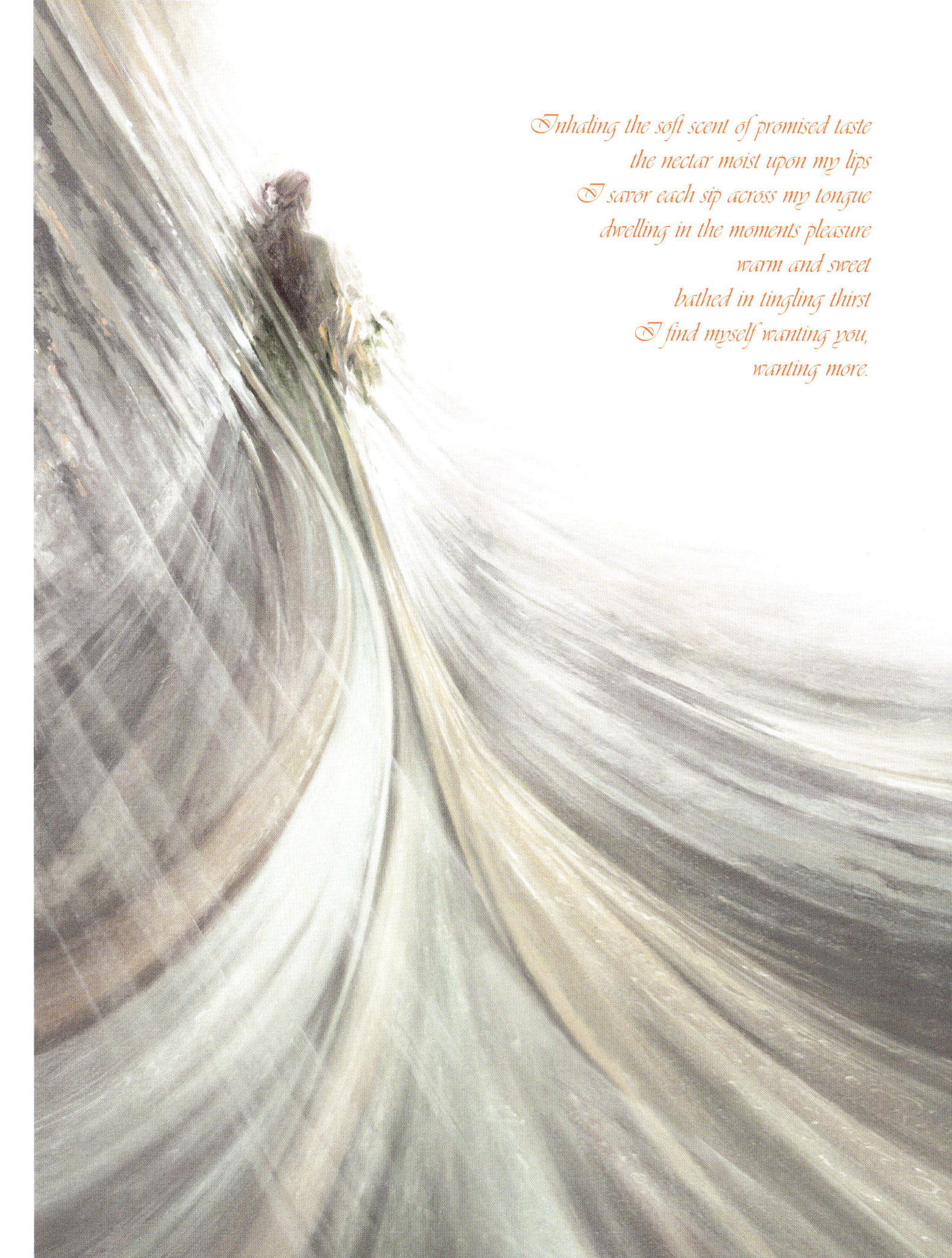

Inhaling the soft scent of promised taste
the nectar moist upon my lips
I savor each sip across my tongue
dwelling in the moments pleasure
warm and sweet
bathed in tingling thirst
I find myself wanting you,
wanting more.

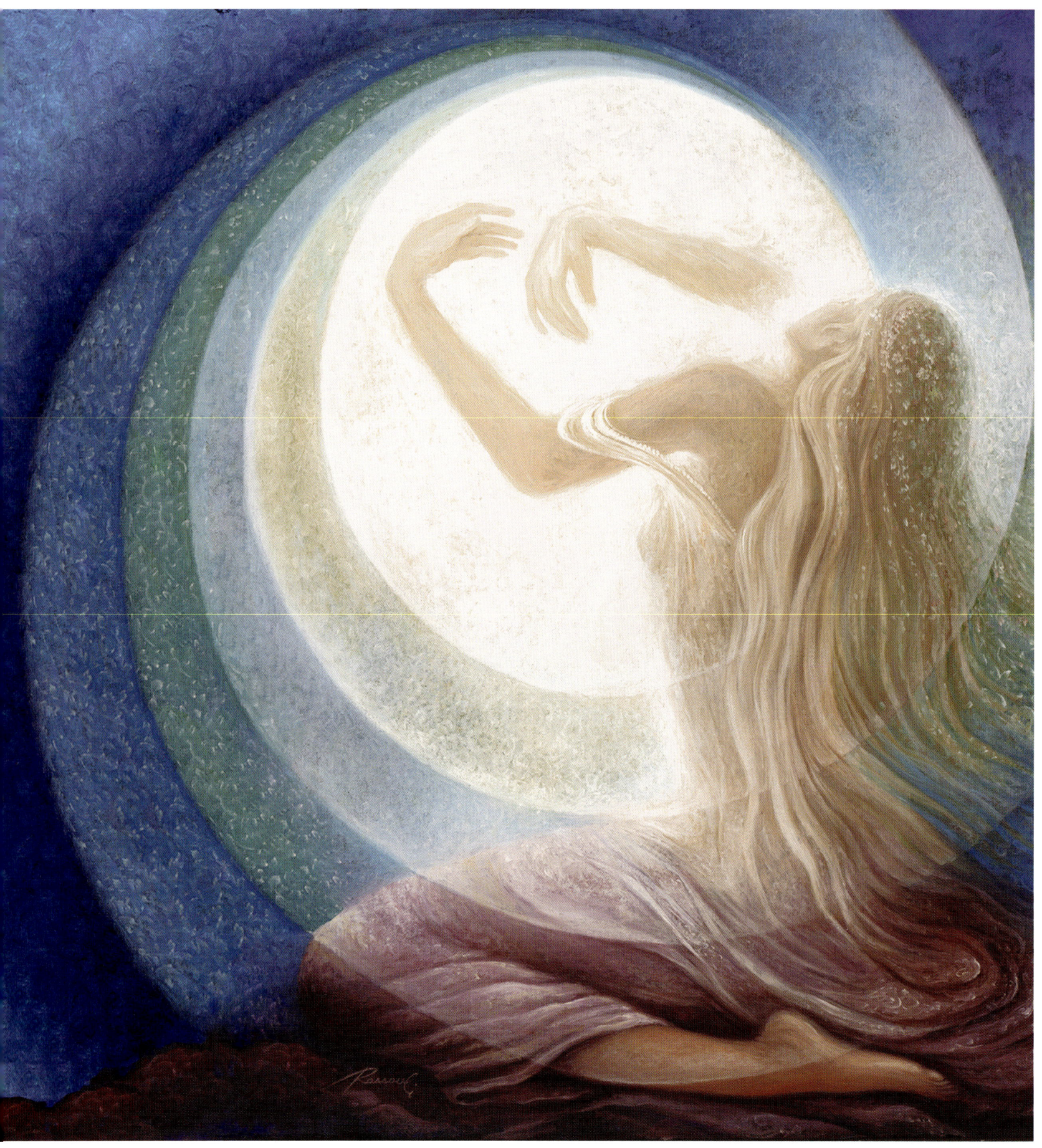

*A state of being,
allowing,
receiving,
becoming one,
with*
all that is.

Waiting

These moments are precious
like jewels on the crown of life.
They beckon my heart
forming memories
that sparkle with joy
and like the longing of a sweet caress
they draw me near, melting into one
showing what is possible
on the journey of life
waiting for the season's change.

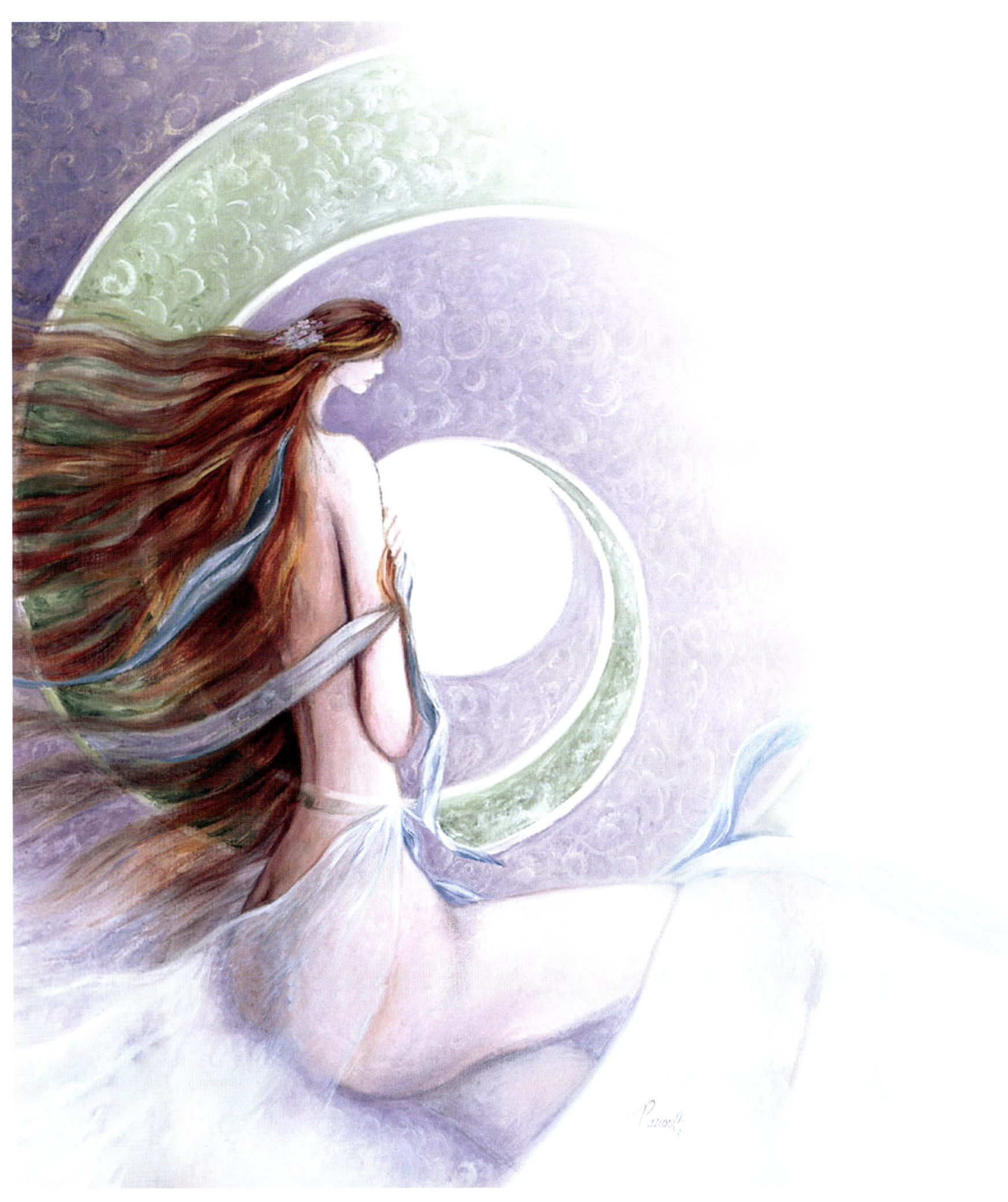

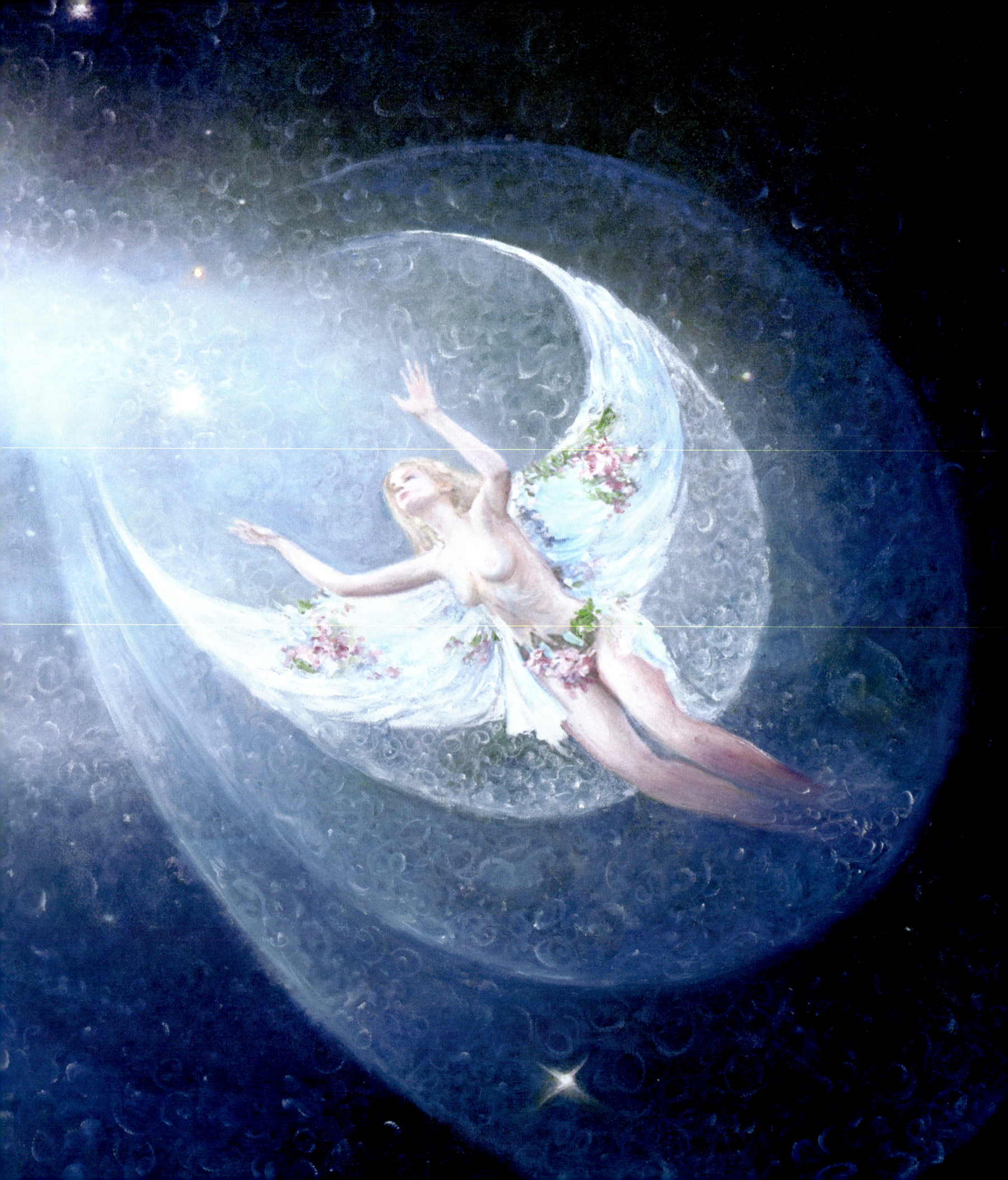

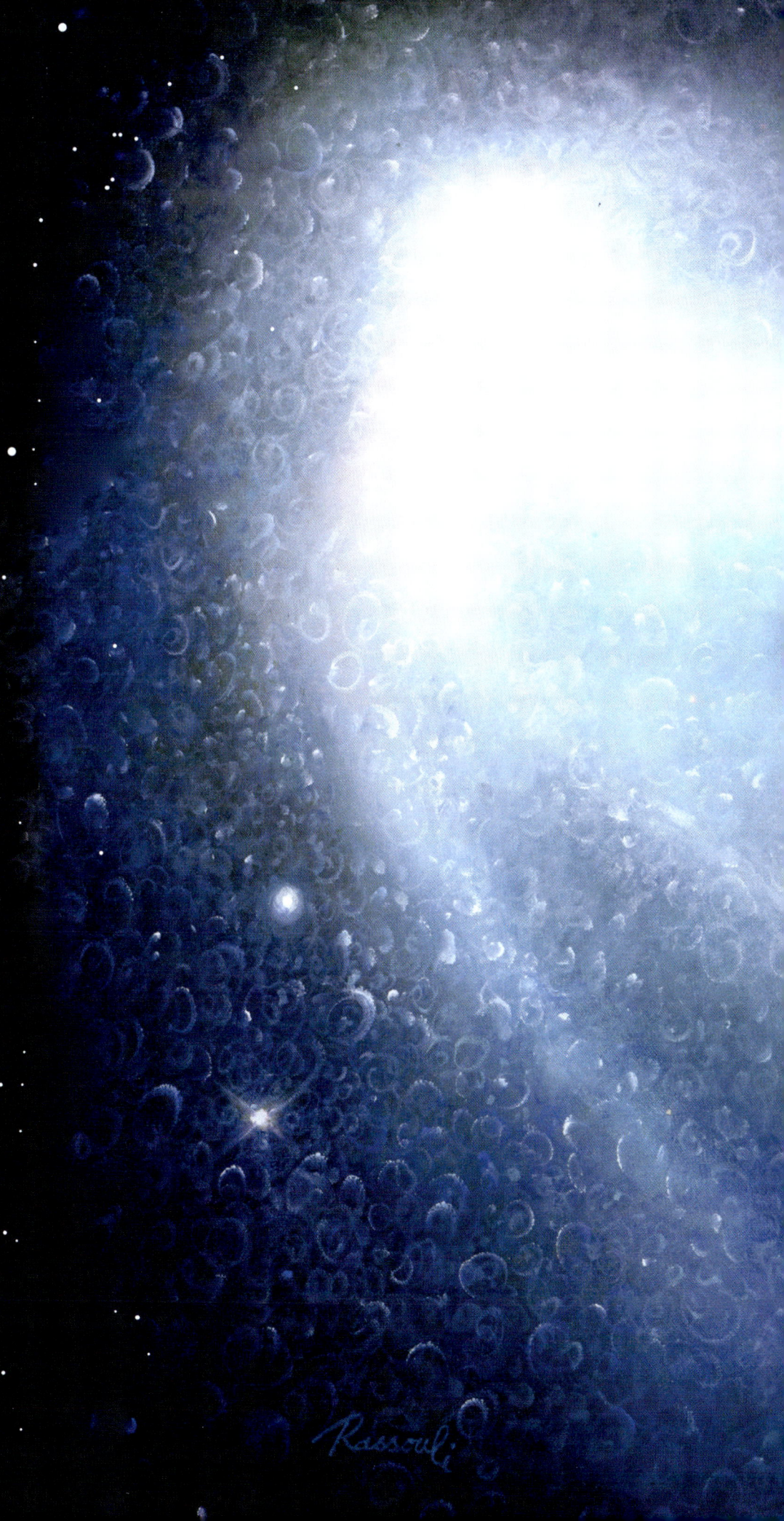

With innocence I share my heart
a smile expressing with a tear
sweet words and feelings that impart
everything that I hold dear

The promise of a blossom high
the air is bathed in fragrant scent
to reach the sun you have to fly
desire wells with love that's meant

To wait for heaven's soft embrace
a fruit so firm and succulent
God's promise must remain so chaste
while passion's glow is slowly spent

Such patience born with time's insight
my soul doth burn in ember's light
and savors fresh and moist and ripe
the gift of love when it is right.

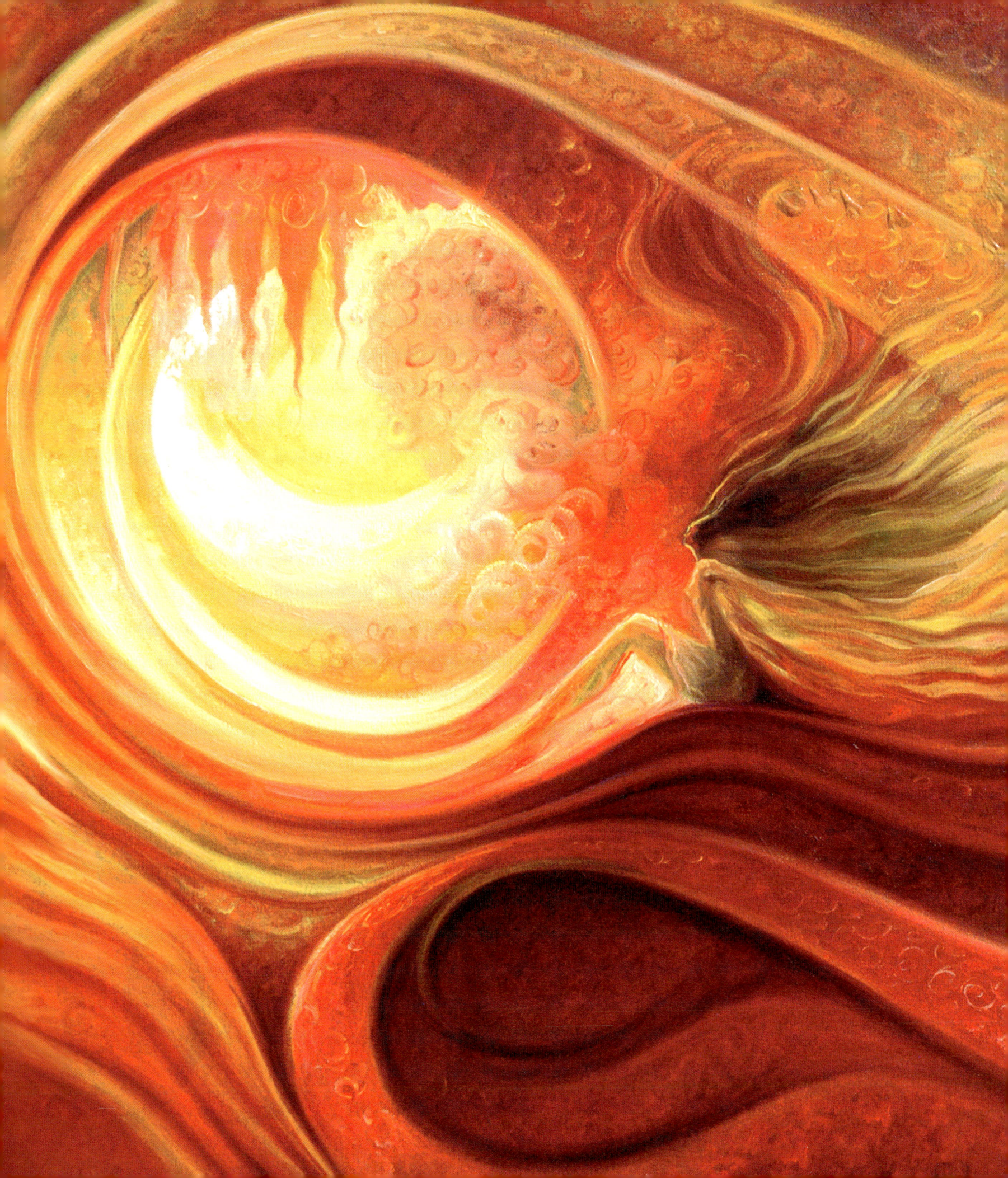

I have watched you hurting
and felt helpless to make life better for you.

Loving you is having to make choices
to let you be who you are,
who you become
and all the who's yet to come.

To love you is to ride the waves
of your passionate embrace of life,
ever mindful of the change in the wind
and the occasional tempest brewing.

Loving you is having to make choices,
knowing it isn't my fault
I can still choose to take it personally,
or, just be,
while I listen and watch you unfold.

Your heart is a beauty I will always love.
It's the part of yopu
that hasn't changed much over time.

When I lie beside you and hear you breathe,
when I touch your skin,
or caress your hair,
you are timeless
and I choose loving you.

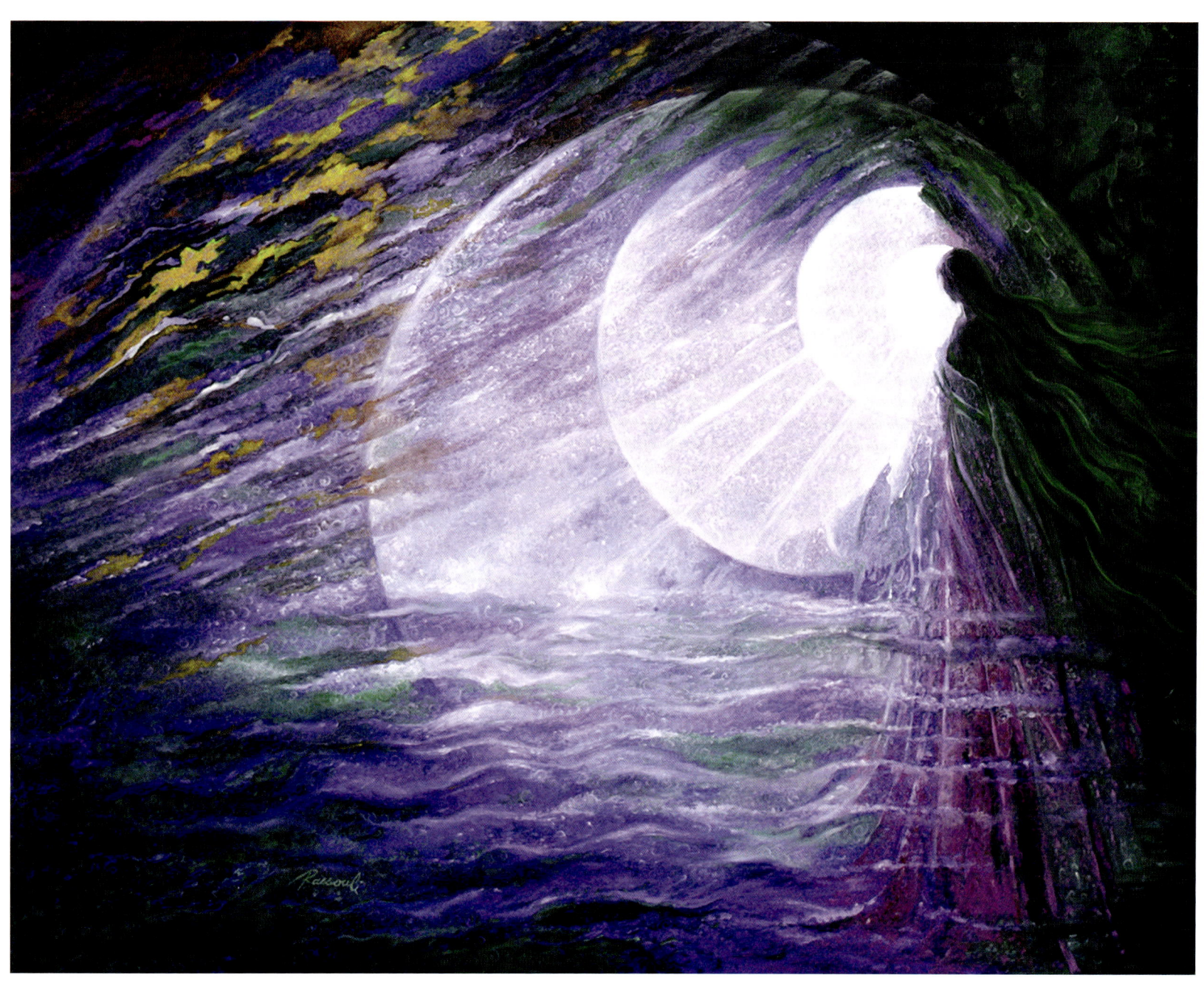

I waited for dawn, not wanting to go,
but knowing I soon would have to leave.
I waited for the first light, listening,
joining with you on each breath
and each exhale.

I watched as morning came
and you gently stirred,
knowing our love was not measured in time,
not the minutes that quickly passed,
or the hours as departure approached.

How I wanted to linger.
How I wanted to tell you
that this moment would last forever
and whisper one more time, I love you.

And then you held me
and said it first
and goodbye no longer mattered.

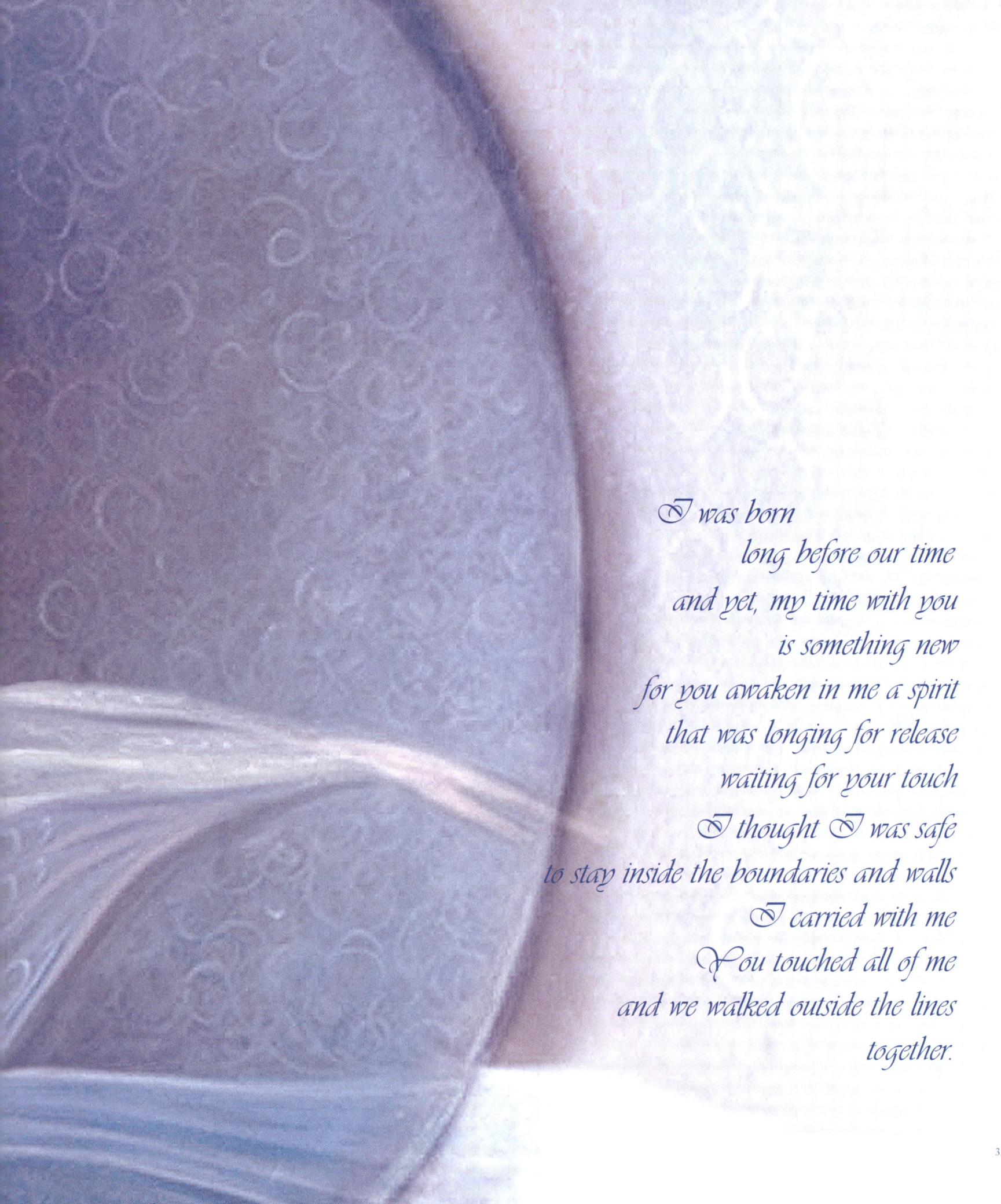

I was born
long before our time
and yet, my time with you
is something new
for you awaken in me a spirit
that was longing for release
waiting for your touch
I thought I was safe
to stay inside the boundaries and walls
I carried with me
You touched all of me
and we walked outside the lines
together.

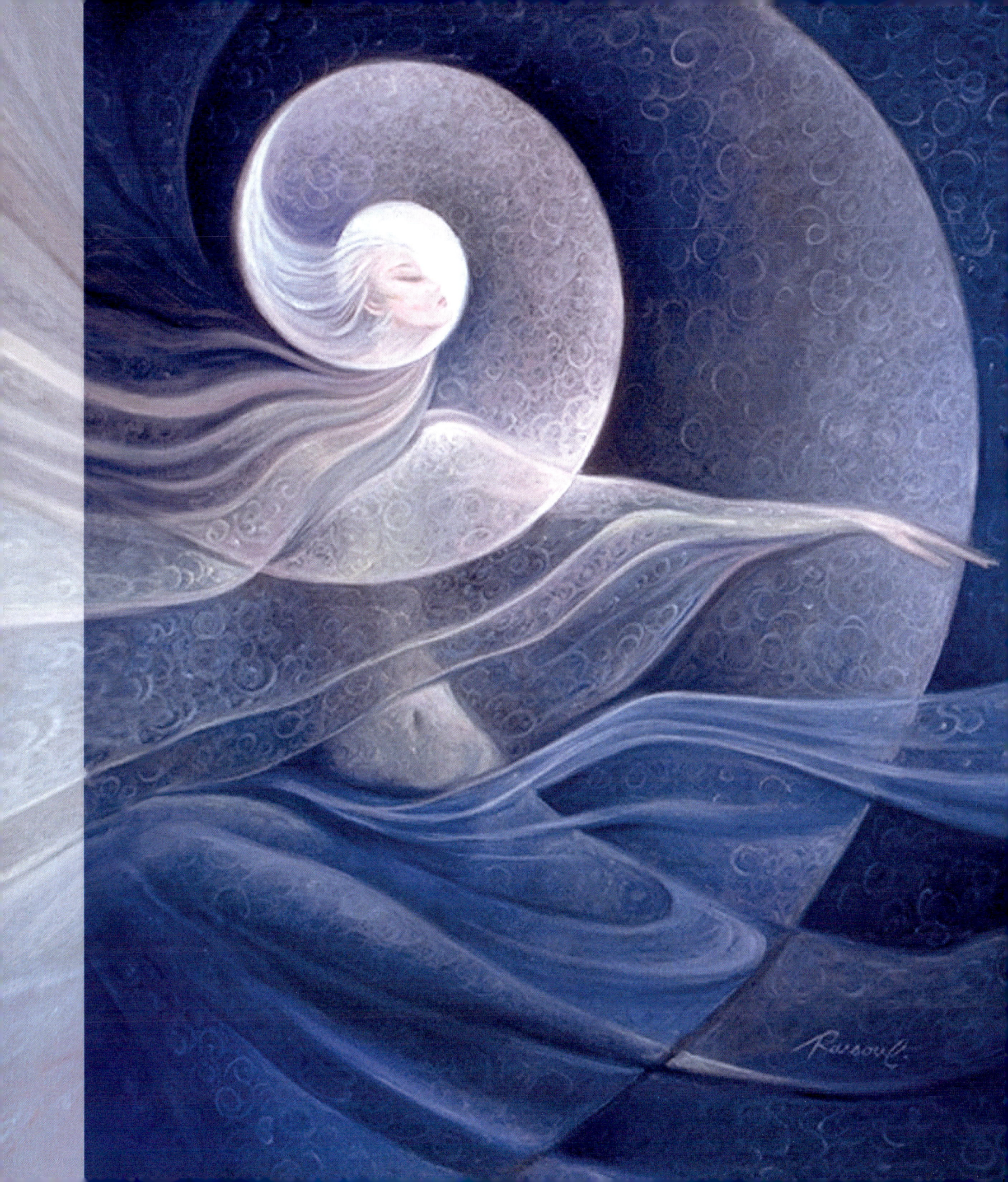

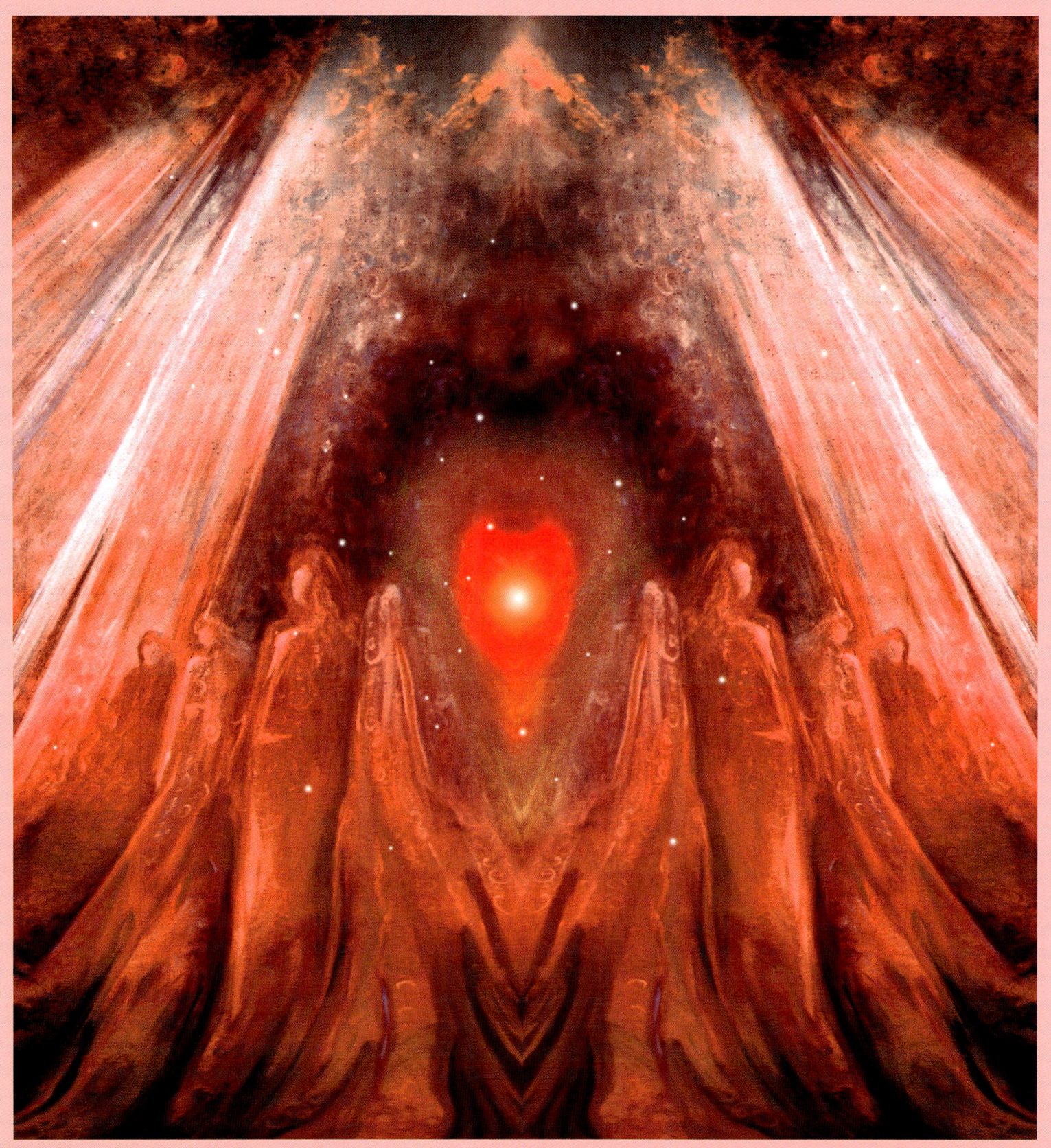

Expression of Love

Love provides the opportunity to express
the core essence of our very nature.
It touches us at a level of feeling beyond the human norm
and renders our beings incapable
of a feeling with greater depth, or wonder.

Love is the fabric of life.
It is the substance that holds it all together
and the magic that opens the unknown.

It is the quality that speaks to our soul,
that opens our heart,
that excites our spirit and allows us in its presence
to become something greater than ourselves,
something more than we are alone.

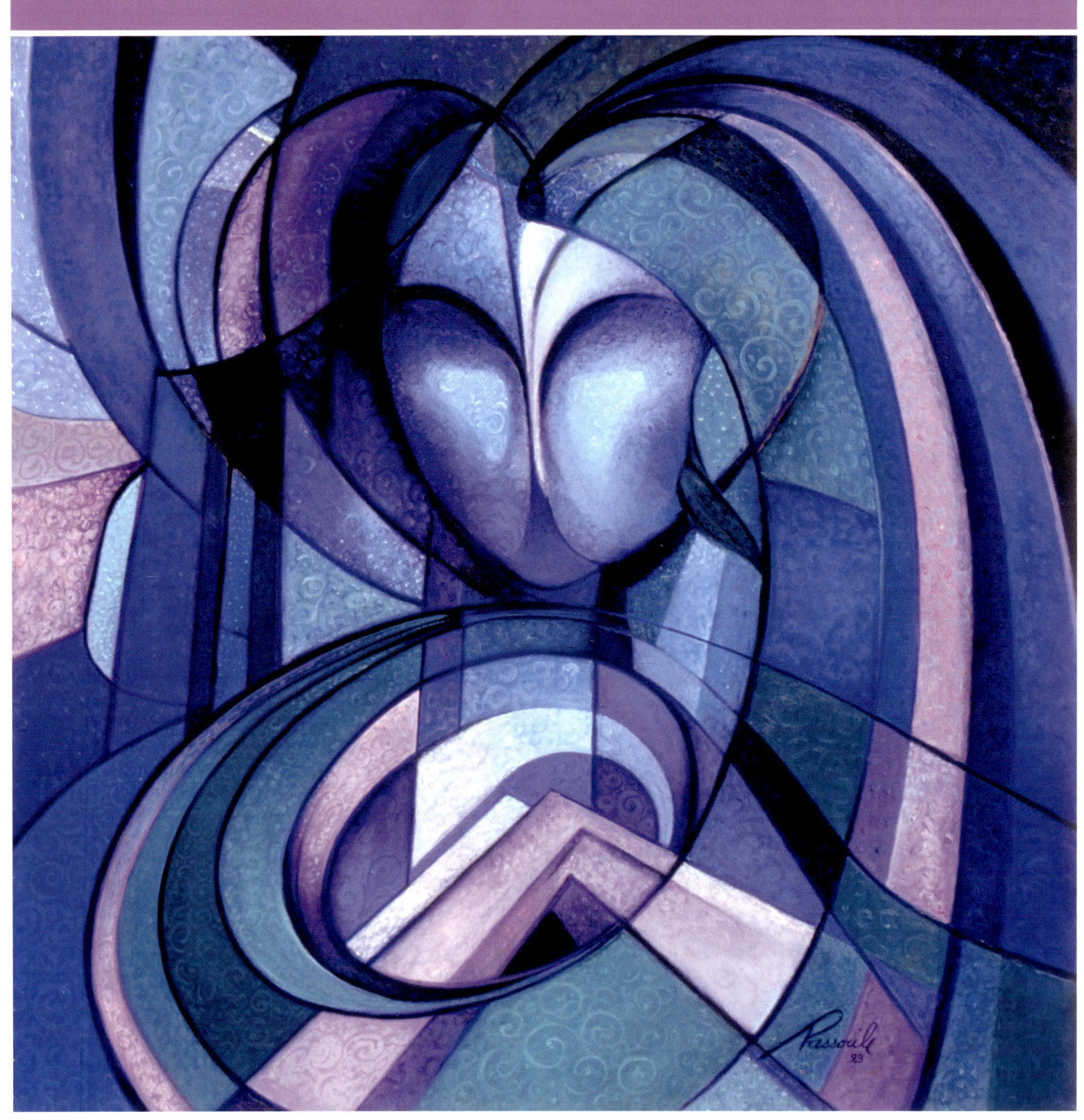

I love you,
holding your breath in my kiss
your heartbeat in my arms
driving home
I could see you sitting beside me
not with my eyes
but I knew you were there
your beautiful legs crossed
your coat open and inviting
the soft scent of you
brings a smile to my lips
and to my heart
because I know
you are still here.

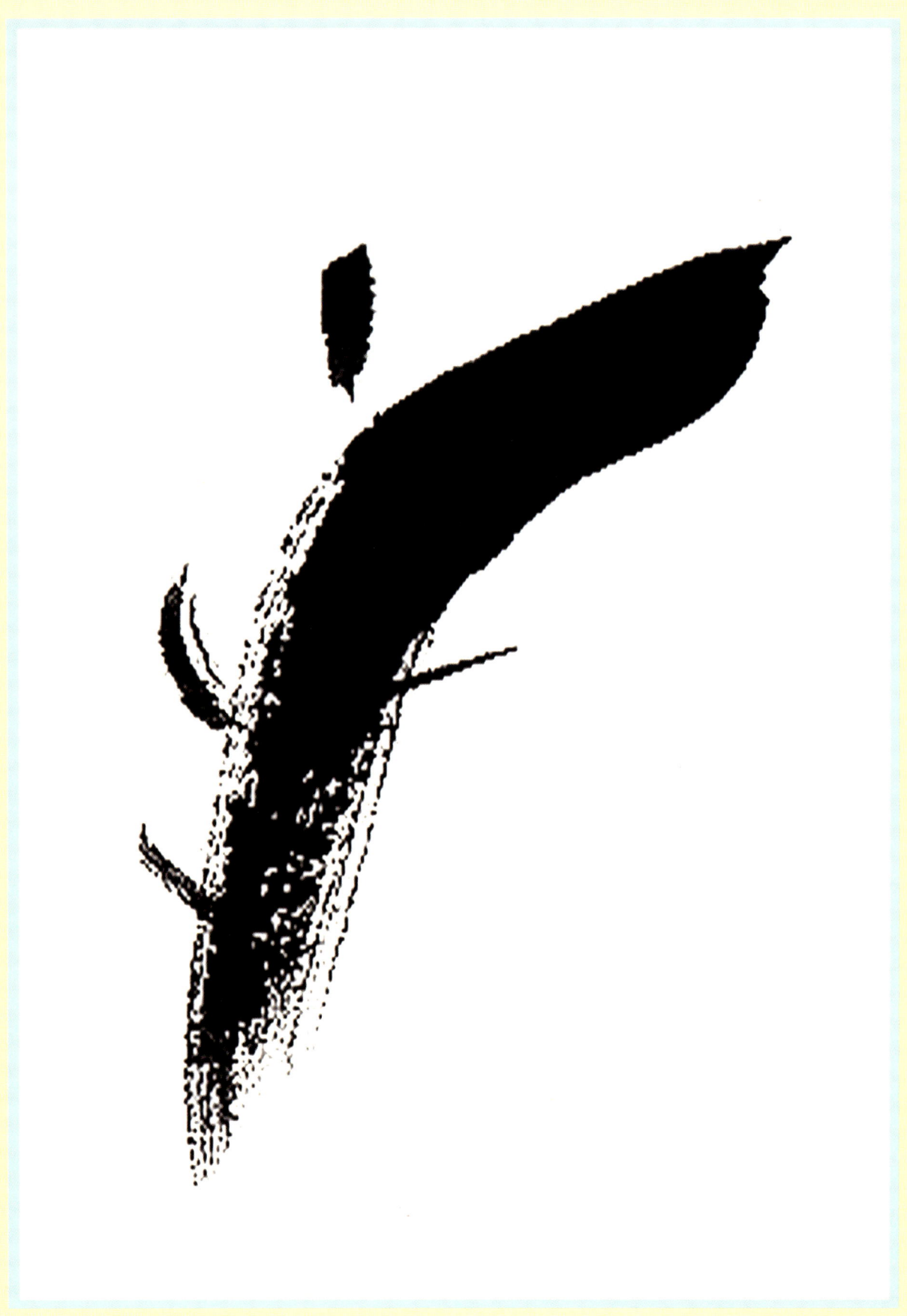

*Is it wrong to love
to feel what I hold inside?
The answer must wait.*

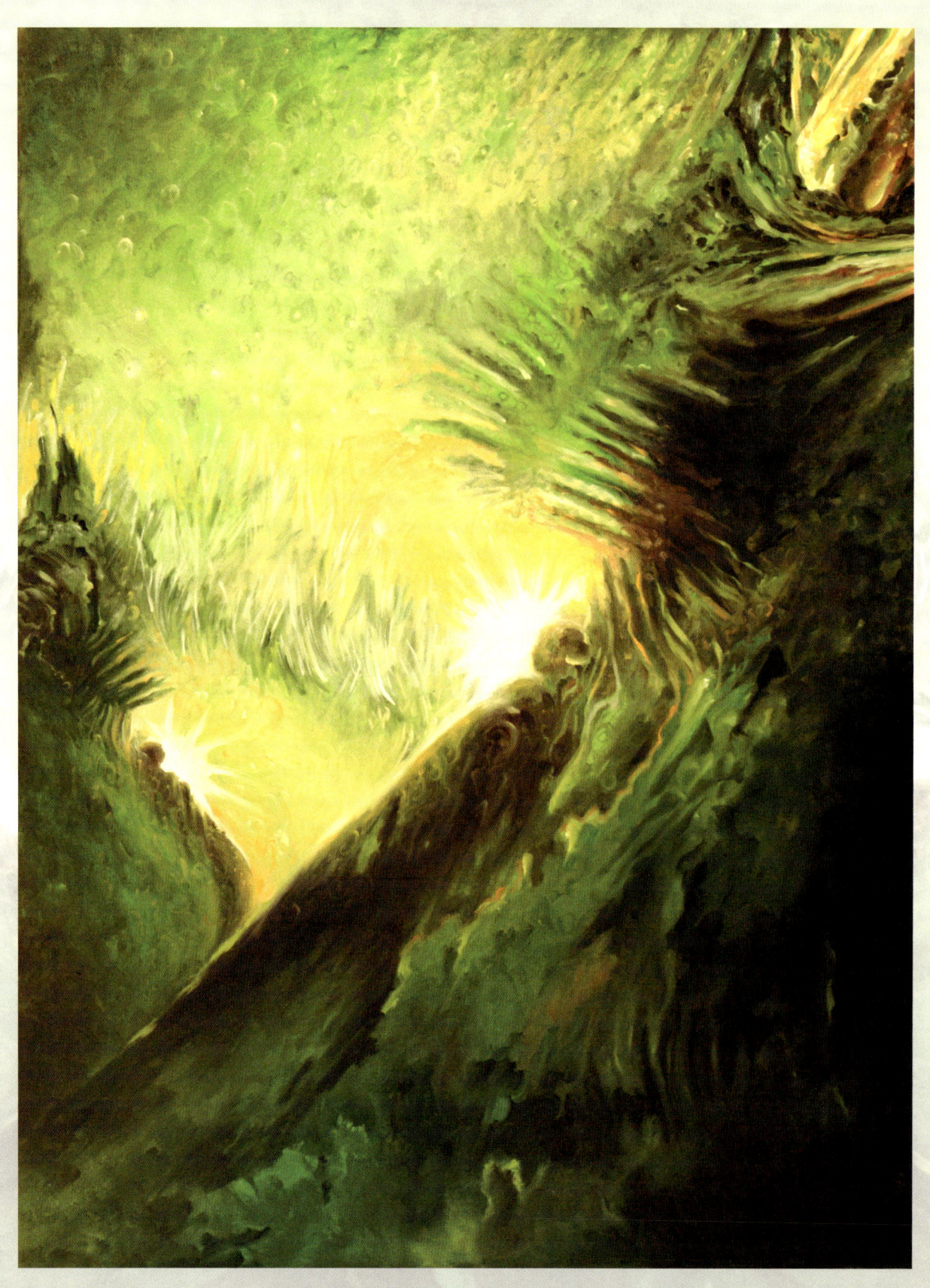

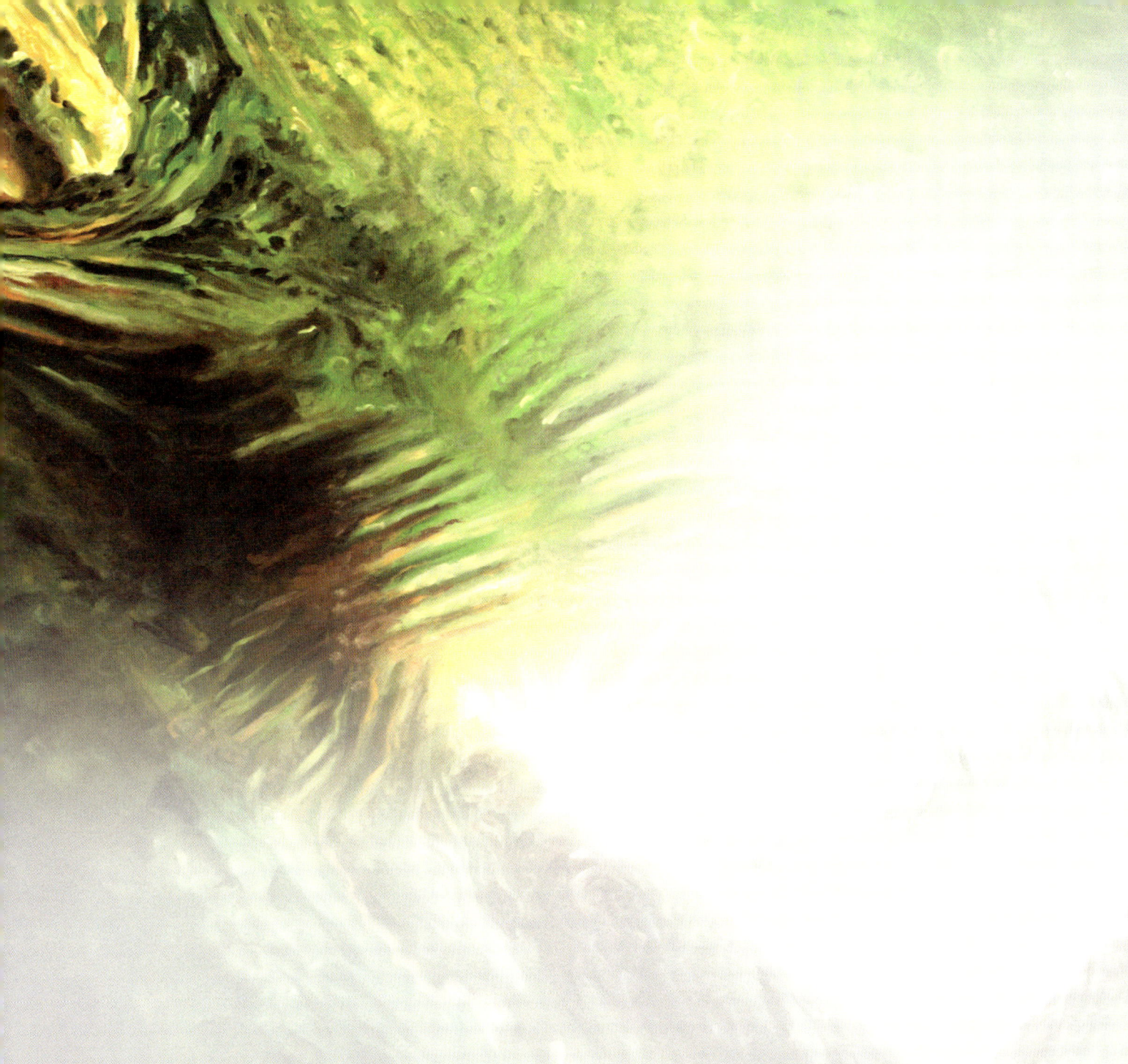

The wind blows softly
  through grass and my open heart
        love unexpected

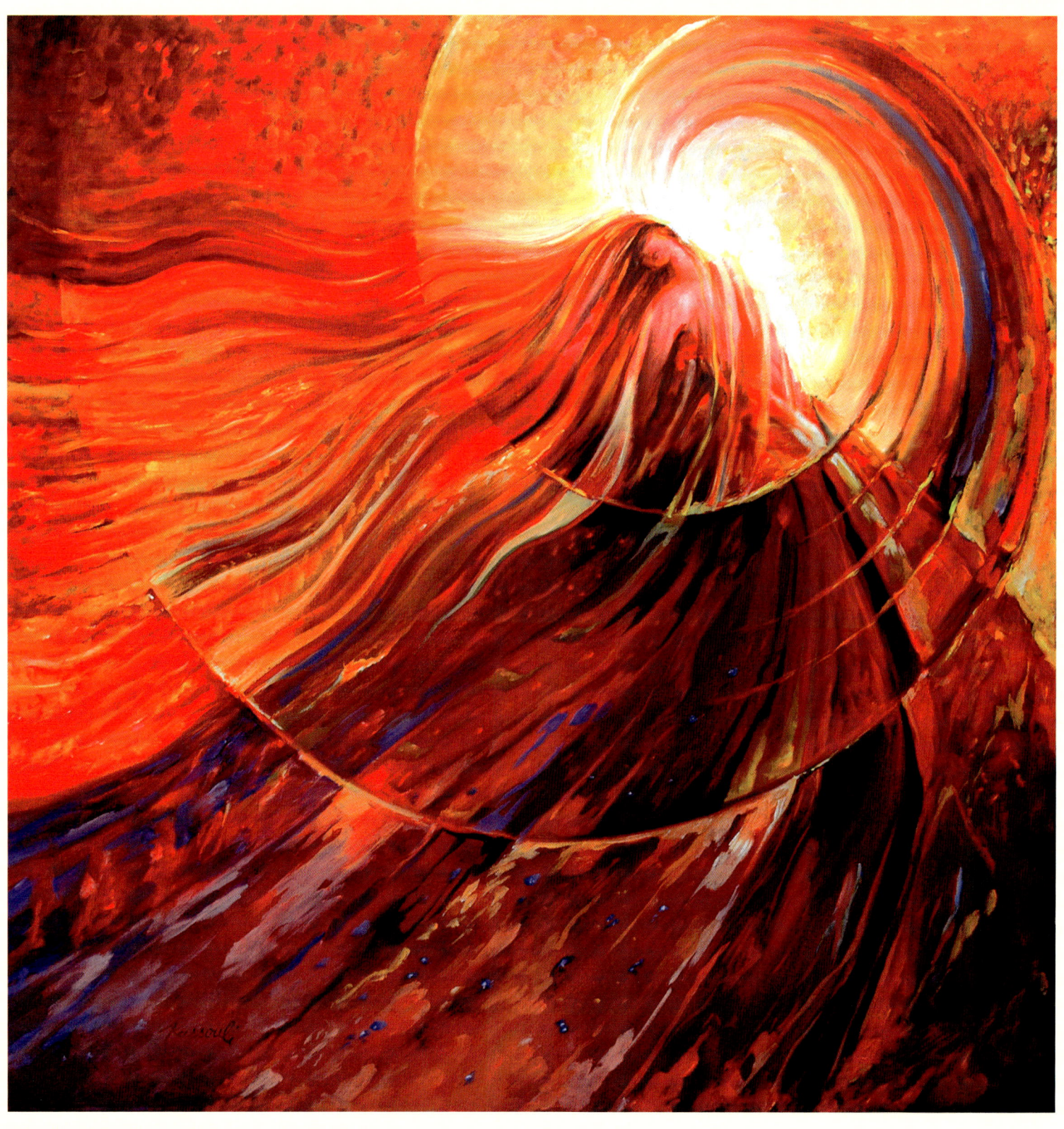

How easy to love
The words flow when it is right
I dare not tell you

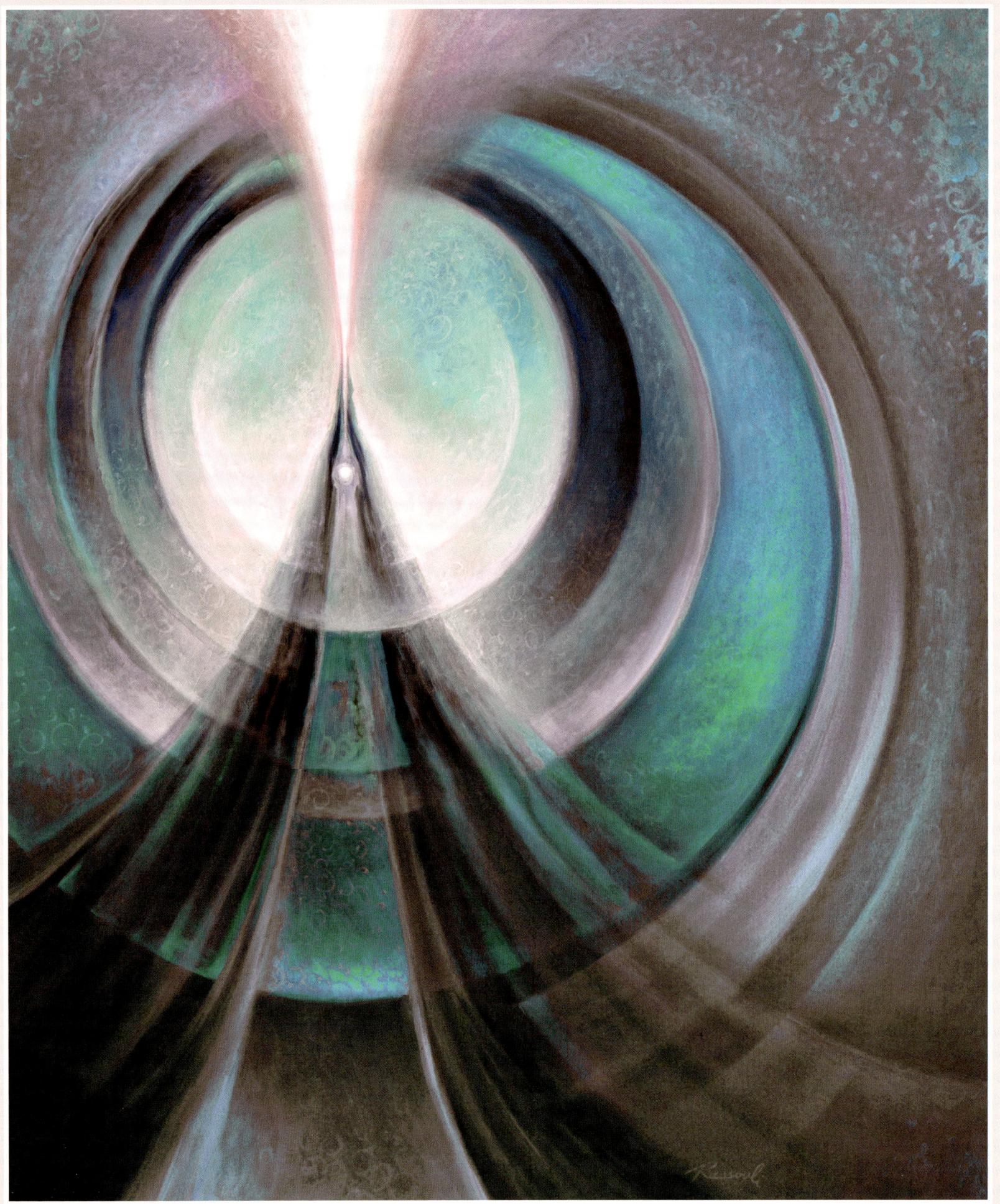

Life begins with *Love*
to complete itself again
Symmetry
is
born

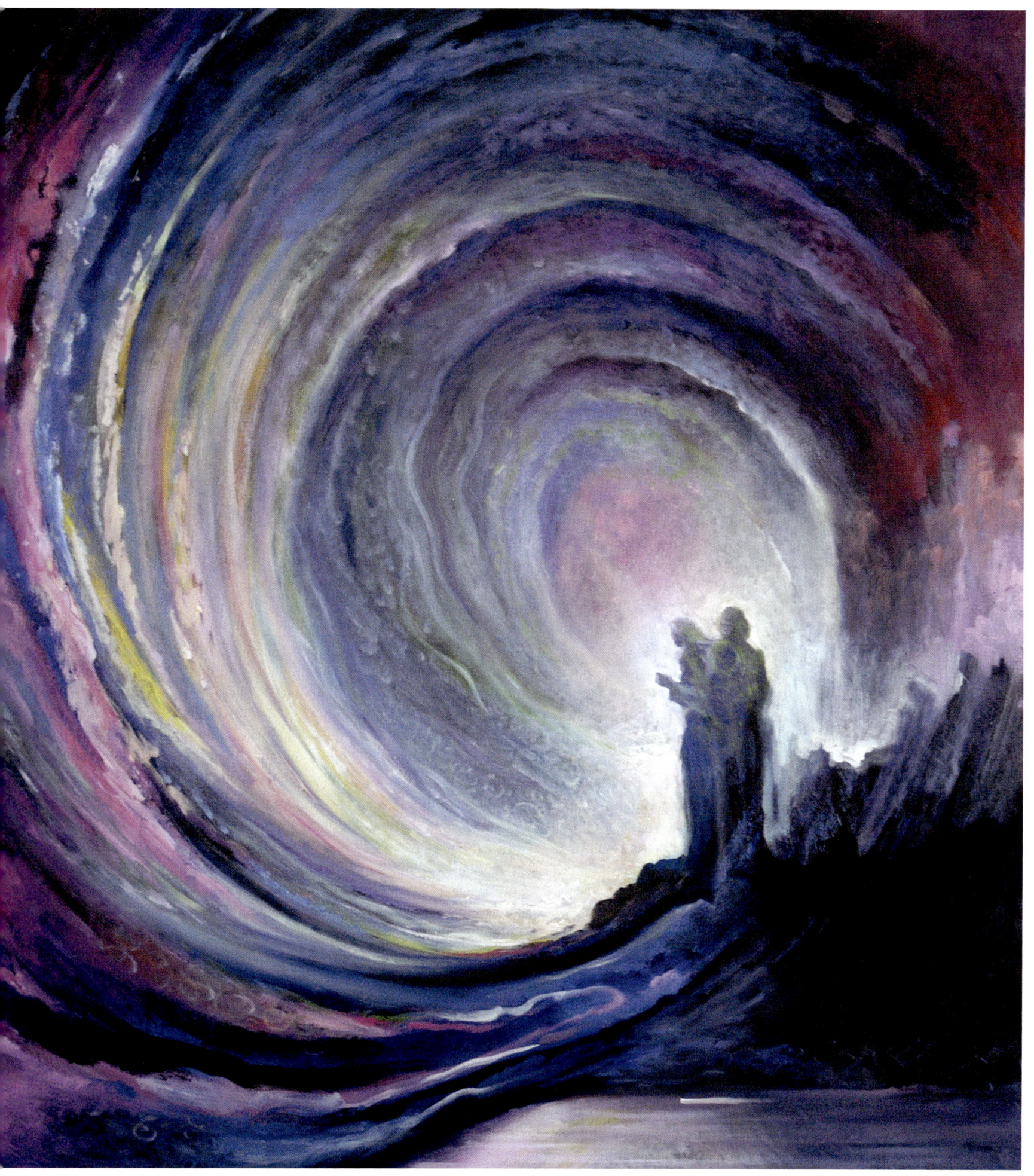

Love

      is what makes the heart beat faster.
          The lump in my throat
the feeling of missing you so much
that I can't wait to be with you again
and then we are
and I look in your eyes deeper
and I know
the unspoken words that say I love you
         and feel words in return

How short each lifetime seems
    but what I feel with you
        lasts forever.

May love be the compass
      that guides you
        on the course of a lifetime.

When souls are touched with love sublime
            and hearts unleash the wonder found
a promise made somewhere in time
            of words that speak without a sound

In gratitude we transcend space
            and bless the gifts we now can keep
                  of thoughts caress in soft embrace
                  and eyes allowed in joy to weep

The moment's song that we compose
            will leave this life with no regret
                  and carry forth what we impose
            to chart again a course once set
                  for what we have is ours to own
each breath a step we measure sweet
            together now, we wait alone
                  and walk in peace, our hearts complete.

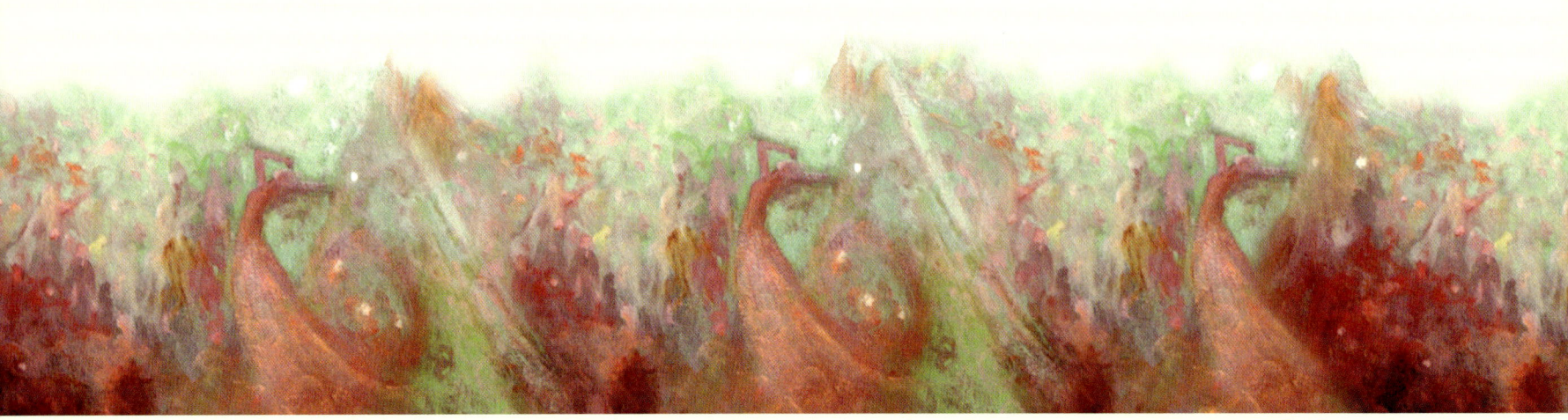

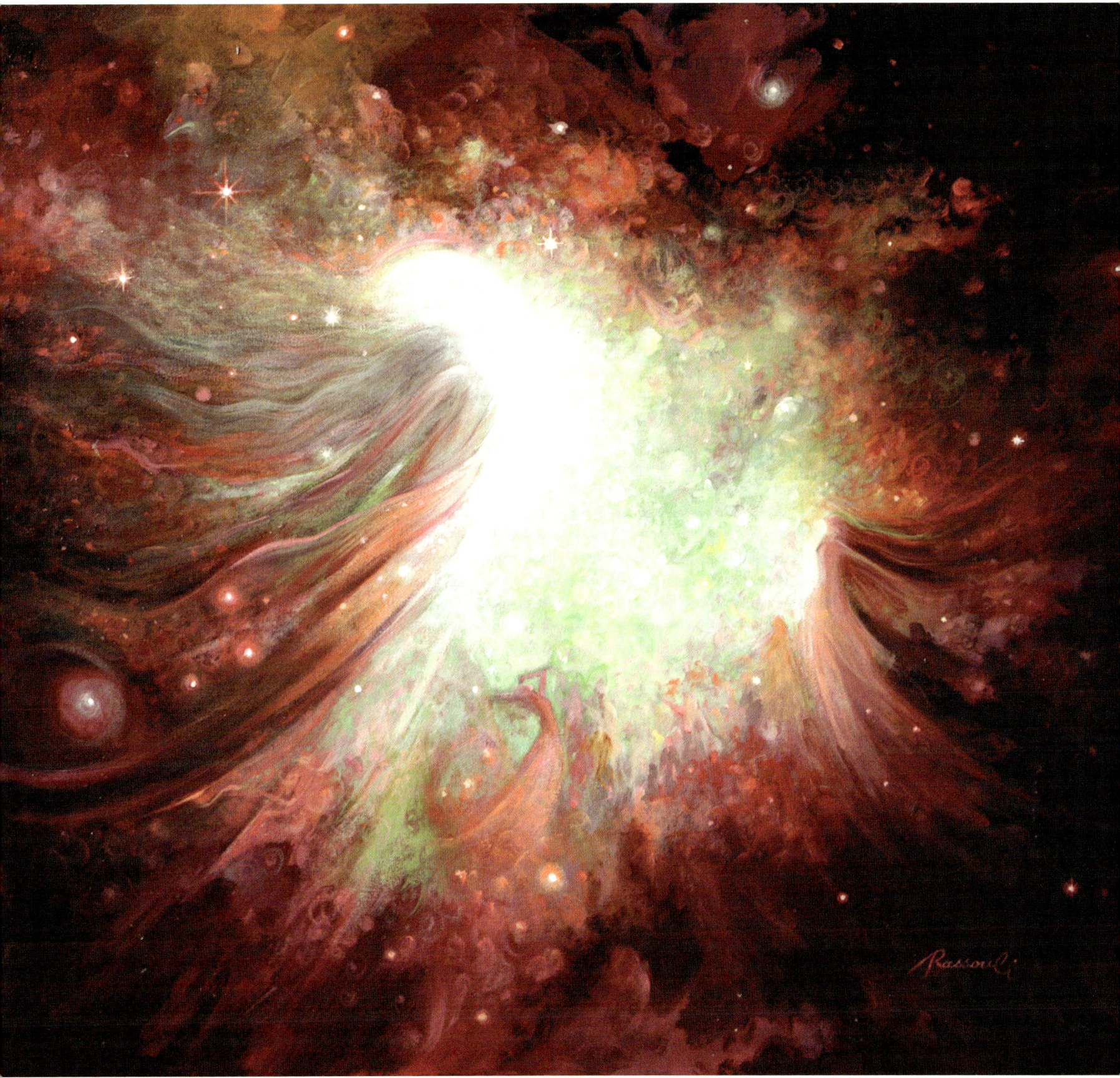

*The moment when to fill my heart again
is measured not in time or sweet remorse
nor tears that wash away unbridled pain
or morning's light which sings its soft retort*

*Such love has slept through storm and winters long
no call could break the stillness' embrace
or hasten change before the season's song
unfurl its melody and words so chaste*

*Empowered thus I found my self compelled
to cast aside emotions dormant still
my feelings spoke from depths the answer welled
no need or past the emptiness to fill*

*At one our touch has opened hearts anew
of patience born there waits a love so true.*

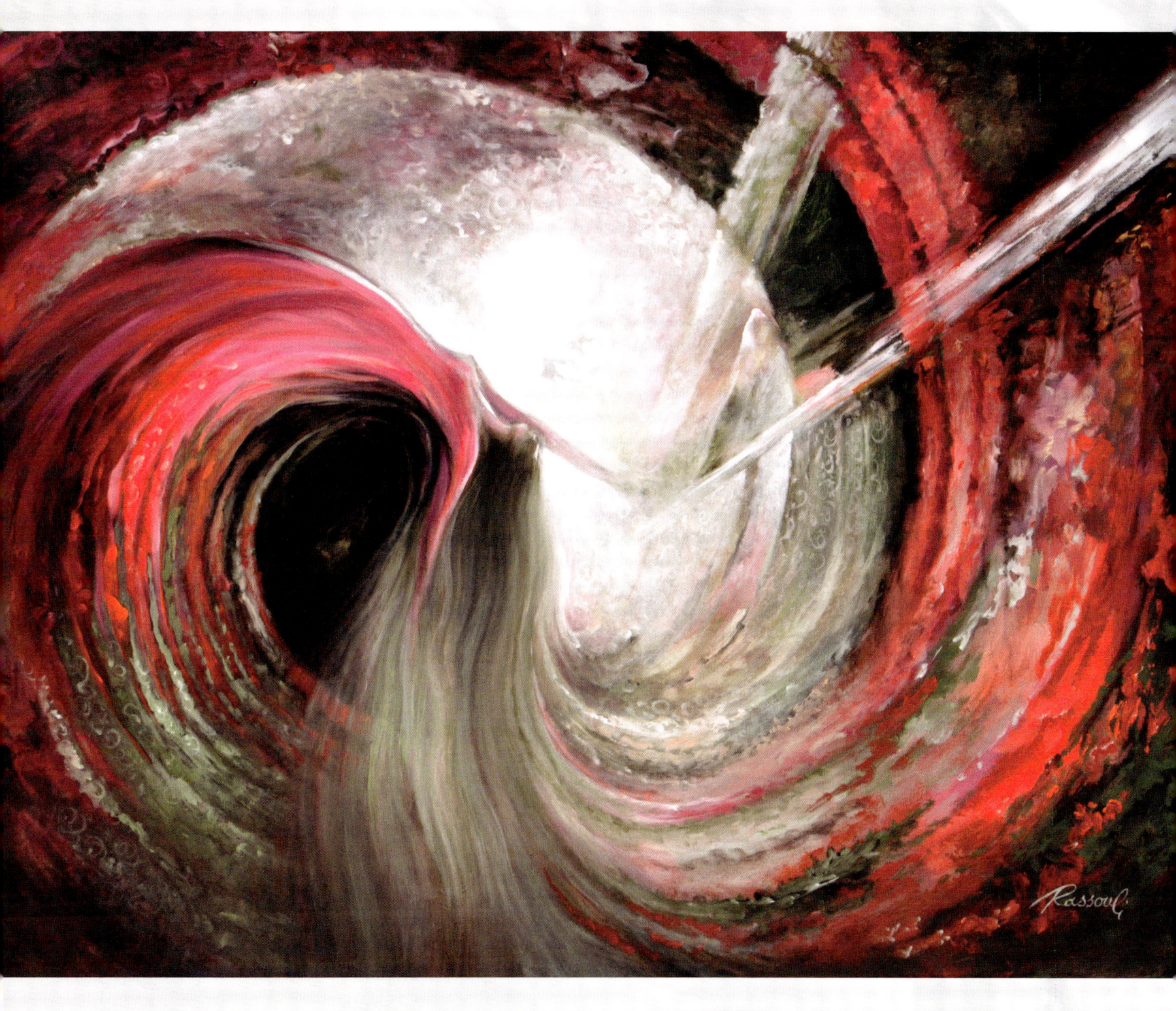

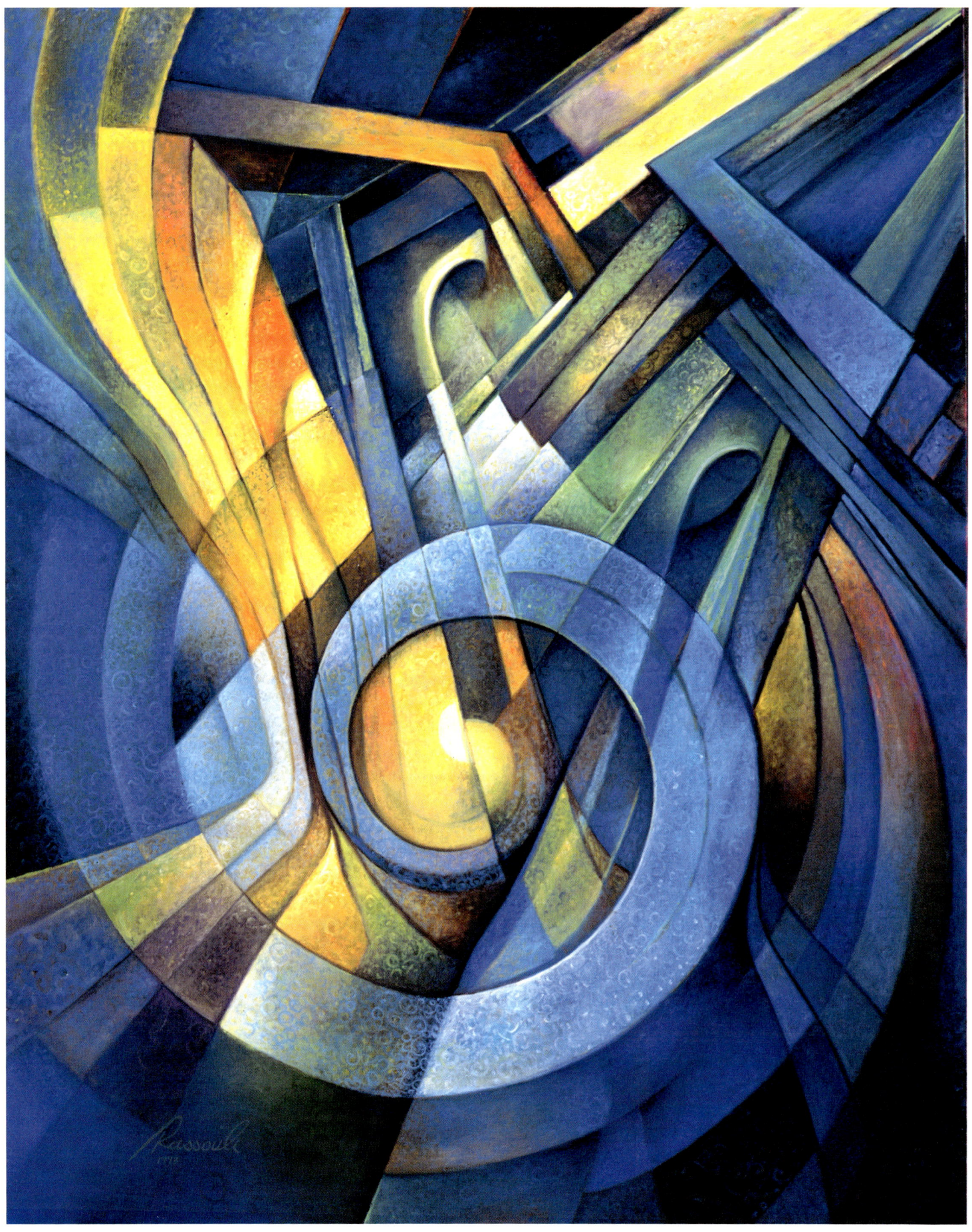

The Dream

The taste and touch of you within,
Thoughts linger on a sweet caress.
You come to me, no sounds distract
The night's embrace of innocence
The artist's brush across my lips
The pallet rich in colors deep
To flow with feelings now renewed
And blend as one in breath and hue
Entwined, our bodies bathe in love
And weep with longing's slow release
Emotions song and soft refrain
Awaken dreams that never cease.

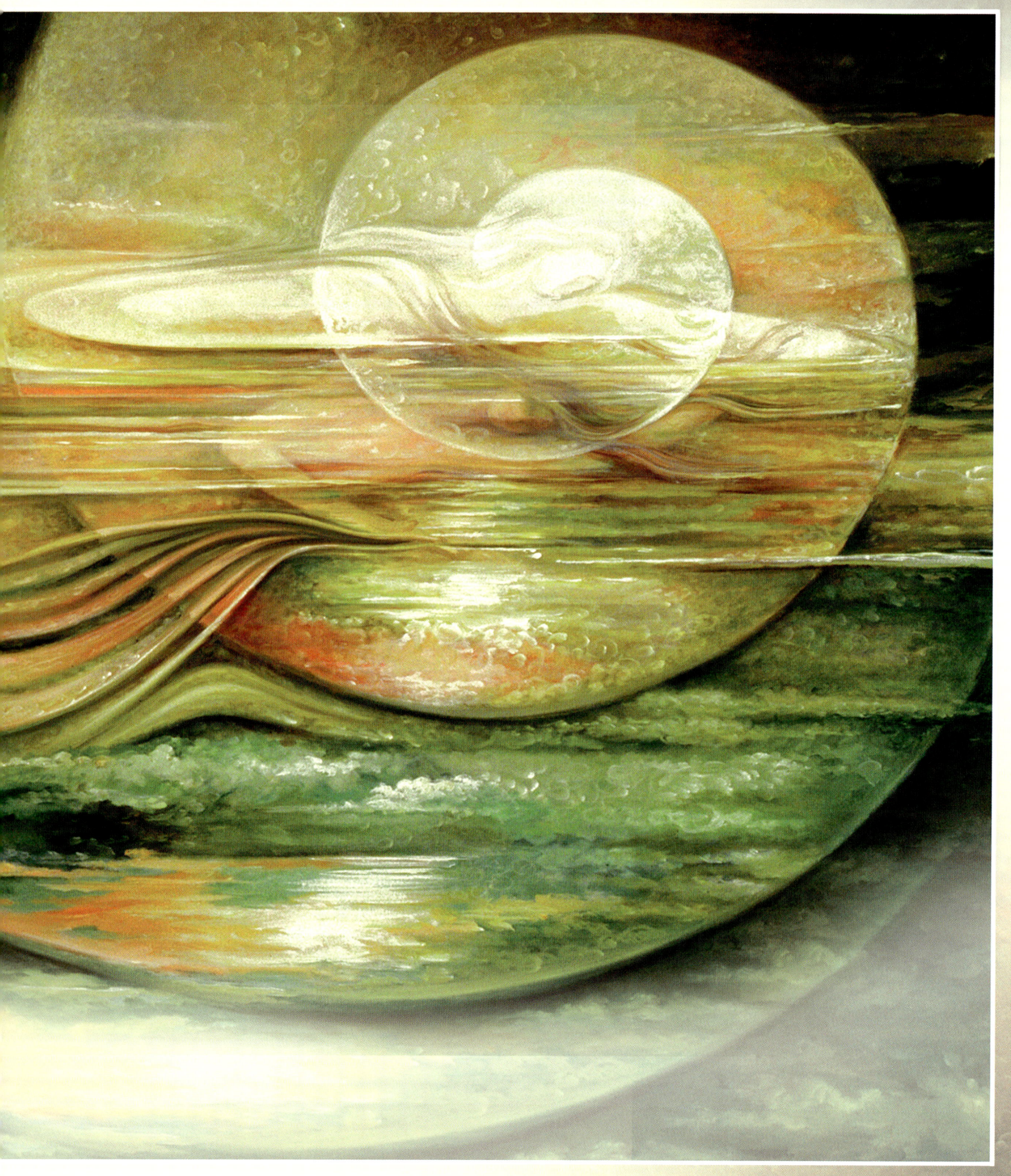

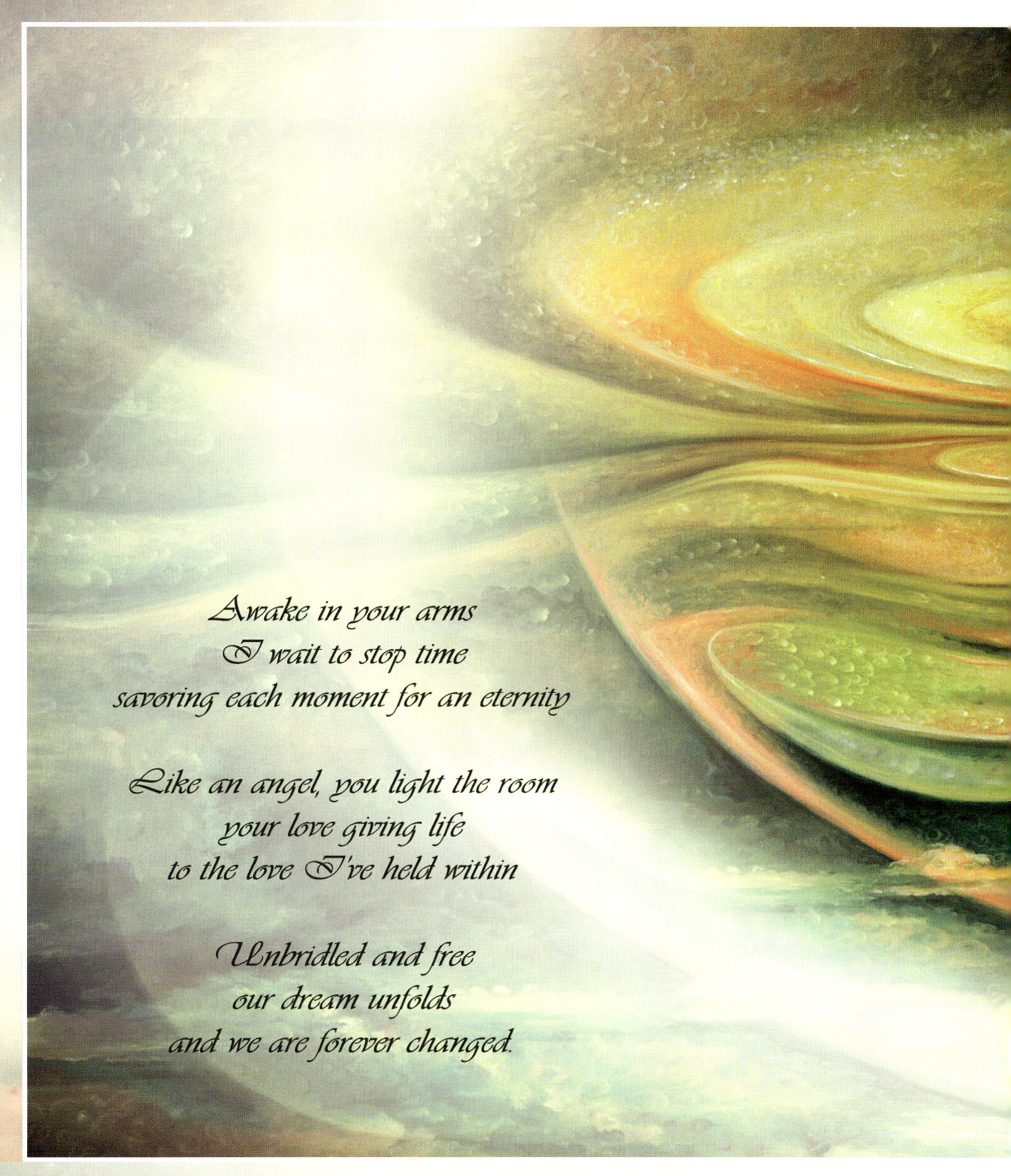

Awake in your arms
I wait to stop time
savoring each moment for an eternity

Like an angel, you light the room
your love giving life
to the love I've held within

Unbridled and free
our dream unfolds
and we are forever changed.

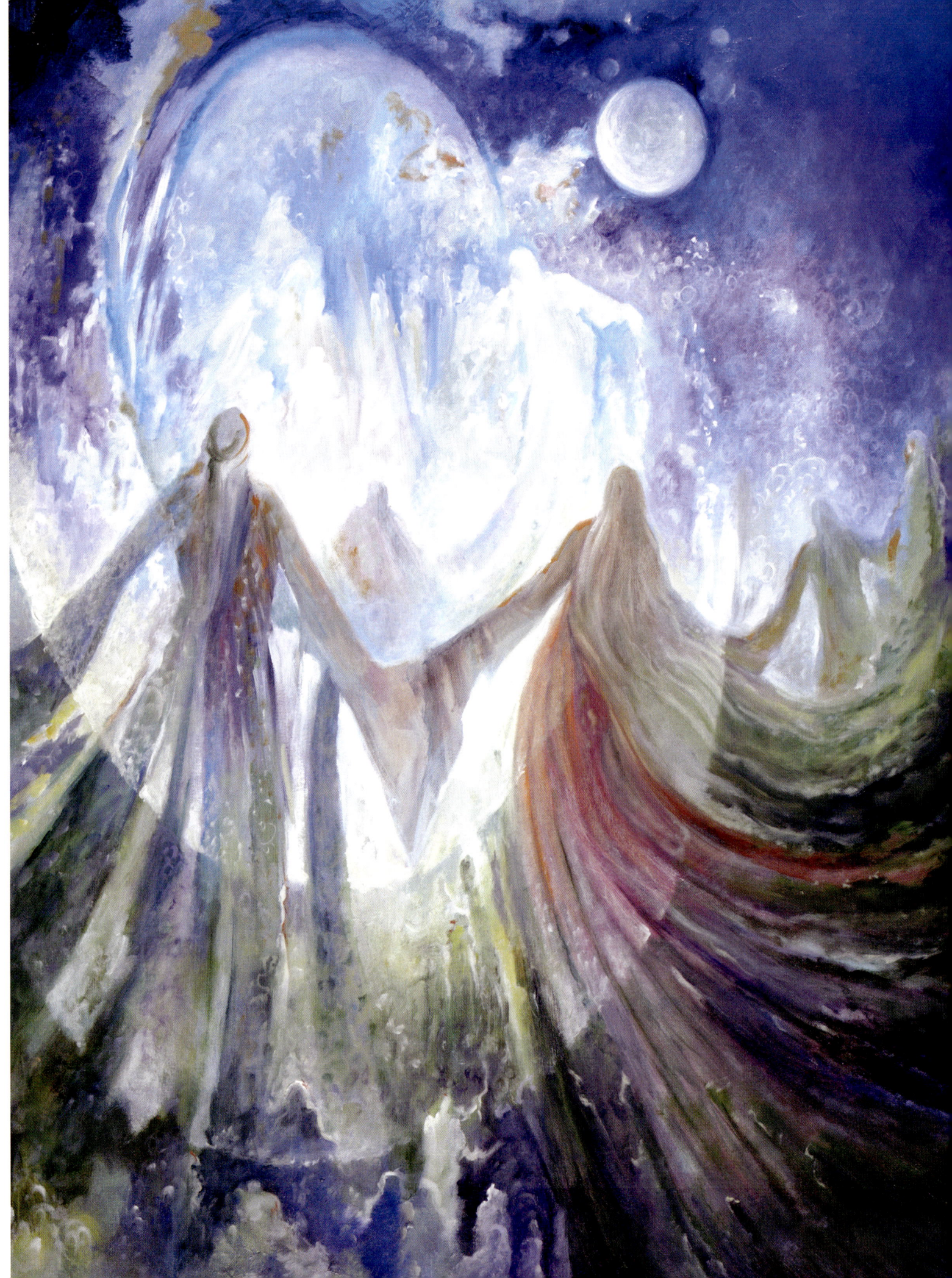

When I stood in front of you
I knew something was in store
I could feel the excitement
of our journey ahead
for I had been that way before

Each person comes into our life
with lessons we may see
and in the reflection of that other self
is the person we can be

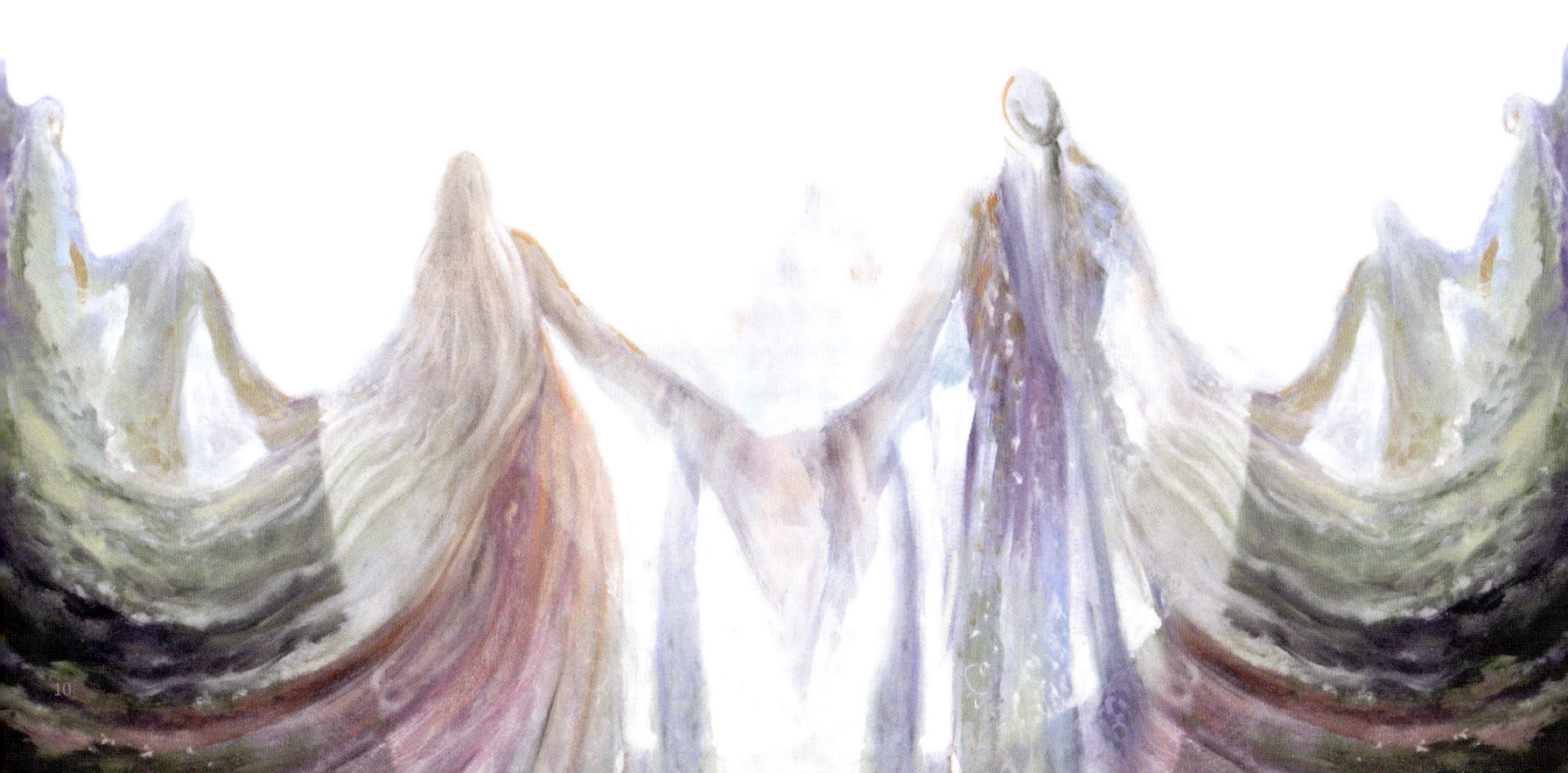

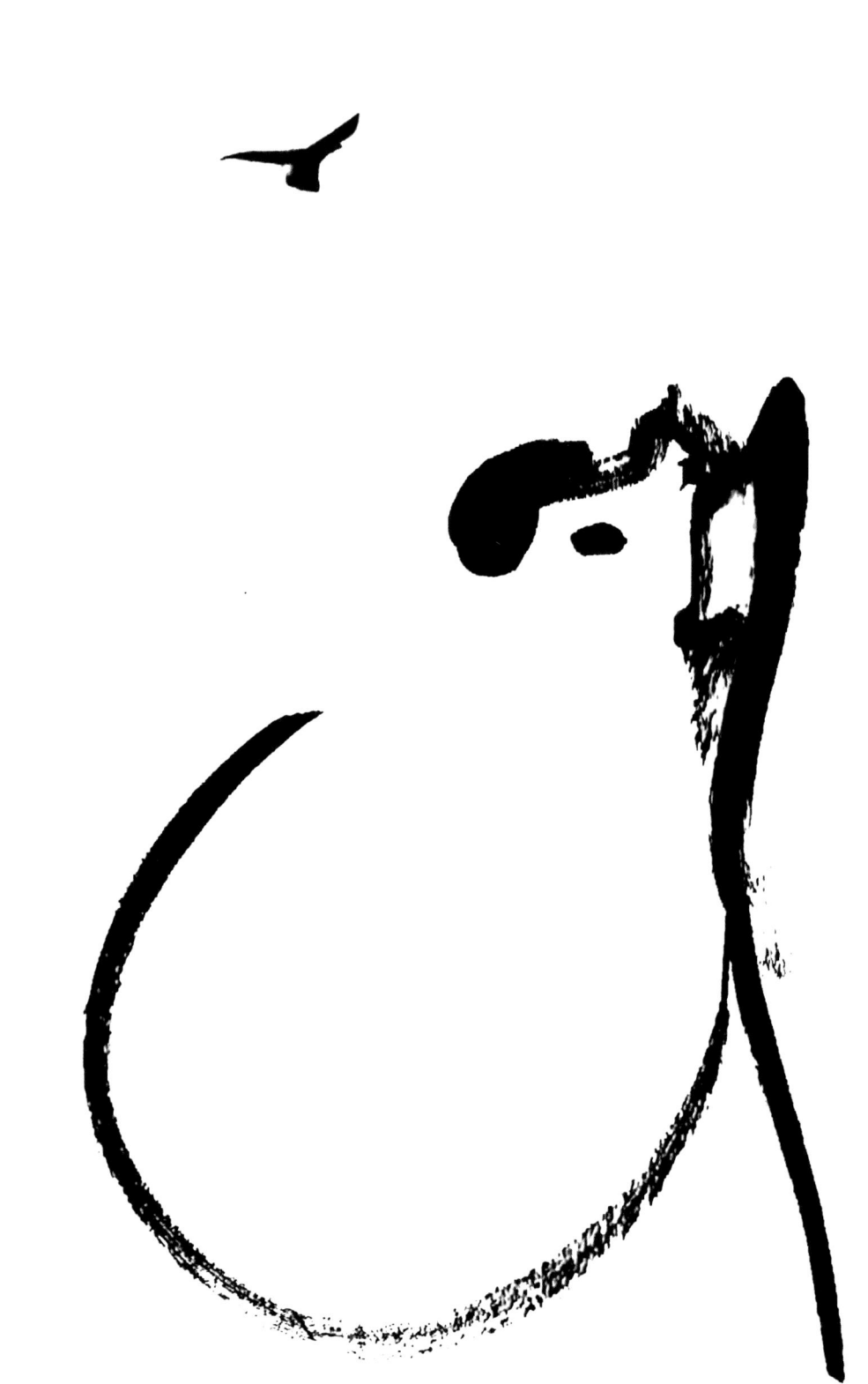

There is peace
for one
whose heart is

open

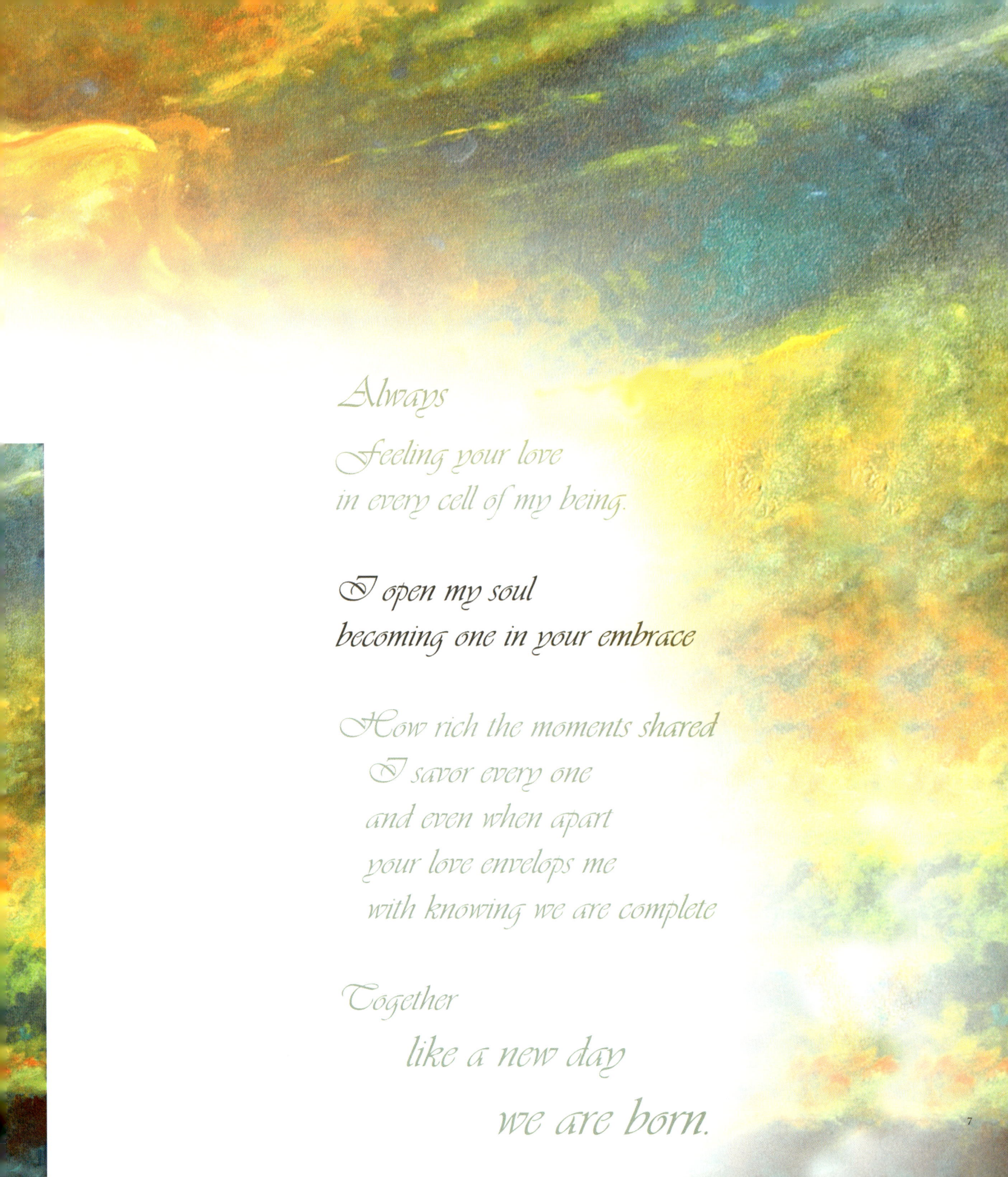

Always
Feeling your love
in every cell of my being.

I open my soul
becoming one in your embrace

How rich the moments shared
I savor every one
and even when apart
your love envelops me
with knowing we are complete

Together
like a new day
we are born.

Always
Always
Always
Always
Always

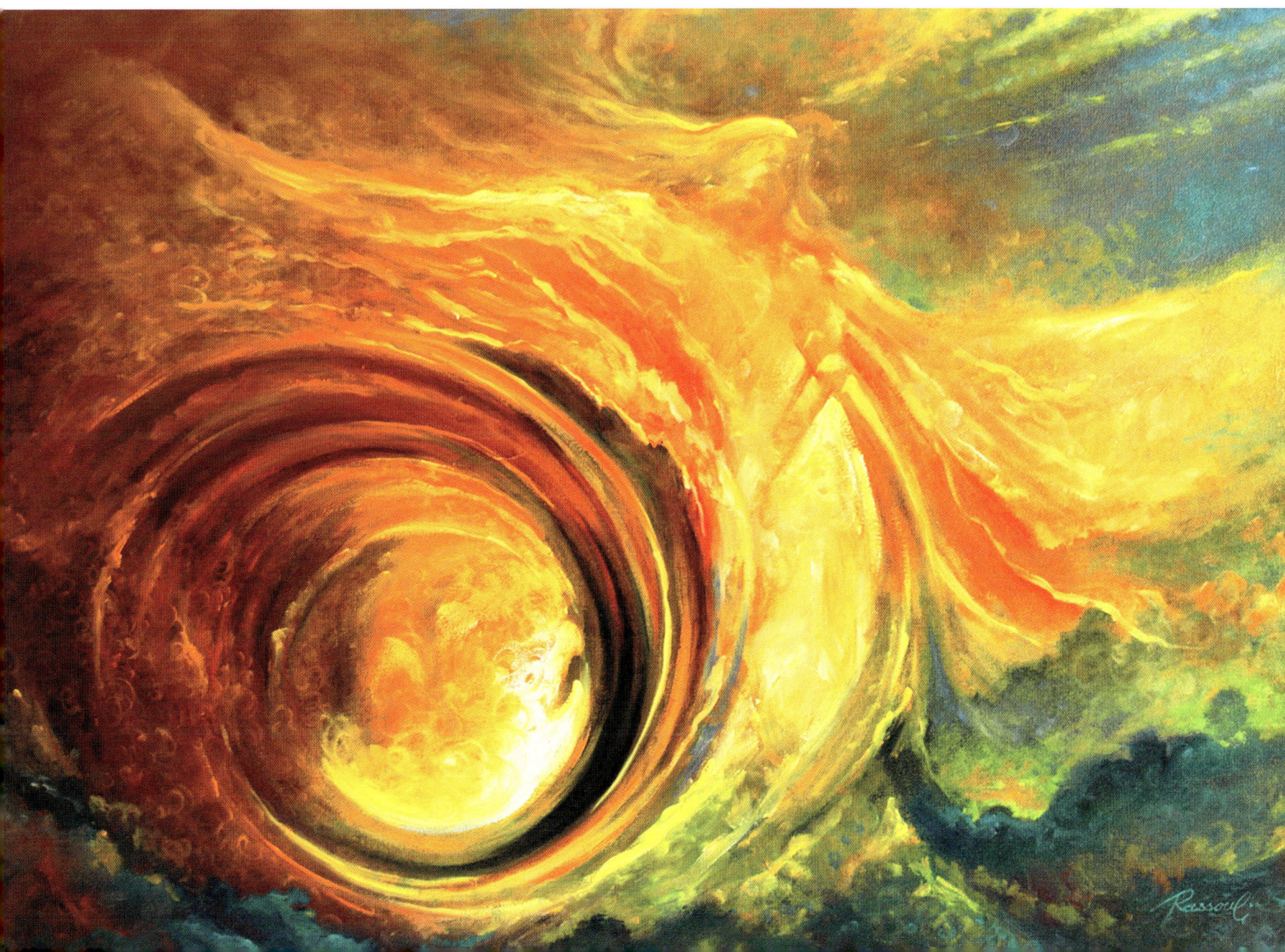

*The wind moves gently
through trees quiet water flows
life's song calls softly*

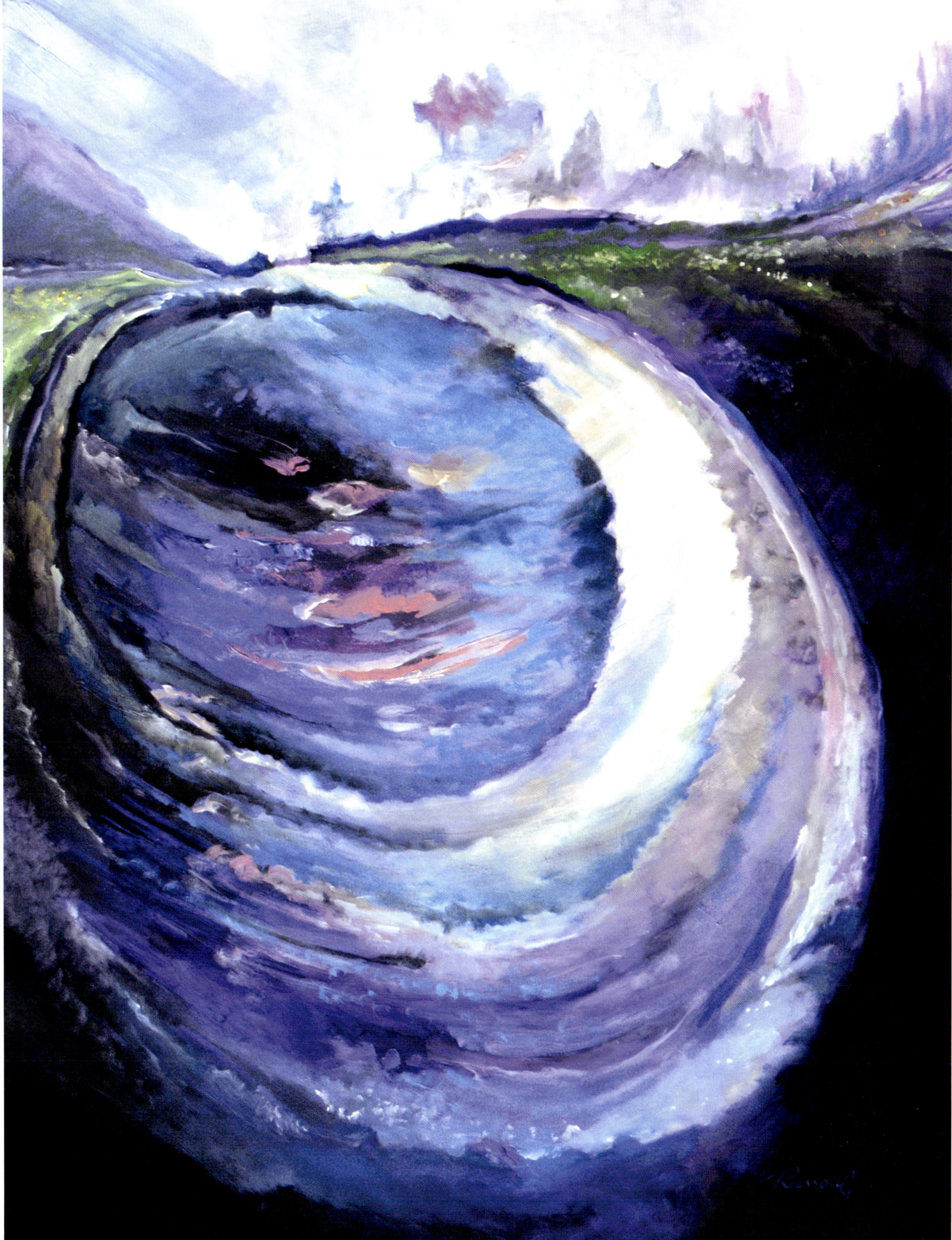

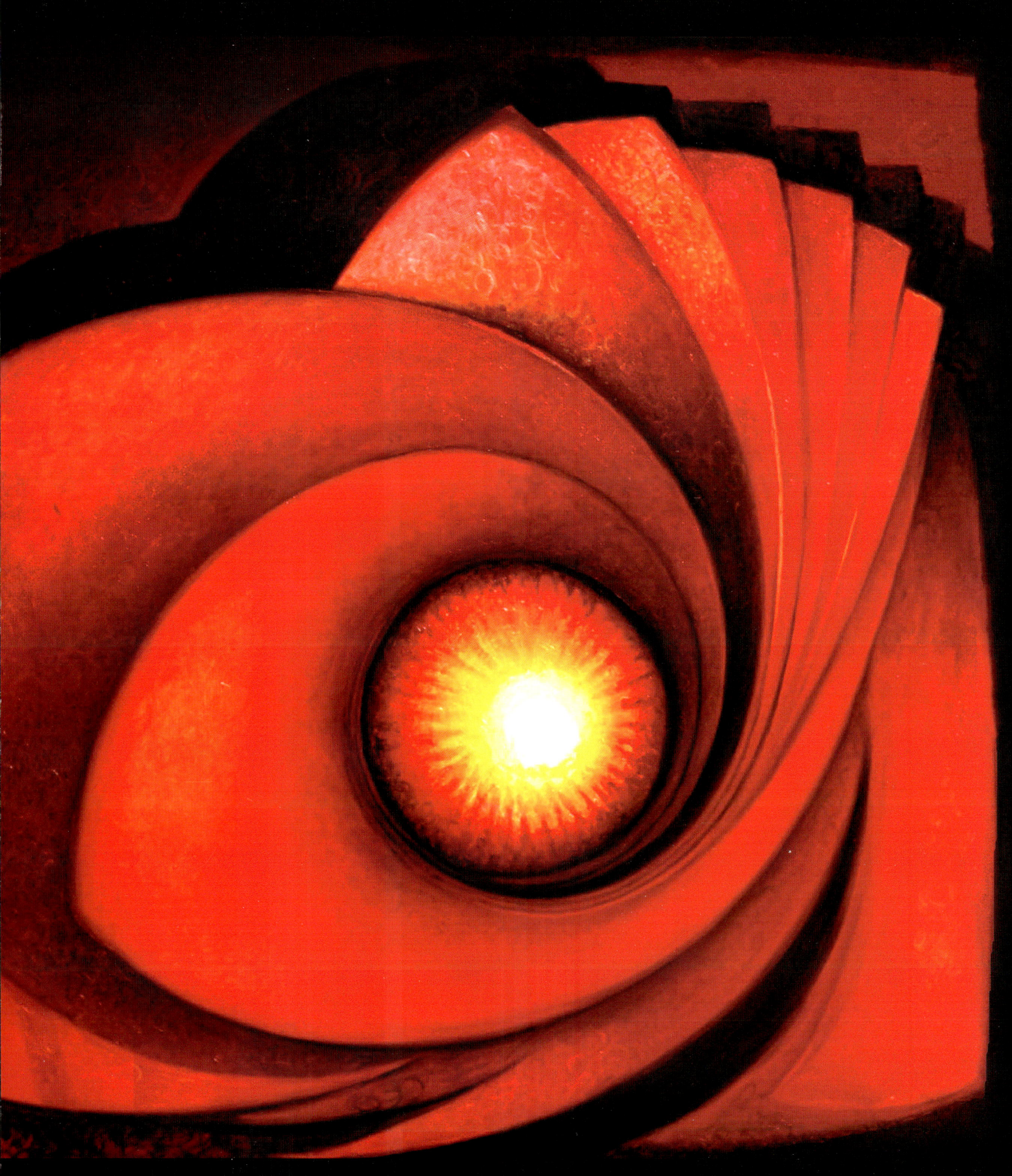